Life and Labor on the Border

LIFE AND LABOR ON THE BORDER

Working People of Northeastern Sonora, Mexico, 1886–1986

Josiah McC. Heyman

The University of Arizona Press   Tucson

The University of Arizona Press
www.uapress.arizona.edu

Printed in the United States of America
21   20   19   18   17   16   7   6   5   4   3   2

ISBN-13: 978-0-8165-1225-6 (cloth)
ISBN-13: 978-0-8165-3278-0 (Century Collection paper)

Parts of chapters 2, 3, 4, and 5 of this book are reprinted by permission
from the *American Ethnologist*, volume 17, number 2.

Library of Congress Cataloging-in-Publication Data
Heyman, Josiah McC. (Josiah McConnell), 1958–
    Life and labor on the border : working people of northeastern
Sonora, Mexico, 1886–1986 / Josiah McC. Heyman.
        p.   cm.
    Includes bibliographical references and index.
1. Working class—Mexico—Sonora (State)   2. Working class—
    Mexican-American Border Region.   I. Title.
    HD8119.S662H49   1991
    305.5'62'097217-dc20   91-12782
                                                                CIP

British Library Cataloguing-in-Publication Data are available.

♾ This paper meets the requirements of ANSI/NISO Z39.48-1992
(Permanence of Paper).

This book is dedicated with love to Merlyn and Robert.

Contents

Illustrations

Acknowledgments

This book imparts a message. The people of the United States have a moral obligation to protect and even increase the legal, secure channels of immigration from Mexico because, as the book shows, North Americans, for their various purposes, have created a way of life in Mexico that requires immigration and that people cannot readily change. This is even more compelling than the fact that large numbers of Mexican citizens are employed in the United States at any given time.

My wife, Merlyn DeLuca Heyman, shared my experiences in Agua Prieta and Douglas, and contributed many observations and insights. She has given me her fullest love through years of research and writing. I also want to thank my parents and my brother and sister, the DeLuca family, the Schiller family (especially Hillel, for looking at the manuscript), and my friends Tom, Dave, and Pete.

I owe the most profound debt to the principal families and their individual members who generously told me of their lives so I could write a book. I have debated long and hard about identifying these people. Surely many of them would be honored and eager to see their names. Yet I do not want inadvertently to cause any one person embarrassment, so I decided not to thank them by name. I hope they understand that I thank them first, before everyone else, and I hope they are proud of what I have done.

There are many other persons who helped us in Agua Prieta and Douglas—so many I can name but a few. Merlyn and I want to thank our good friends Fernando and Bertha de la Vega, Ramón and Juanita

Venegas, Henry and Guadalupe León, Alvaro and Olivia Arellano, Hector Salinas and Mary Vega, and Ben and Petra Wilson. I also want to thank all the members of the club Viejos Amigos, who took us into their convivial midst; the Committee for Justice; Father Antonio and the Sacred Family parish; Fathers Joe, Henry, Liam, and Carlos in Douglas, and Nelly Jo Hendricks of the Loreto School; the Vikingos baseball team; the United Steelworkers local 6305; and the Sociedad Mutualista de Obreros Mexicanos. I thank Dr. Alberto Durazo and his wife for their hospitality and insights into Cananea. I thank Victor Torres, the Mexican counsel in Douglas, for his gracious help and interest. I especially thank my transcriptionist, Moisés Ibarra Abril, for his dedicated work and his considerable insight into the social life of his hometown.

I thank the staff of the Centro Regional del Noroeste of the Instituto Nacional de Antropología e Historia in Hermosillo for their help in this study. I salute the valuable work being done by Sonoran historians and anthropologists, admirably supported by the state government of Sonora; my debt to these scholars is obvious. I also thank Cochise College, especially David Pettes, and the students of Anthropology 198, "The Border: From Heroic Past to Present Controversies," where I first presented much of my field research.

Eric Wolf, my teacher, has been helpful, penetrating, and wise. June Nash offered her rich understanding of working people, and from Ed Hansen I learned how to analyze politics in a realistic fashion. Sidney Mintz introduced me to the study of working people, and the late Herbert Gutman taught me the rudiments of how to think in historical terms. Roger Owen generously shared his knowledge of rural Sonora with me. Carlos Vélez-Ibáñez, Tom Sheridan, Jane Schneider, and Sydel Silverman also helped at various times. I want to thank my colleagues at Michigan Tech, among them Pat and Susan Martin, Jesse Tatum, Carol MacLennan, Terry Reynolds, Bruce Seely, and Larry Lankton.

Among my teachers I owe a special debt to James Greenberg, who introduced me to Douglas and Agua Prieta, taught me fieldwork, and most generously shared both his field site and data with me. He has given me many important ideas and suggestions that are scattered throughout this book, a contribution citations can never fully reveal. Eva and Jim Greenberg have been most hospitable to Merlyn and myself in Tucson.

As we know, graduate students largely teach each other; and while

I worked on the original dissertation, I learned much from Luis Loyola, Gustavo Ribeiro, Teresa Rubin, Jon Poor, Chris Leonard, Alessandro Scasselatti, Beatriz Morales, Wendy Hoefler, Susan Ikenberry, and Kye-Young Park. I also want to thank Rosemary Gianno.

In writing this book, I had the help of Gregory McNamee, Beth Wilson, Alan Schroder, and the University of Arizona Press, as well as very good advice from two anonymous reviewers. All errors of fact and interpretation are, of course, my own responsibility.

This material is based upon work supported by the National Science Foundation under grant BNS-8403884, a fellowship from the Doherty Foundation, and a student grant-in-aid from the Wenner-Gren Foundation for Anthropological Research. The first draft of the book was written under a Richard Carley Hunt Post-Doctoral Fellowship, also from Wenner-Gren. I thank them all.

1. Introduction

Not yet fourteen years old, Pedro Durazo left his mother's home in the northern Mexican state of Sonora, crossed the U.S. border, and joined his uncle in California. Though he had no visa, he had no fear of being caught, for there was no Border Patrol and no meaningful penalty for undocumented entry in 1921. Pedro was to work in the United States for parts of nine years, bothering to apply for a visa (which cost eighteen dollars and required simple health tests) only at the very end. Pedro's son Tomás also worked in the United States without a visa, from 1965 through 1975. It was the era of strict border control, though; Tomás joined the anonymous statistics of undocumented Mexican immigrants after he was caught and "voluntarily" departed three times.

Luis Aguirre worked alongside his father and brothers in an American-owned gold–silver–copper mine not one hundred miles from the international border. The mine closed so suddenly that men were left in the tunnels when the electricity was shut off. Luis resettled his family in the Mexican border city of Agua Prieta, joining the human tide that created the urban border of today. Luis found on-again, off-again employment as a bracero, a temporary contract laborer working in the fields of California and Arizona. Luis's wife, Angelita, also worked—for the first time since she had married—sewing confirmation dresses on a machine purchased years earlier in Mexico from a Singer sales agent.

The Córdoba family likewise moved to Agua Prieta when the father's mine job came to an end. There the younger Córdobas would find employment in American-owned factories springing up in Mexico's border cities. Teresa and Luisa Córdoba worked on the line, soldering electrical connections; their brother Francisco was a mechanic, and their brother Jorge rose to supervise a department. Though the weekly paycheck was puny, families like the Córdoba's tried to make ends meet by combining the earnings of children still living at home.

In overview, these three families are undeniably working class. They gain wages by hard manual labor, in part in major industries such as mines and factories. With their earnings they have to buy every item of their daily existence, for they own little property that could yield them either subsistence or profit. But over time jobs changed, industries stopped and started, and families moved. Households relied on multiple strategies, partly wage earning and partly tiny enterprises, extensions of unpaid household skills. Employment spanned two nations, and U.S. citizenship policies redefined types of labor and fates of persons.

An anthropologist, as a student of comparative societies and cultures, uses such basic generalizations about people as "working class." But an anthropologist must respect the complications of people's lives, and therefore not override the ethnography with abstract labels. The challenge presented is to work with the ethnographic details, even as they depart from the initial generalities, in order to see if this more complicated view of people's lives still coheres in distinct fashion. I will therefore examine the course of life histories to show that the sequences of personal events and changes do indeed have a social order. This order relates to involvement with wages, with purchased consumption, and, most important, with relationships to the more powerful. That is, I will search for the "working classness" of life stories.

Loyalty to the details of working people's lives contrasts with the highly abstract and structural tendency in the social sciences (though not in history) in which working people are considered only as carriers of paid labor power. The ideas that arise as we think carefully about ethnography can, and should, challenge this well-worn assumption; they can, and should, demand stronger and richer theories to encompass the diversity of working classes. Anthropology makes this distinct contribution to the study of the many peoples of the world whose lives have been touched by wage work.

Three important works demonstrate what an anthropology of

working peoples can be. Sidney Mintz, in *Worker in the Cane* (1960), relates one man's life story to the rhythms of economics and labor; it is not so much a matter of determination but, as he says, "history within history." In *Chinese Working-Class Lives* (1987), Hill Gates confronts the diversity found in any urban working class outside single-industry communities. Gates declines to split hairs about modes or sectors of the working class because she is dealing with family economies and life histories that join many seemingly disparate phenomena into a larger whole. In a powerful ethnography of Bolivian tin miners, *We Eat the Mines and the Mines Eat Us* (1979), June Nash roots the working class within the complex history and cultures of the Andes, in contrast with Euro-American labor history. Eric Wolf sets forth in general the task facing anthropologists when he argues that we should expect "working classes" to be diverse in time and place, and complicated in their daily relationships (Wolf, 1982:358–360).

Following these teachers, this book, however flawed, is offered as a sustained analysis meant to elucidate the distinctively anthropological understanding of working peoples. Earning wages, buying things, and moving in response to fluctuating labor markets ramify throughout the personal history, every dilemma, all the weighted emotions of being older or younger, woman or man, citizen of Mexico or of the United States—the force of social class seen as powerful ordering patterns rather than as the neat categories of labor force demography, workplace and occupation, consumption, residence, and consciousness so often used as parameters of working-class life. As anthropologists move toward the study of the many working peoples of the world, our understanding should not become simply a localized, humane version of the "working class" that other social scientists have already produced. We have to deal with politics, economics, and social aggregates, of course, but we should not unthinkingly slip into the assumptions and terminologies inherited with these topics until they have proved themselves useful; the close-grained attention to what people say and do should give us new points of departure.

I approach these questions of complex patterning by applying a specific method to life histories. The life course can be considered as a series of "key junctures." Key junctures are posed either by the larger economy (such as the mine closings of the Great Depression) or personal events such as widowhood. At these times, people are presented with several alternative courses of action. The alternatives lie among basic ways of making a living and crucial choices of residence, such as proximity to the U.S. border.

Such actions are, of course, taken by individuals or family groups, at times with conflicting internal desires. At the individual level though they may be, the decisions among alternatives are not completely open. They are structured by accumulations of work habits and skills, needs for cash and consumer goods, changes in roles among household members, and so forth. The reasons for alternative courses of action at key junctures therefore can be explained. Such explanations in turn address fundamental structures of unequal power, the earning of money, and the dependence on purchased necessities. That is, the key juncture approach aims to uncover the order underlying the history of waged lives.

The method of key junctures brings together the macrohistorical level and the ethnographic level. The key junctures are frequently major events in the regional or national economy and politics. The dates of key junctures in life histories frequently coincide with the dates marking the boundaries of major regional and even world economic–historical periods. The movements by persons and families among various alternatives are, in fact, the crucial movements of populations and classes seen in wider history. The method of key junctures is a useful and concrete manner to bridge the gap between the anthropologist's desire to address large-scale issues and the fine-grained knowledge of people's lives.

REGIONAL AND HISTORICAL FRAMEWORK

This book seeks to explain the origins of a distinctive way of life along Mexico's border with the United States. The rise of the modern "border" as a geographic area and a way of life reflects a profound change in Mexico's history. Much progress has been made in understanding the border in recent years. What we still need, and what I have tried to address through the specifics of the Sonoran case, is an account of the manner in which this border life emerged, the power of the United States in the region, and what Mexicans have made of it in their families, communities, and daily culture.

The simplest definition of the border is the boundary line itself; a little more broadly, the populations living alongside it, especially in the twined cities of the Mexican and U.S. sides. There is also reason to define a wider border, the zone of northern Mexico penetrated and transformed from the U.S. side. Another usage of "border" is the institutional form of nation-state boundaries, such as the Border Patrol within the U.S. Department of Justice. My working definition of the "border" for the purposes of this study is an ordering or structuring of a people's way of life in Mexico caused by the U.S. power over economics and immigration, specifically delineated by proximity to the international boundary.

This research is based on Agua Prieta, Sonora, a small city across from Douglas, Arizona, and in the general area of Tucson (Map 1.).[1] Agua Prieta was a good location to study the industrial working class of the border. Among the seven border cities sampled by Seligson and Williams (1981:14) in 1978, Agua Prieta had the highest proportion of *maquiladora* assembly plant workers (4,000) to total population (40,000)—that is, one in ten of all men, women, and children worked in one of the factories. Northeastern Sonora, the small, well-defined area that surrounds Agua Prieta, contains the largest industrial copper mines in Mexico. Agua Prieta, though not a copper city itself, is the railroad border crossing that unifies this district and links it to the U.S. economy. It was an opportune vantage point over a distinctive region of the border.

The image of a border city like Agua Prieta focuses on its tourist and commercial aspects, from the souvenir shops to the red-light district. Yet such trades, while economically important, tell us more about the American tourists who support them than about Mexican residents. To learn about the people of the border, one has to go into the vast expanses of working-class and middle-class neighborhoods stretching away from the port of entry. This urbanism appears as a symbol of Third World poverty, simply because it is the part of Latin America juxtaposed to the United States. Yet this does not tell us about the actual quality and aspirations of people's lives in Mexico's border regions; the stereotype of uniform impoverishment makes intelligent questions and understanding impossible.

Mexican border culture is clearly influenced by proximity to the United States, yet we cannot assume that culture mysteriously diffuses across the boundary. We need concrete studies of the causes for cultural rearrangement in the pay, credit, and consumer systems of the border regions. Each time we ask a question about today's border, our inquiry pushes back in time and deeper into Mexico's northern borderlands.

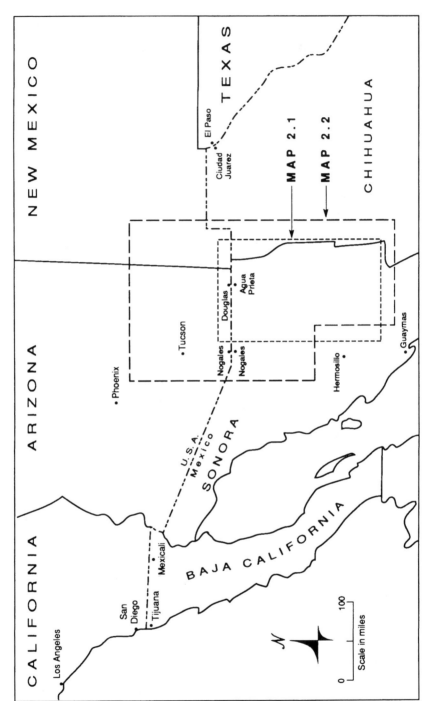

Map 1.1. Location of study area

Friedrich Katz neatly sums up the history of northern Mexico as a change from a "frontier" to a "border" (1981:7). Northern Mexico, like the American West, was a zone of aggressive European expansion against Native Americans. Northeastern Sonora, one of the most isolated regions of all northern Mexico, was a hard-fought frontier with the Apaches. It was peopled in small riverside villages by a mixture of the Opata indigenous to the area and mestizo immigrants attracted by gold and silver finds. ("Mestizo," though originally a term denoting mixed Spanish and Indian ancestry, in fact refers to Mexicans who hold to a fundamentally European way of life; it does not imply a connection of biological descent with culture.) *Norteño* (northern Mexican) society was forged from the frontier economic and cultural complexes of mining and cattle ranching (León-Portilla, 1972).

Amid this frontier a boundary was laid, the result of the Mexican–American War of 1845–1848. The current Arizona–Sonora border, including Douglas and Agua Prieta, was determined in 1854 after the Gadsden Purchase. Although the boundary was surveyed within a few years, the border was made a reality through decades of slow social and economic conquest by Anglo Americans of what became the U.S. Southwest. By the late nineteenth century, a true "border" had emerged in the sense that the American economy had reached the edge of the U.S. territory and was poised to leap the international boundary and penetrate northern Mexico (Fernández, 1977).

The Apache frontier closed in 1886. At nearly the same time national and state governments in Mexico encouraged foreign, mainly U.S., purchases of land and minerals. The aggressive capture of resources uprooted Sonoran frontier settlements. Gigantic cooper mines—Cananea and Pilares de Nacozari—were installed along with their associated complexes of mills and smelters, which provided thousands of wage-paying jobs. Railroads were built south through the vast desert expanses, and commerce turned to U.S. sources.

Similar rapid changes took place all over northern Mexico, giving rise to a large and mobile group of laboring folk. The introduction of a previously preindustrial population to wage labor and factory discipline has been termed "working class formation" (Thompson, 1963; Gutman, 1977). In northeastern Sonora, this process started in the 1880s and accelerated in the first decade of the twentieth century.

Mine employment, though subject to brief, severe depressions, generally sustained a high level until 1929. Meanwhile, labor protest coalesced around inequality between foreigners and Mexicans in company towns and pay policies; during the 1910–1920 revolution, northern Sonorans, both peasants and miners, actively lined up behind such major revolutionary figures as Álvaro Obregón, Plutarco Elías Calles (both from Sonora), and Pancho Villa. With the onset of the 1930s vigorous unions took hold in the copper mines at Cananea and Nacozari. Successive generations of workers in a continuous setting and the development of institutions such as labor unions can be referred to as working-class crystallization.

However, in most of Sonora the mine community was uprooted rather than allowed to crystallize. The Great Depression brought a series of mass layoffs beginning in 1930 and culminating in the final closure of Nacozari in 1949. To this uprooting was added the massive repatriation of people from the United States to Mexico. From their initial refuges in farm villages, ranches, and prospecting camps, families gradually made their way to border cities such as Agua Prieta. The displaced working people were joined by others of rural origin. Like Agua Prieta, all the Mexican border cities grew greatly after 1940, stimulated by the post-World War II boom of the U.S. Southwest. They filled with families mainly immigrating from the Mexican states close by (Urquidi and Méndez Villarreal, 1978).

The period of resettlement beginning around 1940 was a "working class transformation," an established wage-working population undergoing a fundamental rearrangement of their labor and lives (Montgomery, 1979; Gutman, 1984:195–196). Because it was a transformation, it is particularly diverse and interesting. New combinations of local and migratory, U.S. and Mexican, men's and women's effort had to be worked out family by family.

A new wave of light assembly factories, called the Border Industrialization Program or maquiladora industry, emerged after 1965 right along the border. The process consists of importing U.S. manufactured parts, putting them together with Mexican labor, and returning the completed or partially completed product to the United States. Most factories either are owned by U.S. companies or depend on them for orders. The maquiladoras have reached great importance on the border; nationally, a quarter of a million persons were employed in them as of 1986 (Stoddard, 1987:20).

The first maquiladoras arrived in Agua Prieta in 1967. This phase has characteristics of both a transformation of the earlier working population based on heavy industry, and the initiation of a new working class, since these factories characteristically hire young women workers, a group not previously in the paid labor force. Setting maquiladora workers in a longer historical and regional context is the particular emphasis in this book.

During the 1980s Mexico suffered from a hundred billion dollar foreign debt, economic contraction, and severely declining real wages and standards of living. The devaluation of the peso to a hundredth of its value against the dollar especially hit border communities. Yet exports to the United States continued to grow, driven by the outflow of debt dollars, and Agua Prieta factory employment expanded, as employment did along the rest of the border. Ironically, then, the border boom brought an insidious increase in effort with no compensating reward.

To make a complex history yet more complicated, we must consider the history of U.S. border policies, a chronology with different rhythms and powerful repercussions. The movement of Mexicans northward is by no means a new phenomenon. Despite the Gadsden Purchase of 1853, Sonora and southern Arizona continued their intimate historical connection, and Hispanic Sonorans and Arizonans readily moved across the international boundary. As the United States developed its own border economy, however, the nature of the movement changed from one of frontiersmen to labor migration. The change lay not only with the Mexican immigrants, for in the course of the twentieth century the U.S. government has repeatedly redefined who could come from Mexico, and under what terms.

Until 1917 there was virtually no restriction on immigration from Mexico, and relatively little before 1929. This was an era of large—and largely uncounted—population flows across the border. Many of the Sonorans came to work in the copper mines and railroads of Arizona. I label this the "open border" period.

The year 1929 witnessed the first attempt at closing off Mexican immigration by denying visas, and it was soon followed by a massive repatriation of people of Mexican origins from the United States to Mexico. After World War II began, however, the rapidly growing U.S. Southwest resumed its dependence on Mexico to provide laborers. The demand for temporary labor was institutionalized in the 1942–1965 bracero contract labor program. The renewal of employment in the U.S. Southwest came at the time when unemployed mine and repatriate families were searching for new sources of income, and helped make modern border life possible.

Throughout the post–1929 period, however, the bulk of immigration has proceeded outside the formal control of the nation-state. The United States has responded by steadily escalating the means of legal and forcible restriction at the border. I refer to the period since 1929 as the "controlled border" because of the combination of legally restricted immigration, contract labor, and physically constrained border crossing. This term does not imply that the U.S. government has complete control over the boundary, but it usefully contrasts with the fluidity of the earlier period of border history. The U.S. border system will be viewed as an instituted series of power actions that control access to the very valuable resources of legal residence, and temporary and permanent employment.

Besides constituting periods of local and national history, the mine enterprises and the maquiladoras are representative of two important periods in global economic history. Since in each era industrialists sought to establish designs for labor and community organizations that resemble forms found far from the U.S.–Mexican border, exploring patterns discerned in other ethnographic studies will further our understanding of the local material. For example, the mine towns of Cananea and Nacozari were a local manifestation of a global pattern that occurred around the turn of the twentieth century, when the world's industrial centers sought agricultural and mineral raw materials throughout the rest of the world. They implanted huge, technologically sophisticated but economically isolated productive operations, in the process creating new wage-laboring populations (Furtado, 1970:47–49; Zapata, 1977).

Western corporate executives of the time used a similar social "template"—company housing, company stores, racially isolated white management set off from the indigenous work force, direct interference in or colonial control of local government and police—in widely dispersed places: South American mines (DeWind, 1975); southern African mines (Onselen, 1976); Appalachia (Eller, 1982); and the Canadian and U.S. West (Knight, 1975; Byrkit, 1982). Some of the characteristics of this period were captured in A. L. Epstein's label "unitary structure" (1958:122–124), by which he means to convey not that the mine towns were harmonious but, rather, that the extension of the mine enterprise through every aspect of production and daily life caused all community issues—not just workplace issues—to become labor/company issues.

The post–1965 maquiladoras are a manifestation of a cycle in the world economy that has been called "the new international division of labor." This fancy label indicates that the Third World is no longer limited to sources of raw materials or outmoded manufacturing for local markets, but provides advanced production of goods consumed not locally but in the wealthy areas of the globe (Frobel, Heinrichs, and Kreye, 1979). An increasingly sophisticated ability to centralize knowledge and spread out operations has facilitated the placement of manufacturing in dense population centers of poor nations, where an unusually hardworking, poorly paid work force is obtained among young women.

The consistency of the corporate template in these industries is striking (Nash, 1983). Gender is used as a criterion to select a labor force from more complex populations, either urban working classes or nearby peasantries. A social–political form, the export processing zone, occurs either in formally designated districts or in key ports of entry for world trade, such as border towns. Production is not fixed upon the location of a natural resource, as it was in the mines; indeed, mobility is valued in a competitive, cost-cutting world. Local production zones host many firms and no one company is fixed to the locality; unlike the mines, the community and the workplace do not form a "unitary structure."

The case of northeastern Sonora is special because it encompasses important examples of both types of industrial system. In fact, mines and maquiladoras are linked together in the generations of families, the copper workers being the fathers or grandfathers of the female factory operatives. This allows us to contrast two types of labor with very different characteristics, and yet understand one as the historical transformation of the other.

FIELDWORK, DATA ANALYSIS, AND PRESENTATION

This study is based on twenty-one months of fieldwork in Agua Prieta, Sonora, and Douglas, Arizona, from 1984 to 1986, while I was residing in Agua Prieta. Six histories of grand-families, the kin group formed by an elderly couple and all of their children and grandchildren (Lomnitz and Pérez-Lizaur, 1984), are the core. These families were selected opportunistically, on the basis that they came from the region of Sonora around Agua Prieta, and that at different times members were involved in the major forms of wage labor: copper mines and smelters, migratory labor in the United States, and maquiladoras. However, each family had its own labor history, and no single family entirely conformed to the overall sequence. The purpose of this research was in-depth analysis of a few family histories, rather than an attempt to obtain a large, representative sample.

A number of different bodies of data were gathered for each family and combined in the overall family history. I collected year-by-year residential and work histories for the adult members of the "core households" in the six grand-families: the elderly couple at the head, and their resident children and grandchildren. The work history included position, skills, and pay; the residential history included location in Mexico or the United States. I inquired about the work histories of women as well as of men. I also gathered basic data such as date and place of birth, marriage, and death.

Sonorans themselves readily recognized key socioeconomic distinctions. In farming, for instance, they quickly differentiated cattle ranches from small plots for planting accompanied by a few head of cattle in pasture. They also distinguished landownership, sharecropping, and day labor. Likewise, in terms of urban occupations, people differentiated supervisors and supervised, white collar and blue collar, and owners (such as small workshops) versus employees.

Using the base chronologies as guides, I then collected open-ended oral life histories from selected members of the grand-families. My criterion in selecting informants was to obtain histories from both genders and each adult generation of these families. This included the young people now working in the border factories. The topics discussed included youth, family of orientation, work experiences, migratory experiences (both in Mexico and the United States), marriage and family of procreation, housework, housing, material culture, politics, and general perceptions of the world. Some interviews were tape-recorded, and others were set within more informal conversations, but the informants were always informed of the purpose and potential uses of the interviews. All the interviews in Agua Prieta were in Spanish (some interviews done in Douglas were in English). All of the direct quotes are minimally edited from tape-recorded and transcribed interviews; the translations into English are my own.

I collected basic information about the kindred surrounding these core families, a very large number of persons, from key informants who were the eldest, apical women and men in these families. I inquired about their children, grandchildren, great-grandchildren, parents and grandparents (when they remembered), parents' siblings, parents' siblings' children (first cousins), sometimes (when they knew) first cousins' children, their own siblings, their siblings' children (nephews and nieces), and any of their children if they knew them. For each of these people I also asked about the spouses so that I had information on the occupations of women's husbands or men's wives. Since I did this for kin on both the wife's and husband's sides, I assembled twelve kindreds in all. The inquiries about residence and occupation paralleled the chronologies described above, though in less detail.

These kindred charts were not flawless, but I had the chance to check on kin living in Douglas and Agua Prieta and I found consistent confirmation. One should not underestimate the kinship knowledge of the elderly women who are the synapses of family communication. There were gaps, areas of absent knowledge, that were themselves useful social facts (as discussed below).

I collected household incomes and budgets (as well as appliance histories described below) for each of the core households, and selected branch households of the grand-families. My wife and I visited these families frequently; at times I was able to visit each family weekly. The core households of the grandparents were centers for family visiting and interchange. They were effective bases for making the acquaintance of the entire family.

The names used in the family histories are pseudonyms; these people would be readily recognizable to local residents of Douglas and Agua Prieta on the basis of the details I provide. I have therefore used discretion in reporting private and potentially embarrassing items, even when at certain points it would clarify events in the family history. There are, at any rate, few such cases.

The family and individual histories here are my synthesis and are largely presented in my own words, rather than through narratives by my informants. I collected and weighed many sources of evidence about each family. I used versions of the same events from men and women, older and younger people, and people with very diverse viewpoints, experiences, and interests. In response to the inevitable partiality of oral history, I followed Peter Winn's (1979) advice that oral sources have to be read critically, with an understanding of the particular point of view, just as if they were documentary sources.

A life history interview is carried out in some present moment, never in the past to which it ostensibly refers. Recent attention in anthropology has centered on the interview as a meaningful construction of the past for the purposes of the present (Langness and Frank, 1981). Another question, equally present-centered, has received less attention: How did the informants, through a sequence of historical happenstance, realignments, commitments, and abandonments, come to live in the place, the manner, and the relationships they now find themselves? I find myself more interested in the logic of events than in the construction of meaning, though both sides of oral remembrance can be found at various points in this book.

I have attempted to treat the family histories (given the limits of a chapter-by-chapter presentation) as analytical subjects in themselves, set within the context of a larger historical framework. This can be contrasted with using case studies as illustrations of generalizations derived by other means. The virtue of this strategy is that it diminishes the problem of representativeness. Whereas particularistic life history data offer only examples of uncertain validity for macrohistorical generalizations, they form a rich and powerful body of data for cause and effect in lives of small groups of people. This approach concentrates attention on the analytical problem of sequences of events in people's lives, rather than positing "stages" that a working class has to go through (Rosaldo, 1980).

There are two strategies for presenting change across time. It can be presented as a sequence of period after discrete period. But these are human lives, after all, which do not come to an end at the demarcations of historical periods. We can think of change between periods as major rearrangements of ongoing human groups. Our attention will be directed to the times when people move from one place and social order to another, rather than moments typically in the middle of periods; evidence will be found in the redistributions of kin and reorganization of men and women, or of parents and children.

I used four major methods to analyze the individual and family histories: key junctures and alternatives; distinguishing between life cycle and historical time; the branching patterns seen in bilateral kindreds; and the analysis of gender and productive activities. The rationale for the method of key junctures is described above.

Key junctures are defined as historical and personal events that confront the existing arrangement of people's lives; they may bring about a patterned return to an older way of life, or they may force a break with the past. Some examples of historical key junctures are loss of land in the late nineteenth century, the construction of giant mines and smelters, mass layoffs of miners, the 1929–1935 repatriation, the post–1940 reopening of U.S. immigration, and the beginning of the maquiladora program. Some examples of personal key junctures are neolocal marriage and household formation, maturing of children (either possible continuation of education or entry into the labor force), partible inheritance at the death of the father, widow/orphanhood, individual job loss, and cessation of a migratory trip (for example, deportation of an undocumented entrant from the United States).

One of the valuable results of using key junctures is that it realistically keeps the stream of industrial working people in Sonora and Arizona in close contact with other classes. This is because these nearby classes are alternatives that can happen within one's own life or among close relatives. Specific types of alternatives used to analyze family histories include rural northeastern Sonora, where rural production (peasants and ranchers) is combined with external wage labor as a temporary or periodic resource; mine towns, which are centers of male employment, some business opportunities for women, and good places for consumer goods; the border cities of the United States and Mexico, also wage and consumer centers; and the giant agro-industrial cities of Sonora, Baja California, Arizona, and "Alta" (U.S.) California, which can be both end points of long-term family proletarianization and attractive places for temporary labor migration. An important question is whether people move along a gradient tilted toward the U.S. border that is composed of wages/cash income, manufactured goods (both consumer goods and work skills), and national citizenship.

One cannot do life histories without some concept of a culturally patterned sequence of life stages. In anthropology, this has come out of Meyer Fortes's (1949) idea of the "developmental cycle" of domestic groups, which is usually inferred from synchronic distributions and applied as if it were constantly recurring. In the situation of nonrecurrent change, we need to distinguish "life-cycle time" and "historical time" methodologically while combining both in order to analyze life histories (Elder, 1978; Hareven, 1982). In addition,

Roger Sanjek (1983) has pointed out that men and women have very different developmental cycles, even though they are linked in the cycle of the domestic group. In order to understand, therefore, the significance of actions and alternatives in the life history, it will be necessary to delineate both the particular problems posed by the historical context and the life stages of the persons involved.

The analysis of kinship is one of the most powerful tools anthropologists have for discovering the workings of different social orders. In *Pul Eliya* (1961), Sir Edmund Leach shows how kinship is created over time by recognizing or losing ties, and the basis of this process lies in organizing access to resources. Leach specifically treats formal, named groups in a situation of controlling access to land and water. But his insight that "kin" are created and lost over time remains very useful for urban workers, producers, and consumers. They do not control most major resources, and may not form named kinship groups, but these people do align themselves informally to pull each other into institutions (corporate employment offices; the U.S. Immigration and Naturalization Service) where resources are controlled.

The analysis of kinship data starts by looking at the distribution of branches in the kindred (descendants of siblings, or, more broadly, of cousins). The distribution was categorized among the several alternative socioeconomic locations summarized above. The instances of branching were studied in particular historical contexts. For example, a set of siblings at the turn of the century confronted two alternative paths: mine labor markets (in both nations) versus small landholding with access to community resources. The "splits," the lines of division of kindred branches, represent the movement of persons at this period between two possible economies.

One productive approach to kinship analysis takes advantage of the problem of missing kin information. The assumption was that up-to-date kin knowledge is distributed according to who was relevant to the informant in a specific resource context.[2] Therefore, losing track of particular lines of descendants and keeping up with others, or absence of detailed knowledge about persons (their names, children, jobs, properties), was used as evidence about periods in history when the kin branches split into different locations or economies.

Women's housework in border regions of Mexico has not been "traditional" for nearly a century. It was transformed by stoves and sewing machines—manufactured goods purchased with cash—just as paid work was transformed by industrial technologies. Widows, the victims of the early industrial economy, were motivators and carriers of new technologies through their own businesses and the skills they taught their daughters.

Unpaid labor in the life histories can be studied as a sequence of changes just like wage labor; both are integral parts of the ethnography of working people (Tilly and Scott, 1978). Even in the most completely wage-earning settings, not all activities are bought and sold (Bennholdt-Thomsen, 1984). Households that receive an input of wages must also have persons performing tasks that "reproduce" (Rapp, 1983) the household and its workers, such as caring for children, feeding workers, gathering gossip information, and otherwise making useful the hard cash or purchased commodities that workers bring in. Men do some reproductive work, such as house repair, but by far the greatest amount of work is done by women, for reasons explored by Maureen Mackintosh (1984).

But how do we reconstruct the hidden labor history of housewives? One method was "histories" of appliances in people's houses.[3] Talking about stoves and sewing machines sparked lengthy reminiscences. Even more important, it exposed the unpaid work activities that accompanied these appliances.

I selected a set of major material possessions. These included stove; refrigerator; washing machine; sewing machine; kitchen, living room, and bedroom furniture; television and radio; car or truck; men's tools; and the house. One set of questions I asked focused on how the items were acquired—price, credit arrangements, purchase on the U.S. or Mexican side, gifts. This addressed consumption and the relationship to the wage economy. I asked the date and occasion (e.g., marriage) on which the item was obtained. This could be coordinated with the chronology of jobs and migration, as well as with domestic cycles. (I asked similar questions about a selected set of displayed pictures, mementos, and religious objects.)

Another major set of questions was who used the object, how it was used, and who owned it. This addressed the labor activities of the household, in particular the assignment of objects and operations by gender. I asked what was the first example of that type of item the person used, and how he or she learned to use it (including who taught him or her). These questions provided valuable information about gender-based learning. Appliance histories helped date the earliest use of purchased commodities when I discussed the items used by (and sometimes inherited from) the parents of my oldest informants.

Underlying the appliance histories is a concept of items as purchased material culture. The virtue of thinking of manufactured items as material culture is that it directs our attention to the practical uses, bodies of knowledge, and symbolism of these objects, issues that come together in analyzing the connection between material goods and gender. The term "consumption" implies a passive view—objects coming in—while "material culture" implies a positive concern with the activities and skills associated with objects.

INTRODUCTION TO THE BORDER

My wife and I were well-treated Anglo American guests while living in Mexico. This was a curious situation, for, as I have said, the border is basically a power relationship. Our hosts were well aware of the many divisions and inequalities between the United States and Mexico. Indeed, they knew the United States from several sides. At times it was fulfilling, both materially and in terms of life courses that demand periods of migration north of the border. Yet they also knew that they might have to cross into the United States outside of the law and, once there, they might be looked down on.

The usual manner of defusing the tensions involved in this situation was a structure of cordial, public visiting and formal provision of information. But sometimes feelings broke out in expressive language and culture. I spent much time practicing with a local amateur baseball team. At the end of the long afternoon, the group of men started to tease me in a good-natured way. They accused me of being a *mojado* (illegal alien) inside Mexico (in fact, my immigration status was proper). Later, they pretended to escape across the nearby border fence while making rude gestures at an imaginary Border Patrol. These were young men, all prime candidates for undocumented immigration, several of whom had told me of their times spent north of the border. People in Mexico, I realized, live out their lives in a profound tension with the United States.

2. Historical Synopsis of Northeastern Sonora and the U.S.–Mexican Border, 1886–1986

REGIONAL DEFINITION

Northeastern Sonora is demarcated by the Sierra Madre Occidental to the east, the district of Sahuaripa to the south, the Rio San Miguel to the west, and the U.S.–Mexican border to the north. Small rural settlements are irrigated by the upper Yaqui, Moctezuma, Bavispe, Fronteras, and upper Sonora rivers, which tend to run along north–south axes (Map 2.1).

The regional form of northeastern Sonora was strengthened by the industrial economy (Map 2.2). It was isolated from the rest of Sonora and the Mexican nation as a whole, and turned northward toward the United States. The alignment of railroads was crucial: One line ran directly from Agua Prieta to Nacozari; the other ran from the border at Naco to Cananea. Though a link was added from the latter to the main west coast trunk line, both roads directed traffic to the border. Each railhead pulled ore and cattle from farther within highland Sonora, and in turn provisioned the interior with imported consumer goods. Douglas—a U.S. city—became the keystone of this small corner of Mexico. Charles Gildersleeve's research on commercial geography shows that Douglas had a trade zone extending far into northern Sonora, surprisingly farther than larger border centers such as Nogales, Arizona (1978:199). I was repeatedly struck by how strongly northeastern Sonorans of all classes were oriented to Douglas; the historian Ramón E. Ruíz (1988) emphasizes the combined power of economic and psychological dependency over Sonora.

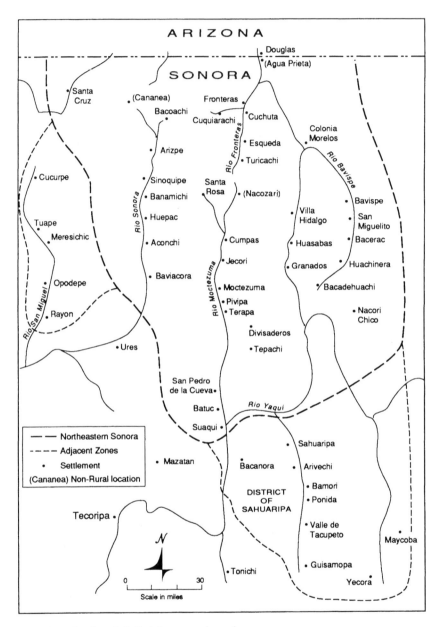

Map 2.1. Regional definition: rural settlements

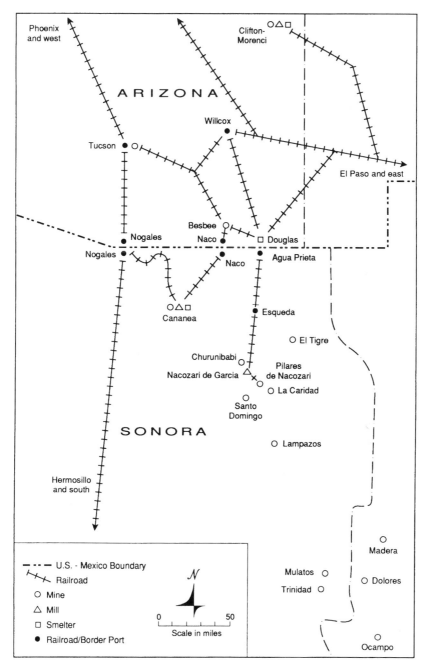

Phoenix and west

Clifton-Morenci ○△□

ARIZONA

Willcox

Tucson ●○

El Paso and east

Besbee ○

Nogales ●

Naco ●

□ Douglas

Nogales ●

Naco ●

Agua Prieta ●

○△□
Cananea

Esqueda ●

○ El Tigre

Churunibabi ○

Pilares
de Nacozari

Nacozari de Garcia △

○ La Caridad

○
Santo
Domingo

○ Lampazos

SONORA

Hermosillo
and south

○
Madera

Mulatos ○

○ Dolores

Trinidad ○

--- U.S. - Mexico Boundary

Railroad

○ Mine

△ Mill

□ Smelter

● Railroad/Border Port

N

0   50
Scale in miles

○
Ocampo

Map 2.2. Industrial complex: copper mines, railroads, and border ports

The south-to-north shape of the region helped determine the movements of people that are the subject of this book. The bonds between northeastern Sonora and southeastern Arizona, focused on Tucson, are especially intimate. Economic and human ties also link this hidden mountain region with the great farms and cities developed, with the aid of irrigation water, in the low deserts of the United States and Mexico: Phoenix, Los Angeles, Mexicali, and Tijuana, and the Sonoran coast of the Gulf of California (Fernández, 1989:Chapter 2).

NORTHEASTERN SONORA BEFORE THE 1880s

Selected aspects of history before the 1880s are helpful in understanding the antecedents of northern Sonora's industrial revolution. The Opata, an Uto–Aztecan people, and affiliated groups inhabited northeastern Sonora, and many current rural settlements are derived from Opata towns of the Jesuit era. The Opata have disappeared as a recognized group (Johnson, 1950; Hinton, 1959, 1976; Owen, 1959; Spicer, 1962). Their descendants now partake in northern Mexican mestizo culture.

The Opata were missionized by Europeans in the mid seventeenth century. Thomas Sheridan (1988:7–8) suggests that the Jesuits sheltered and probably strengthened community-bounded land tenure. Cynthia Radding de Murrieta argues that beginning with the orders of Juan de Galvez (1769) to split up lands, and culminating in the 1828 state law to individualize titles, a sustained assault on the holdings of former mission communities brought about the first steps of the Opata move toward mestizo identity (1984:80; see also Quijada, 1985:67–69). Their homes were overrun by outsiders in the mid eighteenth century. Edward Spicer writes that "no important part of Eudeve or Opata territory was without Spanish inhabitants" (1962:97; see also Radding, 1981; Balmori, Voss, and Wortman, 1984:83–84; Escandón, 1985:264–267).

Many "outsiders" retreated from Sonora when Apache warfare worsened after Mexican independence in 1821, exacerbated by state civil wars and the war of the French Intervention (Balmori, Voss, and Wortman, 1984:94–100). As the Apache threat gradually weakened in the 1870s and 1880s, nonindigenes surged back to the Sonoran highlands, again implanting ranches on community lands (see Dunnigan, 1969:42–43, 49–52, on the Pima Indian areas of Yecora and

Maycoba). Aleŝ Hrdliĉka (1904) found that in the San Miguel River valley the Opata did not wish to distinguish themselves or speak the language; his visit in 1902 (Hinton, 1983) coincides with the time when rural Sonorans were leaving for the mines. The relationship between industrialization and the change from Opata to mestizo cultural identity remains unknown, but there is no question that the uprooting of Opata communities and the influx of fortune-seeking mestizos contributed to the potential for a wage-earning population in Sonora.[1]

Twentieth-century Sonoran working people retained substantial European legacies in the cultural repertoire that Jesuit missionaries and secular ranchers and miners had brought to the area (following Spicer, 1962; 1969). These included reallocation of tasks in agricultural work between men and women; the complex of cattle herding, horsemanship, and masculinity; and a distinctly Mexican tradition of prospecting and mining technology. Each of these will be discussed at length in subsequent chapters.

IMMIGRATION AND LABOR IN EARLY INDUSTRIAL ARIZONA

The Gadsden Purchase of 1853 severed the geographic unity of southern Arizona and Sonora (see Officer, 1987). It lopped Tucson, the northernmost Hispanic settlement of Sonora, from the rest of the state, and placed a border directly in the midst of Sonora's Apache frontier. The placement of an east–west international boundary across the north–south routes from Sonora to Arizona had two consequences. The northward movement of population would continue, aided by the gradual military defeat of the Apache— around four thousand persons came from Mexico to Tucson in the twenty years between 1860 and 1880 (Sheridan, 1986:76–77). As Arizona's industrial economy developed, it would draw on the natural connection of northern Sonora and southern Arizona. But this was now an international immigration, even if not at first very closely watched; and so over time Sonora and Arizona would diverge through formal citizenship with entailed residence rights.

One of the legacies of the Mexican–American War era was a strong, bitter sense of nationalism and distrust of the United States among Sonorans, reinforced by a series of filibuster invasions, gunboat incidents, and speculation about yet more territorial takeovers during the 1850s and 1860s (Park, 1961). Mexican nationalism would reappear in subsequent decades, though the issues would shift from territory to the privileged treatment of Americans in Sonora.

Industrial development of the U.S. side of the border initiated social change in northern Sonora before industry came to that area itself. Americans wanted a cheap labor force, and railroads and the opening of the Arizona–Sonora frontier made it possible for Sonorans to respond. The use of electrical wire during the 1870s created a large demand for copper, which previously had been secondary to gold and silver. Improvements in copper concentrating and smelting permitted the mining of massive amounts of low-grade ores; this in turn moved work organization from skillful extraction of good ores by experienced crews (often Mexicans) toward highly engineered mines with huge, mainly unskilled labor forces.

In Arizona, the composition of the labor force was determined region by region according to the balance of a three-cornered battle involving copper companies, Anglo American miners, and Mexican miners (including Americans of Hispanic ancestry) who were paid the bottom tier of a "dual wage." The mine companies imported Mexicans district by district to undercut the power of Anglo miners; Anglos tried to exclude Mexican workers; and Mexicans, the weakest in terms of formal power, moved from mine to mine and staged independent strikes. The result was that the southeastern zone of Arizona, especially Douglas (located, not coincidentally, on the border), Clifton–Morenci, and to a lesser extent Bisbee, were heavily staffed by workers of Mexican extraction (Park, 1961; also see Barrera, 1979; Byrkit, 1982). Other economic sectors in Arizona— cotton farming and railroads—employed similar labor strategies (see Sheridan, 1986, on railroads and the urban labor market of Tucson).

Railroads, which linked the interior of Mexico to networks crossing the western United States, were the single most important factor initiating Mexican labor immigration, according to Lawrence Cardoso (1980). In 1882, the Southern Pacific crossed the border at Nogales. Two branch lines, one leading Sonorans to Bisbee and the other to Douglas and points north, were added by 1904. Railroad construction within Mexico pulled workers away from haciendas and sharecropping by offering higher wages, paid in cash, while making further movement toward the U.S. border much easier. At the border, Mexican immigrants were met by employment agencies or corporate recruiters, many of them seeking track crews for the vast

U.S. West. After spreading through the rail network, laborers abandoned track crews in great numbers because of low pay, hard work, and poor living conditions (García, 1981).

The U.S. border was open during this entire period. Before 1917 there were no significant requirements to immigrate from Mexico, and even after 1917 legal immigration was quite simple: Immigrants from Mexico needed two copies of birth and marriage certificates, a certificate of good conduct, good health, and a fee of eight dollars—eighteen dollars after 1924. The 1924 National Origins Act that blunted European immigration did not include the Western Hemisphere within its restrictive quota system. Entry without even these nominal papers was little constrained—the Border Patrol was created in 1924 to prevent Chinese immigration through Mexico—and those who were caught were asked to pay their fees and reenter legally. It was only in 1929 that visas were severely restricted and border enforcement was strengthened (Hoffman, 1974).

PORFIRIAN SONORA: 1883–1910

In Mexican history the presidency of Porfirio Díaz witnessed the rapid development of mines and railroads, and forceful encroachment on older land and resource rights. In Sonora, a series of related events in the 1880s opened the state for industrialization. The end of the Apache wars, conventionally marked by Geronimo's surrender in 1886, brought to an end the frontier violence that had blocked development and the free movement of people. The twenty-seven-year rule, beginning in 1883, of the Porfirian governors Luis Emeterio Torres, Ramón Corral, and Rafael Izabal provided Sonora with the administrative power and legal chicanery needed to start growth. In 1884, for example, a wide-open mine law initiated a massive mineral boom. In 1883 the Southern Pacific had completed the first section of the Mexican west coast trunk line, increasing the commerce and cash circulating within the state. In this book the year 1886 represents the start of a distinctive epoch that has continued, in mutated form, through the present.

With the open approval of governors Torres, Corral, and Izabal, foreign and domestic speculators claimed huge tracts of minerals, pasture, water, and timber, thus breaking land rights of communities or groups of heirs. The national "Ley Lerda," providing for the individualization of title to corporately held land, was passed in

1856, but the brunt of its application occurred late in the nineteenth century. Alejandro Figueroa lists the towns in the Sonoran sierra that were affected by this law; they comprise the vast majority of important rural municipalities (1985:156). Though the mechanism for distributing titles seemingly was fair, Figueroa found that if indigenous inhabitants were even mentioned in land records, it was to complain that they were not getting their proper share.

North Americans were a major motivating force in land expropriation. Mine operators needed water and timber, while cattle producers found a growing export market to the United States after 1900 (Ruíz, 1988:134, 141–142). William C. Greene assembled 440,000 acres of grassy pastures and timbered ranges around his mine at Cananea. Part of the ranch came from the Pesqueira estate, from which the mines had been purchased. Greene also used the land claims process to pressure the descendants of frontier military colonist José María Arvallo to sell the land grant "Ojo de Agua." This gave Greene's companies control over the bountiful spring that was the source of the Río Sonora. Partly diverted from farming villages along the river, Ojo de Agua provided 1.5 million gallons a day to the mine and town of Cananea. Similarly, Greene claimed thirty-seven units of the land grant given to the community dwellers of Santa Cruz; he obtained over five thousand hectares from them (Aguirre, 1958:30–32, 117–118, 166–169; Sonnichsen, 1974:98; Gracida, 1985:48; Peña and Chávez, 1985:276). Phelps Dodge supplied meat to its company store at Nacozari, and Ramón E. Ruíz cites several other American-owned ranches adjacent to the principal mines (1988:136ff.; see also Radding, 1985:275).

Mexican-owned estates in the northern districts of Arizpe and Moctezuma boomed during the Porfiriato because of commerce in wheat, flour milling, and cattle, first to Arizona and then to Sonora's own expanding economy (Gracida, 1985:45; Balmori, Voss, and Wortman, 1984:109–110). Ironically, the internal boom of rural Sonora placed more pressure on peasants rather than bettering their livelihoods.

The Sonoran peasant economy is based on a triangle of resources: river-bottom farmland, water for irrigation, and extensive, low-quality upland cattle pastures. Rights to water and pastures were attacked during the Porfirian boom. Grazing more cattle, ranchers used legal claims and barbed wire to encroach on community pasture, a process that Thomas Sheridan found had occurred in

Cucurpe (1988:21). For sparse, scattered resources like pastures, peasants relied on open, shared access. Fencing made villagers' small herds of cattle less viable. Small farmers who had lost access to irrigation water or river-bottom lands were forced to plant rain-fed plots in ravines. These were much more vulnerable to dry years in this desert zone. A stroke of bad luck meant that families would have to leave the land.

The large ranches did not replace the rural livelihoods they took away. Only ninety full-time cowboys worked on the nearly half-million acres of the Cananea Cattle Company; added seasonal laborers brought the maximum to two hundred men (Peña and Chávez, 1985:275). The effects of the Porfirian boom on other rural occupations are ambiguous. As the frontier was closed, land was fenced; and, herds of feral cattle and horses finished off, the skills of the Sonoran frontiersman were no longer in demand: hunters and rustlers of wild cattle, horse breakers, gold prospectors, Apache fighters. Mule and horse teamsters were alternately encouraged and displaced by industrial development. They were in demand for hauling supplies and ore for early mines; Henry León of Douglas recalled hearing that his grandfather drove a horse carriage between Cumpas, Sonora, and Tombstone, Arizona, key towns at the very beginning of the mine boom (interview, Douglas, January 16, 1986). However, the railroad from Agua Prieta to Nacozari caused the disappearance of carriages, teamsters, and blacksmiths in the Fronteras area (Aguilar Camín, 1977:98). The Cananea–Naco railroad replaced nine hundred horse teams in 1902 (Sonnichsen, 1974:75).

On the whole, many rural Sonoran farmers and frontiersmen lost their livelihoods—or were subject to greater pressures and risks—while mines opened on both sides of the border, and industrial jobs beckoned. A population was available locally for the labor market.

INDUSTRIAL MINES IN SONORA

Sonorans had always been miners. The nature of the occupation changed dramatically around the turn of the century, however. The older tradition of mining had concentrated on silver; it was small scale (as late as 1894, the average number of miners per mine was ninety-two); and it was centered in the Alamos district in the far south of the state. Then the market for silver collapsed and was supplanted by copper. Copper was mined in bulk; it employed a mass labor force; and its extraction mostly took place in the northeastern corner of the state. Copper brought with it a true industrial working class.

Sonoran mining, especially large- and medium-scale mining, shifted from domestic to foreign, mostly American, ownership; Sonora received 7.3 percent of the foreign investment in Mexico during the Porfiriato, ranking it third among states and making a particularly dramatic impact on this sparsely settled frontier (Bernstein, 1964:27–28; Gracida, 1985:39–41, 92; Figueroa, 1985:154).

Nacozari, located due south of Agua Prieta, eventually came to be the major Sonoran operation of Phelps Dodge, the firm that already dominated Arizona copper production. The mine, located high in the mountains at Pilares de Nacozari, was linked by narrow-gauge railway to the mill, concentrator, and company stores at Nacozari de García, and thence by standard railroad to the U.S. smelter. When Pilares de Nacozari reached full operation in 1905, the mine alone employed two thousand workers (Leland, 1930:2–3; Bernstein, 1964:59–60; Gracida, 1985:92).

Nacozari, as a railhead, mill, and supply center, stimulated other mines in the region: Lampazos, Churunibabi, Santo Domingo, Transvaal Copper in Cumpas, and the rich silver–copper–gold mine at El Tigre, bought by the Lucky Tiger Gold mining company of Kansas City in 1902 and employing roughly seven hundred men (Bernstein, 1964:70–71).

The railroad line linking Arizona to Nacozari was started in 1900 and completed in 1904. Where the railroad crossed into Mexico, the town of Agua Prieta grew to serve customs and export businesses, and as a bedroom community for workers in the smelters across the international boundary. Two smelters were built (starting in 1901) at Douglas, one for Phelps Dodge, serving Nacozari and Bisbee, and the other for the Calumet and Arizona Company, also of Bisbee. Together they employed seventeen hundred men in 1913 (Dumke, 1948; Jeffrey, 1951).

Cananea, which lies to the southwest of Agua Prieta, had long been exploited as an ore field. Its modern era dates to 1896, when it was purchased and developed by the famous (or infamous) speculator William C. Greene. By 1907 Greene had lost control of the mine to Rockefeller-backed interests that became Anaconda; his family, however, kept the surrounding ranch. The Four C's (Cananea Consolidated Copper Company) by 1907 had installed, expanded, and rebuilt several multilevel mines, a mill, a concentrator, and a smelter, all at Cananea, as well as a railroad spur to the nearby U.S. border port at Naco, adjacent to Bisbee. The mines were in full production by 1903, and had 5,360 Mexican and 2,200 foreign (American) employees in 1906—without exaggeration, a massive installation.

Cananea is famous in Mexican history because of a strike in 1906 that was one of the direct antecedents of the Mexican Revolution. The central issue in the strike was pay scales that gave Mexican workers less than comparable American employees. Because the Sonoran state governor allowed Greene to bring armed irregulars from Bisbee into Mexico, the strike focused nationalistic discontent against the United States on Mexico's own subservient regime (Aguirre, 1958; Bernstein, 1964; Cockcroft, 1968; Sonnichsen, 1974; Meyer et al., 1980; Ruíz, 1988).

Mine cities, large by the scale of the era, were injected into a thinly populated frontier where the Spanish tradition of urban life had barely survived in the defensive walls around town or ranch center. In 1891, Cananea had 891 people; in 1901, 3,500; and in 1910, 14,800 people lived there, when it was the largest city in the state. Nacozari, which in 1900 was a prospectors' camp so small it was not censused, by 1910 had four thousand people—a figure, I suspect, that does not include the separate mine site of Pilares de Nacozari (Aguilar Camín, 1977:111–113).

The change was qualitative as well as quantitative, for the mine towns were completely new settlements in different places from the villages whose names they took. Nacozari Viejo (Old Nacozari) lay at the base of the mountains, where the Río Moctezuma disgorged; the developers of the copper mine decided in 1895 to relocate to a gold-washing camp, Placeritos, closer to the ore body. This became the city of Nacozari de García. Pilares de Nacozari was entirely new, a planned town in the mountain heights above the mine head. Corporate Cananea sprawled on top of the famous mesa, mentioned in song, while below, Cananea Viejo became a refuge for disabled and retired miners, small prospectors, and other working people marginal to the mine itself.

The new settlements, except for the border town of Agua Prieta, were company towns. Cananea was owned by Cananea Realty Co., whose 90 percent owner was William Greene, and which was chartered for virtually all functions, including land, transportation, water, factories, and hotels. The Cananea Cattle Company controlled roads and permission to travel, as well as the slaughterhouse and the meat supply; the bank was the Cananea Mercantile Bank; and the largest store by far was the Cananea company store (Aguirre, 1958:36ff., 157; Ruíz, 1988:77). Phelps Dodge's control of Nacozari did not differ except in detail. Douglas, though not a formal company-owned town, was controlled by real estate speculators who were Phelps Dodge company executives and their insider friends (Jeffrey, 1951).

Before the 1910 revolution, mine companies controlled the political and civic life of these cities by paying the salaries and costs of municipal government, specifically law and education, the key institutions of social control (Ruíz, 1988:80–83). The Lucky Tiger Mining Company (El Tigre) received its mining concession in exchange for paying the costs of the town school and police force, and a similar agreement was made with Phelps Dodge at Nacozari— agreements that made sense for towns in remote places but had the obvious effect of tying municipality to management (Aguilar Camín, 1977:113). The first mayors of Cananea were chief officials of the company, and Greene cultivated relations with erstwhile independent Mexican officials (see Balmori, Voss, and Wortman, 1984).

Company stores were overpowering commercial intrusions relative to the existing scale of highland Sonora. The Cananea company store had sales of 145,000 pesos, compared with 20,000 by its nearest competitor; Phelps Dodge Mercantile in Pilares and Nacozari de García had annual sales of 30,000 pesos versus 8,000 of the next firm; and that of the Lucky Tiger Mining Company in El Tigre sold 25,000 pesos versus 2,100 (Aguilar Camín, 1977:114–115). Stocked almost entirely from across the border, these stores were important conduits for North American material culture.

NORTHEASTERN SONORA IN THE MEXICAN REVOLUTION

The Mexican Revolution, which lasted from 1910 to 1920, was caused by increasingly closed circles of leadership in Porfirian Mexico, the assault on well-understood rights (especially land), and the activation of society by rapid economic change. The events of the revolution were complex, and took place region by region. Sonora was one of the critical areas in the revolution, and the men who ultimately triumphed over the nation as a whole—Alvaro Obregón,

Plutarco Elías Calles, and Adolfo de la Huerta—came from this state.

The Sonoran leadership was connected, sometimes marginally, to elite families—Maytorena, Elías Calles, Obregón Salcido, Bonillas, and Pesqueira, among others (see Aguilar Camín, 1977; Balmori, Voss, and Wortman, 1984). It was not a unified clique; bitter personal rivalries culminated in an internal war for Sonora between Plutarco Elías Calles and José María Maytorena, allied with Obregón and Pancho Villa, respectively, at the national level. These men concentrated on shattering the political monopoly of Porfirio Díaz's clique and replacing it with themselves. Their proposals for social reform were limited to the distribution of unused land to promote private agriculture and the arbitration of disputes between labor and capital (Ruíz, 1976).

The common people of northeastern Sonora were an important source of armed men. At the very earliest stages of the revolution, rebel bands formed from the heterogeneous population of early industrial Sonora—miners, farm villagers, prospectors, cowboys, teamsters, and bandits from desert interstices. Constant movement of laborers between Sonora and Arizona made Mexican neighborhoods in Arizona, including Douglas, bases for recruitment and operations.

Yet we cannot say that Sonoran workers fought as a class; rather, they seem to have split into groups following various revolutionary chieftains. For example, while Maytorena offered to support the miners of Cananea after Calles sent three hundred troops to repress strikes in 1914 (Aguilar Camín, 1977:407), Calles drew on miners of Pilares de Nacozari and their kin in nearby peasant villages in the Batallón Pilares. The absence of a popular program in the Sonoran part of the revolution at a time when there was considerable mine labor unrest and unofficial seizures of land in highland Sonora points out the need to examine working-class politics in terms of specific instances of recruitment. (The Batallón Pilares is discussed in Chapter 3.)

Civilians, especially residents of rural towns, fled the revolution and its side effects by going to mine centers and U.S. border cities. The oral history of Río Sonora villagers assembled by Cynthia Radding (1985:265–266) testifies to terror by bands of wandering hungry soldiers, combined with natural disaster in the form of floods in 1914. The later years of the revolution—1916 and 1917—saw outright starvation and smallpox epidemics in the Sahuaripa district (and presumably elsewhere). During the last years of the revolution there were frequent reports of uncultivated lands in highland Sonora (Radding, 1985:274).

Inflation and food shortages plagued the mine cities, but with a few interruptions by blockading armies, Sonoran copper production remained strong from 1910 to 1919 (Bernstein, 1964). Copper miners stayed in place, and refugees from the countryside streamed into the work force. Therefore the formative working population, which had started in a migratory flux, began to crystallize in the neighborhoods and workplaces of Sonoran mine cities during the revolutionary decade. It was also in this decade, Cardoso argues, that a permanent Mexican American population coalesced in the U.S.–side border cities (1980:49).

Miners' attempts to form labor unions increased in tempo because of the combination of permanent residence, inflation, and revolutionary inspiration. In June 1911 a wave of strikes brought the first real improvements for Cananea workers: the reduction of the workday to nine hours and a pay raise to 3.50 pesos daily (Bernstein, 1964:98–101). An attempt to form a radical miners' union in Cananea was repressed in 1912 by Sonoran revolutionary leaders who were more interested in taxes from copper mines and help in smuggling munitions from U.S. corporations, but the workers did obtain free water, cheaper rent, and contributions to a workers' hospital (Radding, 1985:245).

THE 1920S

World War I was a tremendous boon for the metal industries. After the war ended, U.S. copper companies unloaded their stocks, causing a short but severe depression from 1919 to 1921. Cananea and Nacozari were closed for a year and a half in 1921 and 1922, and the two smelters at Douglas (which had been hiring in Mexico as recently as 1918) closed for nine months. El Tigre stayed open but cut wages (Jeffrey, 1951:111–113; Bernstein, 1964:130–133). As if massive layoffs were not bad enough, during these years (1918–1920) the Spanish flu epidemic hit Sonora, with particular virulence in the crowded and war-torn towns of the northeast.

After 1922, copper production recovered only among the industrial producers; small mines either fluctuated with the production of minor minerals (fluorite, antimony, manganese) or suffered a sustained decline in silver prices. The disappearing small mines had been important sources of intermittent cash wages for the dozens of peasant municipalities in which they were scattered. Now the wage economy was strong only in the major mines and their border ports (Ramírez, León, and Conde, 1985:19–25). The 1920s culminated the tendency toward consolidation of the urban working class that had begun during the revolution. The unionism that arose in the 1930s had its first stirrings in cultural associations of the 1920s, about which little is known.

Immigration to the United States was extensive during the 1920s. Cardoso estimates, for the statistics collected then were faulty, that approximately one million persons of Mexican origin were added to the permanent U.S. population; this does not include temporary immigrant workers (1980:94). Suddenly, in 1929, Mexicans were denied visas, until then easily gotten; Mexicans who had previously been welcomed to the United States as laborers were reclassified as "likely to become public charges" and thus not permissible immigrants. This action took place before the first signs of economic crisis (Hoffman, 1974:32). In the same year the Border Patrol was doubled in size and made effective. The year 1929 marks the end of the open period and the first steps toward border control.

THE 1930S: REPATRIATION, MINE CLOSINGS, LABOR UNIONS, LAND REDISTRIBUTION

The depression of the 1930s was a profoundly disruptive period in northern Sonora, with echoes lasting into the 1940s, 1950s, and even 1960s. There were four major processes at work: the repatriation of persons of Mexican origin from the United States; the closings of mines and massive layoffs in Sonora; the emergence of unions among the remaining miners; and the agrarian reform of the Cárdenas years. These processes were simultaneous and intertwined, but for the sake of clarity we must separate them and consider each in order.

The Great Depression witnessed a massive expulsion of persons of Mexican origin (some of them U.S. citizens, including the U.S.–born children of immigrants) from the United States to Mexico. The best estimate is that roughly half a million persons left through 1935 (Hoffman, 1974:126). At the beginning many families left because breadwinners lost their jobs. As the depression worsened in 1931 and 1932, a decentralized but vigorous campaign emerged in the United States that sought to expel the population of Mexican origin. A relatively small portion were legally deported, but most were coerced into "voluntarily" departing through various means, such as offering transportation to Mexico while simultaneously threatening to cut families off the aid rolls in the United States. After repatriates had left the U.S. side, the new visa policy prevented former residents without citizenship from returning (Hoffman, 1974).

Paul Taylor (1933:45–47), using official counts of existing visa bearers (and my interviews indicate that many persons left without registering), found that 17,760 persons arrived in Sonora during the years 1930–1932. Of these, 6,064 had come from Arizona and another 2,353 from California. Correspondingly, Arizona lost 18,520 repatriates, including the 6,000 who went to Sonora. These figures are a minimum estimate of "repatriates" to Sonora in this period because Taylor's evidence comes from only a part of the repatriation period and because of limits to the visa data.

Many Douglas families were repatriated in 1931 when the two existing smelters were merged into one under the aegis of Phelps Dodge. Only 450 workers were kept on; and though there is no number for those laid off (or "retired"), the total must have been over 1,000 (Jeffrey, 1951). Oral histories collected in Douglas repeatedly state that Phelps Dodge preferred to keep Anglo American workers and paid costs for workers of Mexican origin to depart (Heyman, 1986).

Mexico absorbed the influx of repatriates although its economy was equally depression-racked. The rural geographer Leslie Hewes (1935) found during his 1931 visit to Huepac, a typical highland valley municipality, that it was full of unemployed copper miners from Arizona idling about the main plaza. There were some agricultural colonies on the coast of Sonora sponsored by the state government. Many other repatriates hung about the severely depressed Sonoran mines, prospecting for gold, cutting firewood, and picking over spoil piles.

Within Sonora, miners and their families were subjected to mass expulsions that in their social effects closely resembled the international repatriation. With the exception of Cananea, the mines were emptied by the late 1940s. Copper's price began to fall in May

1930, and it remained depressed until 1937. Sonora's production in 1932 was one-sixth that of 1929. Phelps Dodge closed Nacozari on September 21, 1931. Altogether, 2,000 mine workers were fired; others lost their livelihoods in the commercial center of Nacozari de García. The magnitude of the exodus can be measured in the 6,800 railroad tickets distributed by Phelps Dodge; there were also workers who departed in other directions by mule train, provided by the company. The nearby El Tigre mine nearly closed in 1931, when half the work force was laid off. Its U.S. parent corporation "ate up" its capital, and finally abandoned it in 1938 to the labor union to be run as a cooperative, after which it died a slow death (Jeffrey, 1951:117; Bernstein, 1964:201–211; Ramírez, León, and Conde, 1985:58–62; Peña and Chávez, 1985:255).

Agua Prieta, though not a mine town, suffered a collapse in exports at the same time that men who had commuted to work in the Douglas smelters lost their jobs. In 1932 Agua Prieta shipped one-thirteenth the value of 1930; not only had copper fallen but a 1929 tariff effectively blocked cattle exports to the United States. The border ports recovered at the end of the decade.

Small mining and prospecting grew in the 1930s, for the obvious reason that many miners and repatriates had to scrape out a living. Some idea of the numbers of unemployed men wandering about the state might be gathered from the five thousand who joined the 1940 gold rush at El Mezquite, in the municipality of Cucurpe (Sheridan, 1983:218; interviews with Ramón Romero, Agua Prieta, 1984–1986). State and federal policies aimed to help prospectors: The Mexican government had been accumulating gold reserves since 1931, and large companies were pressed to open up tunnels and buy ore from small miners.

Phelps Dodge restarted Nacozari in 1937 with 1,500 men. Nacozari would remain open for twelve more years, then close for good in 1949. An exodus similar to the first was organized: 1,500 workers were laid off, indemnified, and transported out; up to 10,000 people exited, the entire town of Pilares de Nacozari was depopulated, and the houses were removed by the company. Smaller mines nearby—Santo Domingo and Churunibabi—disappeared within a few years. The last echo of the collapse that began in 1929 was heard in 1965, when the railroad branch from Agua Prieta to Nacozari was abandoned by the Southern Pacific to the Mexican national railroad;

most of the fifty-five workers were retired with compensation (Bernstein, 1964:241; interview with Ruben Villa, Agua Prieta, February 28, 1986).

Cananea, unlike the other mines, never completely closed, but more than half the labor force of 1,700 was laid off between 1930 and 1932 (Ramírez, León, and Conde, 1985:56–57, 59–62). Yet a curiously reversed strengthening of working-class institutions took place there. The union Nueva Orientación was formed in response to the first wave of layoffs during 1930, and it was successful in forcing the Cananea company to rearrange work to limit firings and to pay indemnities to those who did lose jobs. However, the company refused to recognize the union and instead created its own "white union." In 1932, political maneuvers by Sonoran governor Rodolfo Calles forced Nueva Orientación to merge with the "white union," forming the union Martires de 1906. The company finally signed a contract in July 1932.

While the Cananea union continued to fight local battles (they struck again in 1935 to insist on the rehiring of former employees), a national miners' union arose in the interior of Mexico. The Cananea local joined in 1936. Intervening in two strikes in 1936 and 1940, the government of President Lázaro Cárdenas firmly entrenched union power inside the mines (a closed-shop contract for the industry and significant wage improvements) while forcing the union to retreat from its goal of nationalizing the mines. Thus the government demonstrated that the union would be subservient to the political rulers of Mexico.

The local at Cananea, Section 65, remained relatively independent of the interference in the national miners' union by the Alemán (1946–1952) and subsequent administrations. However, municipal politics in Cananea has come under the control of union bosses acting through the PRI, and in the 1980s this brought serious conflicts with municipal candidates from left-wing parties. (This material is summarized from Bernstein, 1964; Besserer, Díaz, and Santana, 1980; Besserer, Novelo, and Sariego, 1983; Peña and Chávez, 1985).

Because research has concentrated on Cananea, little is known about the labor movement at Nacozari and other mines. Nacozari had a union, Sindicato de Obreros de Pilares, affiliated with the CROM labor confederation in the 1920s. This union was also energized by job cutbacks, and was able to block an initial closure attempt in 1930. However, in the very period when the Cananea labor movement consolidated itself, Nacozari was closed. In 1937, the re-opened Nacozari, Pilares, and Santo Domingo mines became part of the national miners' union. Ultimately all these sections disappeared.

A different sort of labor movement also arose in 1930s Sonora, based on unions of the unemployed in various guises—unions of *oficios varios* (diverse trades), firewood cutters, prospectors, and veterans of the revolution. At Cananea these groups arose, for example, in response to a deliberate company strategy of layoffs to cull those who would have to be paid silicosis indemnity. They engaged in a persistent conflict with the Cananea Cattle Company over access to firewood and gold placers on company lands. They participated in the ultimately successful struggle to force the expropriation of the Cananea ranches in 1958, though the activists were denied positions in the official lists of recipients (Peña and Chávez, 1985:273–279). Similar struggles with ranchers over public access were engaged in by a union of *oficios varios* in Depression-era Agua Prieta (interview with Trinidad Loreto, Agua Prieta, October 6, 1985). However, the labor movement of the unemployed faded as people moved into the booming border cities in the 1950s and 1960s.

Because laid-off miners and repatriates were shipped into the Sonoran countryside, it is important to learn about the economy of rural highland towns in the 1930s and beyond in order to interpret the alternatives they faced. Virtually every municipality in highland Sonora has some agrarian reform lands, many of them officially awarded in the 1930s and early 1940s (see the list in Sanderson, 1981). Histories of the upper Río Sonora valley indicate that haciendas which had owned great chunks of the irrigated river bottom had already been broken up or invaded late in the 1910s, and had essentially disappeared by the 1930s (Hewes, 1935; Simonelli, 1985; Valencia, 1986). But the questions of adequacy for that period— quality of land and water, numbers of persons inscribed, and so on— are unresearched; and there has been no study of agrarian politics and the potential involvement of repatriates and unemployed copper miners.

There appears to have been little in the way of a cash economy in 1930s highland villages. The lack of cash was important because, I will argue, cash was necessary to sustain purchased material culture and work specialties. During the 1930s Simonelli found that in Baviacora only two men were producing cattle and three were growing corn and beans to sell. Growers took wheat to be milled in exchange for a share—how much I do not know—and the rest went for food (Simonelli, 1985). Likewise, Hewes found that in the 1930s Huepac was feeding itself and selling a little cheese and dried meat to Cananea and Nacozari (1935:292). Commercial export of cattle to the United States was nil in the early 1930s, then surged in the late 1930s (Ramírez, León, and Conde, 1985).

POPULATION SHIFT TO THE BORDER

Agua Prieta, like the rest of the urban border, witnessed explosive growth during the decades after 1940. Hit hard by the Great Depression, Agua Prieta's population apparently was not affected by the repatriates who returned through the border port. However, its population surged from 1940 to 1950, when repatriated families left their rural refuges for the border, and fired miners from Nacozari and El Tigre arrived in search of employment. The decades from 1940 to 1960 were prosperous ones for the city: soldiers stationed at nearby Fort Huachuca shopped there, the bracero program lasted from 1942 to 1965 (contracting along the boundary prior to 1952 favored settlement in Mexican border towns, but then it was centralized), and for a few key years a meat-packing plant operated in Agua Prieta to compensate for the hoof-and-mouth cattle quarantine (1947–1954) imposed by the United States on Mexico (Machado, 1981). Margarita Nolasco's calculations (1979) show little net immigration to Agua Prieta from 1960 to 1970, but the population again exploded in the decade of the maquiladora industry, 1970–1980.

The urbanization of Agua Prieta after 1940 was part of an overall shift of population in Sonora from the rural, interior municipalities to the coastal and border cities. Nolasco (1979) calculated net inter-municipal migration after deduction for the rate of natural increase for the decade 1960–1970. Of sixty-nine Sonora municipalities, only nine attracted immigration—all but one, San Pedro de la Cueva, were on the coast. Four had an equilibrium of new families and emigrants: Agua Prieta and Nogales (ports of embarkation for the United States), Villa Hidalgo (in the highlands), and Etchojoa (on the coast). Fifty-six municipalities, including all but two of the rural highland ones, were net exporters of people. Flour mills, such as the large one in Agua Prieta, stopped buying wheat from peasants in nearby Colonia Morelos and similar rural towns, opting for cheaper

Table 2.1. Agua Prieta Municipal Population[a]
by Decades, 1930–1980

1930	6,677
1940	6,552
1950	13,121
1960	17,248
1970	23,272
1980	32,691

SOURCE: Instituto Nacional de Estadística, Geografía,
e Informática, 1984:*Cuadro* 2.1.1.

[a] Agua Prieta's urban population has always been around
2,000 to 2,500 less than the municipal population, so it is
reasonable to use the latter to represent changes in the
former. The censused rural population in 1980 shot up to
5,202, but I believe that this is an artifact of counting
urban neighborhoods on *ejido* lands as part of the *ejido*.

supplies from the agroindustrial coast of the state (interview with
Dolores Molina, Agua Prieta, October 20, 1985).

The data also show that migration out of the mine centers, which
had started in the 1930s and 1940s, continued into the 1960s.
Cananea had net out-migration of 6,679 persons, and 1,441 left already depopulated Nacozari de Garcia. Although the mine remained
in operation, Cananea stagnated as a source of employment until
the 1980s. The mine began a new type of production in the early
1940s, when new concentrating methods and the start of open-pit
extraction of lower-grade ore enabled total copper production to increase with a declining labor force per unit of copper (Peña and
Chávez, 1985:259).

POST–WORLD WAR II IMMIGRATION TO THE UNITED STATES

Immigration to and work in the United States had particular importance to the border in the period after the mines had declined and
before significant numbers of border factories were opened. Unlike
the earlier open-border period, in this era the U.S. government distinguished among a complicated set of documented entrants and
created a large, negative category of the undocumented.

Permanent immigration to the United States from Mexico between
1940 and 1965 depended to a substantial extent on employment.

There was no numerical limit on immigration from Western Hemisphere nations until 1965, but potential immigrants had to demonstrate that they had work or support in the United States, or they would be blocked as "likely public charges." During World War II key industries that lost workers to military service, such as the Douglas smelter and the Bisbee mine, were allowed to certify potential employees for immigration from Mexico. Another group of legal immigrants were returning U.S.–born citizens, children of repatriates.

Through a series of alterations in immigration law that began in 1965 and culminated in 1976, Mexico was restricted to the 20,000 person annual quota under six quota preferences, plus close kin. An average of 35,000 legal immigrants came to the United States annually from Mexico during the period 1941–1978 (calculated from Portes and Bach, 1985:79).

Some persons who secured employment-certified permanent residence status (green cards) were allowed through a legal fiction to reside in Mexican border cities but to commute to workplaces on the U.S. side, as long as they recertified their continued employment every six months. This category, though small, is important in Mexican border cities, since their earnings in dollars have a disproportionate value. It is estimated that 250,000 persons in Mexican border cities directly depend on the earnings of commuters (Kiser and Kiser, 1979:215).

The bracero program, a temporary labor contract program, was much larger than permanent residential immigration. It began in 1942 as a wartime labor program, and continued until 1965. During the years 1951–1965 there were at least 100,000 braceros contracted annually, and over 400,000 during the late 1950s (Portes and Bach, 1985:63). The bracero program by design employed Mexicans without permitting them secure settlement in the United States (Galarza, 1964).

Flourishing undocumented labor migration existed side by side with contract labor during the bracero years, and after the legal program was terminated, employers turned to additional undocumented entrants (Kiser and Kiser, 1979:69). It is, of course, difficult to know how many undocumented immigrants have come to the United States; apprehension statistics, which are often cited, may in fact more closely reflect periodic swings in enforcement rather than numbers of undocumented entrants. There have been three campaigns of border interception since the end of the repatriation: 1947,

1954 (a militarized exercise called "Operation Wetback"), and a lengthy escalation since the late 1970s and continuing through the 1980s (summarized from Samora, 1971:50–55; Portes and Bach, 1985:65). In periods in between, notably 1955–1976, undocumented immigration from Mexico has been unofficially tolerated. The overall trend of U.S. policy from 1940 to 1986 has been increased application of force at the border.[2]

THE MAQUILADORA PERIOD

Maquiladoras, assembly plants located mainly in the cities of Mexico's northern border, have since the 1970s become an industry important on any scale. Most of the plants are direct subsidiaries of U.S. corporations; some are locally owned subcontractors. Typical maquiladora industries are electrical parts and electronics, garments, and auto parts. In the maquiladoras, parts and items are put together by Mexican workers, by hand or with machinery that is usually fairly simple. The original pieces are brought from outside, and goods are exported and consumed beyond Mexico. The purpose of the maquiladora is to obtain inexpensive effort at the labor-intensive assembly steps of manufacturing.

The Border Industrialization Program (BIP), the legal underpinning for the maquiladoras, was established by Mexico's government in 1965. The BIP established a zone with special privileges for foreign companies: tariff-free, in-bond importation of parts and equipment; control of land in the face of a constitutional restriction on non-Mexican ownership in a northern boundary strip; 100 percent foreign ownership of plant; and frequent state tax exemptions. Though not per se part of the BIP, the import–assembly–reexport cycle is facilitated by two loopholes in the U.S. tariff code that enable shipping of parts for partial modification outside the United States, and return with tariffs charged only on "value added" (labor costs and other local expenses), not the total import value (Fernández-Kelly, 1983:Chapter 2).

The maquiladoras are notable for a labor force that is largely female and quite young, with the exception of a few predominantly male-staffed factories. In Seligson and Williams's sample of Agua Prieta maquiladora employees, 80 percent were women and 20 percent men; 86 percent were below the age of thirty (1981:30–36).

The first maquiladora in Agua Prieta opened in 1967 (it was

Table 2.2. Agua Prieta Maquiladora
Employment

1971 (May)	800
1974 (first half)	4,000
1975 (January)	2,800
1978	4,000
1982 (June)	2,978
1985 (September)	5,792
1986 (June)	6,434

SOURCES: Ignacio Romero, Agua Prieta state labor inspector; Ladman and Poulson, 1972; Seligson and Williams, 1981; *Arizona Daily Star,* June 20, 1982:B1–2; February 19, 1985:Sec. 4 p. 2; February 25, 1986:E6; Douglas Chamber of Commerce, 1986; Stoddard, 1987:19.

referred to as a "pirate," or unlicensed factory). Since then, there have been three cycles in Agua Prieta maquiladora history. The first wave started in 1969 and lasted until early 1974, by which time the number of workers had risen fivefold. Expansion came to a crashing halt in late 1974, when American companies responded to a moderate U.S. downturn with extreme reductions in Mexico (Peña, 1980). At least 1,232 workers were laid off in Agua Prieta through early 1975. Gradual recovery through the 1970s marked the second wave. As of 1980, maquiladora employment made up the plurality, 38 percent, of the officially censused labor force in Agua Prieta (Secretaría de Programación y Presupuesto, 1983). However, a slumping U.S. automotive industry hit Agua Prieta in summer 1982 with layoffs in large seat-belt and tire-iron factories.

This downturn, though harmful, was short-lived, because rapid and frequent devaluations of the Mexican peso against the U.S. dollar from January 1982 through November 1987 motivated Americans to take further advantage of cheapened Mexican labor. The business newsletter *Twin Plant News* (January 1986:12) estimated that the dollar cost of maquiladora wages with benefits fell roughly 60 percent between August 1982 and January 1986. In keeping with the logic of the world export system, to seek inexpensive labor for a few key points in manufacture, maquiladoras in Agua Prieta expanded in numbers and size to unprecedented levels. By 1986, there were roughly 2,500 more factory workers than in the late 1970s.

John Taylor, a spokesman for Zenith, described in an unusually frank manner the benefit his company obtained in the devaluation of 1982–1983: "It is common knowledge that Zenith suffered a net loss of $21.8 million last year. We had a turnaround the first half of this year. We benefited significantly by the devaluation of the Mexican peso" (*Arizona Daily Star*, September 25, 1983:A20). In 1983, Zenith opened its first plant in Agua Prieta, and by 1986 it was the largest employer there, with 1,200 employed in four factories and a warehouse. Zenith is the biggest overall maquiladora employer in Mexico (*Multinational Monitor*, February 1987:6).

The copper economy in northern Sonora also returned to vigor in the 1980s. Major investments were made in Cananea and in La Caridad, a new development in the Nacozari area. Both are highly capitalized, low-labor-ratio open-pit mine–mill–smelter complexes. La Caridad in particular has a close relationship with Agua Prieta, as Nacozari has always had. Many men work during the week in La Caridad and commute to homes in Agua Prieta on the weekend. La Caridad was the scene of bitterly repressed strikes in 1978–1979 by the contract construction labor force (documented in Besserer, González, and Rosales, 1979). In contrast, Douglas, which had depended on the smelter for so many years, was undermined in the early 1980s after Phelps Dodge invested in a new smelter and offices elsewhere; there was a prolonged national strike against Phelps Dodge starting in 1983, and the old smelter closed in 1987 for lack of sulfur pollution controls.

REAL WAGES AND DEVALUATIONS

Because working people use cash to buy most of their daily necessities, the history of the real wage is essential to interpreting the rhythms of family histories. On the border, purchasing power is directly related to the peso/dollar exchange rate.

At the turn of the century, wages in the large Sonoran mines were the highest in the Mexican republic. At the same time, Mexico suffered a tumble in the value of its once stable silver currency, bringing a devaluation and inflation (Bernstein, 1964; Katz, 1981). The state's working class formed in an environment where, for the first time, common people had access to a large amount of circulating paper currency, and wages were unmoored from their traditional base. The 1910s and 1920s were difficult because of inflated cur-

Table 2.3. Peso Devaluation and Real Wages (Selected Dates)

Date	Pesos per Dollar[a]	Real Wage Index[b] (1978 = 100)
1905	2.0	n.a.
1934–35	3.6	53.2
1940–41	4.85	46.8
1947–48	8.65	29.3
1954–55	12.5	39.5
1964–65	12.5	54.9
1974 (Jan.)	12.5	89.4
1976 (Oct.)	22.5	107.3
1982 (Jan.)	48.5	87.3
1982 (Sept.)	150–200	80.9
1983 (June)	200	67.2
1985 (June)	400	n.a.
1986 (June)	1,000	n.a.
1987 (Nov.)	2,250	n.a.

SOURCES: Martínez, 1977; Gregory, 1986; field notes 1982, 1984–1986.
[a]Pesos/dollars after 1982 are approximate open market values.
[b]Real unweighted average urban minimum wage.

rency and expensive food. However, during the 1930s the Cárdenas administration made a concerted effort to push wages up, reflected in the real wage index, despite problems of foreign exchange that brought several devaluations. Those Sonoran miners who survived the mass layoffs of 1931 particularly benefited from the rise in pay through 1940 conveyed by their new union power (Bernstein, 1964:198).

After 1940, however, the situation was reversed. Post-Cárdenas governments prevented miners from raising wages to recoup inflation (Bernstein, 1964:229). As the position of working people in Mexico declined, the real wage hit bottom in 1946–1947. The peso suffered major devaluations in 1948 and 1953. During this nadir families were abandoning their old lives in the mine centers and starting, amid severe poverty, new lives in the border cities.

For the next three decades (1947–1976) families witnessed a stable peso, which especially benefited border consumers, and a long, gradual improvement in earnings. Decent standards of life took hold, only to come under severe threat. In 1976, the peso was devalued for the first time in twenty-three years.

As the politics of Mexico's upper class broke into open dispute, national capital fled to deposits and real estate in the United States, and the central government borrowed from American banks. The shaky balance collapsed in 1982, and the peso was allowed to fall freely. The bank debt was handled by a series of agreements negotiated through the offices of the International Monetary Fund— agreements that did no more than roll the principal over for another year, and guarantee seemingly endless payment of interest—while domestic consumption was reduced (by devaluations, less-than-inflation raises, etc.) in order to fund the interest payments (Cornelius, 1986).

Purchasing power collapsed, and nowhere was the collapse worse than at the border. The 1983 real wage figure was but two-thirds of 1978; it lay below the level of 1966–1967 (70.3). With the succeeding devaluations and inflation of 1984–1987, it seems certain that the real wage in Mexico today approximates the depth of the Great Depression (1934–1935). The border, though relatively prosperous compared with most of Mexico, is particularly vulnerable to devaluations, which reduced the peso one hundred times relative to the dollar from 1976 to 1987. This was the context of the 1984–1986 field research period.

3. The Formative Working Class in the Mine Period, 1886–1949

When the foundations for two smelters were laid in Douglas, and a narrow-gauge rail climbed the mountain of copper at Pilares de Nacozari, thousands of men walked the fifty or one hundred desert miles from their farmside homes. Some of them stayed, bringing in their sisters and brothers, marrying, and having children of their own. A class and a community formed, seemingly bound within the monolithic plans of the company town; but within the dense networks of these communities unions arose that could, in some ways, contest the power of the company. Not in all instances when classes form does a powerful labor movement arise, and it is interesting to ask why it did happen in the mines of Sonora. This process of class formation took roughly two generations in the family histories. The story of Guadalupe Hernández looks at the first steps, when he became a miner after his village lost an armed battle for their land. The youth and marriage of Luis and Angelita Aguirre in El Tigre, on the other hand, took place during the generation that grew up completely within the world of the mines.

THE HERNÁNDEZ FAMILY HISTORY: ENTRY TO THE WORKING POPULATION

Antonio Hernández, resting at a table after a long day welding a new bed on the back of a pickup truck, talked animatedly of his childhood on his parents' farm. When his mother sent him to the store for kerosene or coffee, he brought a leather sack of chicken eggs to pay

for it. They did not sell wheat—Antonio's father milled it in his
tauna, a horizontal stone mill pulled by a burro, and stored it in the
back room of his house. Antonio's older brother José was more terse,
after years of wearing himself out in the gravel pits and construction
sites of California and Arizona. All he had to say was that he got
tired of working for next to nothing on the farm, and the pay in the
United States looked awfully good.

I interviewed these brothers, as well as their wives, children, and
grandchildren, in a city on the border. Clearly, they came to Agua
Prieta from a rural background. Yet the family story they told in
separate interviews was anything but simple. In fact, it started with
their father, Guadalupe Hernández, firmly in the heart of the industrial work force, a hoist operator in a giant mine. Reconstructing his
odyssey, we will not only join the great drama of the Mexican Revolution, we will discover the intimate interchange between peasant
and industrial milieus in Sonoran lives.

Pivipa, a settlement of no more than three hundred inhabitants,
set apart from the main municipal center of commerce, schools, social visibility, and politics, is dedicated to farming small amounts of
wheat and selling cakes of unrefined brown sugar; nevertheless, it is
a special and fascinating place. Thomas Hinton (1959) showed
Pivipa and its equally tiny neighbor San Clemente de Terapa as two
of the strongest surviving centers of Opata culture. José said that his
great-grandfather (FaFaFa), a teamster who drove a mule cart between Moctezuma and Hermosillo, spoke only Opata, no Spanish.
His grandfather, the father of Guadalupe, spoke Opata and Spanish
but refused to pass on the Indian language or customs. He labeled
his grandfather an *agricultor,* a peasant with reliable access to plant-
able land. Though these items, remote in time as they are, should be
regarded as family legends, certainly Hinton's map supports their
veracity.

Guadalupe Hernández was at the Pilares de Nacozari mine by
1908 when José, his oldest son, was born. Pilares, though only a few
miles up valley and mountainside from Pivipa, was in fact a world
away: a crowded city, a town of money and stores. Two of Guadalupe's brothers were also miners in Pilares. A brother, two sisters,
and the widow of one mining brother went even farther, California
or Arizona, where my informant Antonio had lost track of their
descendants. The oldest brother became an officer in the Mexican
army (Figure 3.1). Whether north or south of the border, a whole

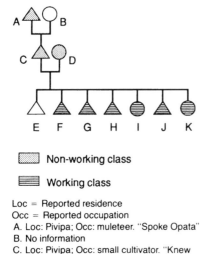

Non-working class

Working class

Loc = Reported residence
Occ = Reported occupation
A. Loc: Pivipa; Occ: muleteer. "Spoke Opata"
B. No information
C. Loc: Pivipa; Occ: small cultivator. "Knew
   Opata"
D. Loc: Pivipa
E. Loc: varied; Occ: military officer
F. Loc: Pilares; Occ: miner, landless laborer
G. Guadalupe Hernández. Loc: Pilares;
   Occ: miner
H. Loc: Pilares; Occ: miner
 I. Loc: California; Occ: agricultural laborer
J. Loc: Arizona; Occ: agricultural and day
   laborer
K. Loc: California; Occ: agricultural laborer

Figure 3.1. Hernández family: formative working class

generation of Hernández siblings had joined the great ebb and flow
of Mexican working people. What caused them to leave Pivipa?

In 1883 there was a lawsuit over the lands of Pivipa between the
residents of Pivipa, led by Guadalupe Velarde, and Genaro Teran and
his mother, Dolores Villaescusa of Moctezuma. The judge in Moctezuma ruled in favor of Teran, but the villagers refused to leave the
land. When public force was sent to remove the landholders, thirty
of them manned a fort at a place called Churivari. Governor Luis
Torres sent state troops to bring Velarde and his band to Hermosillo,
where they were released after a promise to desist from the struggle
for the land. Of course they did not comply. After further legal ap-
peals, Velarde dispossessed Teran from the land. Velarde had raised a
small army of one hundred men, and they had taken to the mountains in "open rebellion," to use the phrase of Eduardo Villa, the
distinguished historian of Sonora.

In January 1886, the 10th State Regiment and some attachments of federal troops were sent after Velarde and the neighbors of Pivipa. In June they killed the prefect of the district, José María Torres, the brother of Governor Torres. In October, Velarde was finally captured and executed. Political opponents of the Porfirian governor started a newspaper in Guaymas called "The Shadow of Velarde." (This account is taken from Villa, 1984:365–366.) The land remained alienated from the residents of Pivipa and San Clemente de Terapa until after the revolution, when Guadalupe Hernández played a part in recovering it.

Guadalupe's wife, María, and her family also joined the formative working population around the turn of the twentieth century. Their kinship history is a particularly interesting example of siblings spreading into the working class as the labor market opened up. María, Antonio reported, was born in Ocampo, Chihuahua, a *mineral* (mine town). Her parents (José and Antonio's MoFa and MoMo) came from Madera, Chihuahua, an active mine town in close communication with Sahuaripa, Sonora (however, María's father was recalled as a *peón,* a laborer, not a miner). María's parents were traveling to Sonora when her father drowned crossing a river—a normally half-dry stream will become a dangerous torrent during Sonora's summer rains. Following this ordeal, the widow came to Pilares de Nacozari, where her grown children supported the family by entering the mine. María's two unmarried brothers were miners, and she and both sisters married mine workers—thus, in María's generation, all five siblings were included in the mine economy by 1908, the year José was born at Pilares (Figure 3.2).[1]

Guadalupe Hernández was a hoistman in the Pilares de Nacozari mine—he drove the elevator that raised and lowered men into the mine. This was a highly responsible position in the work hierarchy, and the general manager of Pilares, Frank Horton, treated Guadalupe as a personally valued employee, almost in the manner of a patron. An identifiable description of Guadalupe and an explicit statement of his relationship to Frank Horton can be found in a book by his wife, Inez Horton (1968:Chapter 18).

Guadalupe's most notable career, however, was that of officer in the Mexican Revolution, on the "Constitutionalist" side that ultimately triumphed. In a document dated January 24, 1916,[2] Lieutenant Colonel Abraham Fraujo testifies that Guadalupe Hernández joined the *guerrilla* Fraujo in September 1914 at Pilares (it also notes

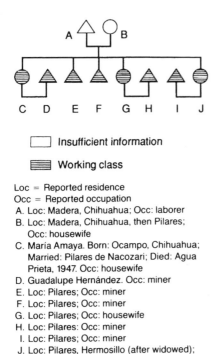

□ Insufficient information

▤ Working class

Loc = Reported residence
Occ = Reported occupation
A. Loc: Madera, Chihuahua; Occ: laborer
B. Loc: Madera, Chihuahua, then Pilares;
    Occ: housewife
C. María Amaya. Born: Ocampo, Chihuahua;
    Married: Pilares de Nacozari; Died: Agua
    Prieta, 1947. Occ: housewife
D. Guadalupe Hernández. Occ: miner
E. Loc: Pilares; Occ: miner
F. Loc: Pilares; Occ: miner
G. Loc: Pilares; Occ: housewife
H. Loc: Pilares; Occ: miner
I. Loc: Pilares; Occ: miner
J. Loc: Pilares, Hermosillo (after widowed);
    Occ: housewife

Figure 3.2. Amaya family: formative working class

that Guadalupe had been in service in 1913, the year of the rebellion against Francisco Madero's killer, Victoriano Huerta, but details about his activities in this period are absent). After testifying that Guadalupe fought in Naco, Sonora, under General Benjamin Hill, the Fraujo document states that in November 1914 Guadalupe was commissioned by General Hill to "go through Nacozari, Pilares de Nacozari, Cumpas, and the commissary of San Clemente de Terapa to recruit people [soldiers], a commission that he fulfilled the best that he was able." Guadalupe returned with eighty men.

Guadalupe's progress from Pilares, as pure a city of miners as could be found in Sonora, through the industrial and commercial Nacozari de García, across the large rural center of Cumpas, and into the hamlets of Terapa and Pivipa (the commissary included Guadalupe's natal village) is a striking recapitulation of the formation of workers from peasants; the fact that Guadalupe did this at the behest of Benjamin Hill, a revolutionary son of the Sonoran elite, is equally worthy of notice.[3]

The troops of Hernández were merged with the troops of Fraujo and Contreras into the "Batallón Pilares." Hernández served as a second captain under Fraujo. These units were part of the forces that sided with Plutarco Elías Calles in his split with José María Maytorena, the Sonoran state governor and ally of Pancho Villa. Hernández fought in eight battles in the northeastern corner of Sonora that culminated in Villa's dramatic defeat when he besieged Calles at Agua Prieta in November 1915. After this time we do not know what Hernández did, except that at some time he returned to work in Pilares.

Calles declared the lands in San Clemente de Terapa and Pivipa restored on January 1, 1916. The official date of possession was February 22, 1920 (Sanderson, 1981:236),[4] but some of the documents held by the family indicate that Pivipa was already in the hands of the agrarians. The grant included 1,503 acres of farmland and 18,400 acres of pasture. Evidently Calles, not otherwise noted for land reform, gave out this terrain to reward his loyal troops,[5] and it seems that his follower Guadalupe had a hand in the distribution. Guadalupe obtained for himself the substantial amount of seven hectares of farmland, which included the use of shares of absent siblings. Antonio recalled that his father, who years later bought a hand-cranked victrola, played for his sons by way of instruction a revolutionary ballad, the "Corrido of the Agrarians."

For several years after the initial land distribution, Guadalupe continued to work in Pilares and commuted to the farm. By 1927, however, the family was residing in Pivipa. But Guadalupe soon fled the area after a political dispute ended in a gunfight.[6] In the meantime, José took responsibility for the farm, directing the work of his younger siblings. Life was harsh, and eventually María took her younger children with her to Nacozari de García, where she found work in a restaurant (later, Guadalupe rejoined them). José struggled by himself, farming and teaching school for a pittance; he even made several ventures to the United States to find work. As José and Antonio each found his own path to the border, none of the Hernández family stayed with the land their ancestors had fought to retain.

THE ANTHROPOLOGY OF WORKING-CLASS FORMATION

Working-class formation in Sonora is unproblematic from the large-scale perspective. A large industry came, and a working class followed. When the structure of capital is in place, and numbers of wage laborers in the new cities can be counted, then working-class formation is assumed to have taken place. In fact, this does not adequately investigate the human organization of the labor flow (Wolf, 1982:359): How did people become available to work for a wage? That question is suitable for anthropology.

Why, for example, did the Porfirian expulsion of people from the land result in siblings moving as a bloc into wage-earning locations? Stating the issue of working-class formation in this way integrates a major structural process, the attack on rural livelihoods, with specific mechanisms of inheritance and kinship relations, and thereby brings us to understand the rapid formation of the working class. Again and again, we ask such questions: How did frontier Sonorans organize work before industries? How did the impersonal market break loose the preindustrial supply of labor? What was the cultural diversity of workers, and what can this tell us about possible paths into the mines? How were border people brought to sell their efforts by coercion and attraction? These inquiries, which regard generalizations such as "labor markets" or "rural out-migration" as open questions rather than answers, arise from studying large events at the anthropological level.

The Emergence of an Impersonal Labor Market

There is little evidence about the organization of labor in northern Sonora prior to the industrial era. To seek such evidence, I read the exploratory ethnographies of Lumholtz (1973 [1902]), Bandelier (1970 [1883–1884]), and Hrdliĉka (1904), not for information on surviving Indian cultural traits of northeastern Sonora but for information on how they organized their expeditions. Lumholtz, describing how he obtained his mule train crew entering Sonora, stated: "In hiring them, only one precaution had always to be observed: never to accept one unless he had a good recommendation from his village authorities or some prominent man in his neighborhood" (1973, Vol. 1:5–6). Similar labor recruitment patterns appear in the 1858–1859 journal of Samuel Peter Heintzelman, who operated a mine near Arivaca, between Tucson and Mexico. He sent assistants several times to Sonora, to Santa Cruz, Altar, and Tubutama "to see a rich Mexican there and get laborers. The cry now is the want of laborers, when some time ago any number could be obtained, as they were flocking to these rich mines" (North, 1980:61; see also 86).

Why were these men seeking workers through local elites rather than hiring them directly? Eric Wolf, in his masterful discussion of the Mexican past, speaks of the manner in which labor was bound within a "personalized" relationship between property owner and laborer (Wolf, 1959:207–209). On the Sonoran frontier, there were many instances of paid labor before working-class formation, but it was always limited to the terms of such relationships.

The new labor market was "impersonal"; people went to jobs on their own, though kinship among workers or relations with managers still played a part in employment. Workers could enter and leave (or be forced out of) any number of different jobs. They were no longer caught within a single relationship with a patron. I hypothesize that more readily available consumer goods, wages paid in portable currency (instead of the local favors of landlords), demand for massive numbers of laborers, and the freedom to leave home for work in the United States broke down the older forms of labor recruitment.

The haciendas and ranches of Sonora felt the North American demand for Mexican immigrant workers in the final decades of the nineteenth century. Park argues that as early as the 1870s the demands of Arizona mines disrupted labor relations inside Sonora. He quotes an Arizona newspaper of 1879:

> Sonora seems to be undergoing a labor crisis, writes *La Sonora*. Ten years ago she paid her *peones* seven to ten pesos per month and cotton clothes. Now due to American influence they want shoes, pants, and flannel shirts, for which the *hacendado* puts them deeper into debt. But the *peones* now run away. (1961:148)

The ability of workers to flee their obligations was a threat to the personalized order of labor relations. Ease of movement characterized northern Mexican workers such as cowboys and railroad crews. Miners were more responsive to far-flung job markets, and proved difficult to tie down. Above all, this was permitted by the proximity of the boundary (Katz, 1981:12–14).

We again see the loosening effects of new labor markets if we look at the terms sharecroppers had to face. Katz found that sharecropping arrangements improved the closer the locality to the U.S. border, as well as to northern Mexican mines and industries, and he reports that debt peonage was much lessened. In the Río Sonora town of Banamichi, due south of Cananea, even when the owner provided seed, draft animals, and tools, the sharecropper kept two-thirds of the crop; without these, he kept three-fourths (Katz, 1980:44–45).

Large construction projects that preceded the establishment of industries exploded the old labor arrangements. They drew thousands of men by offering an outburst of wages, and in this manner created the possibility for a modern labor market (Ribeiro, 1985). Cananea employed between seven and eight thousand men when it was built (Besserer, Díaz, and Santana, 1980:1323). In 1913, the two Douglas smelters employed 1,700 construction laborers (Jeffrey, 1951:25). Railroads in Sonora were built by local, not Chinese, contract labor, in contrast with the U.S. West (Hu-DeHart, 1980:51–52; on the paucity of Chinese contract labor in general, see Hu-DeHart, 1985:195). Oral histories indicate the power of these projects to attract potential labor from large areas: Dolores Molina recalled that his father and uncle traveled over two hundred miles on horseback from the Valle de Tacupeto to work in the construction of the Douglas smelters in 1901 (interview, Agua Prieta, October 20, 1985).

Changes in mining technology caused the labor market to change from a small, differentiated range of skills to a large, impersonal demand. The great Mexican mining tradition dating to the sixteenth century was finally superseded during the last three decades of the nineteenth century, and older crafts were eliminated. Steam- or diesel-driven mechanical mills and chemical leaching processes replaced *arrastra* (mule-dragged) milling and *patio* (mercury) amalgamation of gold and silver chlorides. Charcoal-heated "Castilian" reverberatory furnaces had required high-grade ores to be worthwhile. Smelting in Mexico had been a carefully developed empirical tradition of lead, salt, and soda ash combinations applied to different types of silver ore. This was replaced with much hotter furnaces and applications of scientific chemical engineering that allowed the extraction of low-grade, difficult sulfides—not only of silver but, more important, of the copper now desired for electrical wire.

The new technology of copper smelting permitted the use of low-grade porphyry ores. These were not taken out by the careful chasing of veins by experienced miners, as high-grade ores had been, but were extracted in high-volume operations planned by engineers on structural and cost-efficiency bases. Other changes inside the mine followed the logic of mass ore removal—laying tracks for ore cars, lines for water and electricity, and so on. (This material is sum-marized from Park, 1961; Young, 1970; Gómez-Quiñones, 1979; Jiménez, 1985:176–191).

High-volume mines brought high-volume labor markets, though differences by seniority and knowledge by no means disappeared. In the ten years from 1897 to 1907, the reported mine, mill, and smel-ter work force in Sonora tripled from 5,874 to 17,368 (Flores, Velasco, and Ramírez, 1985:Cuadros 89 and 90). These numbers do not include Sonorans who were working in Arizona, nor does it count family members who were dependent on mining wages. In the three decades from 1880 to 1910 tens of thousands of persons came to depend on the tugs and jolts of an impersonal labor demand. Where had they come from?

Sources of the Working Population

According to Besserer, Díaz, and Santana (1980:1324–1325), Cananea civil registries indicate that the first generation of industrial miners at Cananea came from two sources: experienced miners who moved from interior states of Mexico to fill better jobs, and villagers hired from the Río Sonora valley (and surely the parallel valleys in the same region) for unskilled laboring positions. This pattern is consistent with the genealogies I collected for families at other mines. It seems likely that the majority of Sonoran miners were locally rooted.

We lack a study of the changes that experienced miners, such as men from the southerly silver-mining district of Alamos, underwent if and when they moved to industrial mines near the border. For the mass of Sonoran laborers, however, it is possible to be specific about the processes by which they were made into miners. There were several routes into the formative working class. The paths differed by cultural and geographical origin: former Opata villagers versus mestizo, Norteño Mexicans.

Owen found differences in labor market participation between for-mer Opata and non-Opata as late as the 1950s, half a century after their cultural separation had, on the surface, disappeared. First, the non-Opata (or "whites") had come into the locality relatively re-cently and were nowhere near as deeply rooted as the descendants of Opata villages:

> Another feature that differentiates between many Whites and many
> Indians is that the Indians typically think of Marobavi as their ancestral
> home and have no remembrance or knowledge of their families ever

having lived anywhere else. Half of the Whites are not native to Marobavi and many of these are from some distance away—Tomchic, Ures, other river valleys, or even from Hermosillo. (1959:39)

Owen goes on to correlate this with entry into external wage labor markets:

Possibly related to differences in attitudes toward the village as a place in which to live and to work, are the relative numbers of the three categories who have gone to the United States to work. Few Indians have gone, and none are going now. If the figures on movement to other parts of Sonora were included . . . the differences would become larger. (1959:39–40)

Owen observes that cash for expenses of migrating to work was a barrier for poorer, more Indian villagers.

Under what circumstances, then, would former Opata have entered the early industrial labor market? We can see the answer in the Hernández history. They left the ancestral village of Pivipa only under extreme compulsion, the community's lands having been usurped; indeed, despite his time spent working in the mines, Guadalupe Hernández would seek their restitution.

Mestizos, on the other hand, were more mobile and responsive to opportunities for earnings. Miguel León-Portilla, in his discussion of the historical roots of northern Mexican culture, speaks of the "almost constant" drive to seek "riches and advantages" (1972:110). Mestizos were a fluid, expansive segment of the population in late-nineteenth-century Sonora. I propose that mestizo families involved in the capture of other resources sent branches to the new mine centers, where earnings were high and American consumer goods were sold. This argument and a case study, the Encinas-Acosta family, are analyzed in the following chapter.

Recruitment into the Labor Market

The offering of a wage is a necessary but not a sufficient condition for the creation of a working population. Why should people take payment for their time? An anthropological comparison with literature on miners in other regions of the world permits us to set out possible alternative causes for the Sonoran case. The studies of De-Wind (1975) in central Peru and Van Onselen (1976) in colonial Rhodesia describe labor forces created by coercion, specifically the use of money or goods advanced to entrap men into enforced labor-time contracts. The opposite possibility would be uncoerced attraction by wages or consumer goods. Looking again at Peruvian miners, we see a working class that over a long time has persisted in cycling between a copper refinery and home villages where land rights, business, and political offices are retained (Laite, 1981). In brief, there are two sets of contrasts: coerced versus voluntary entry, and temporary versus permanent tenure in wage labor.

There does not seem to be any evidence in northern Sonoran mining for coercive labor recruitment or contracting by advances. Besserer, Díaz, and Santana (1980) state that Cananea did not employ any labor contractors (*enganchadores*). I asked about labor recruitment; no such material was reported either for Sonoran mines or for the Douglas smelter. Mario García (1981) does write about U.S. labor recruitment in the interior of Mexico, and there were contractors who met immigrants at the border (such as the Southern Pacific at Willcox, Arizona, north of Douglas), but considering the evidence about how difficult it was to restrain the movement of labor near the boundary, it seems unlikely that there was much forced labor north of the Yaqui labor area on the Gulf of California coast.

Although there was no direct coercion, an indirect form of coercion was the severe pressure brought to bear on rural livelihoods. It seems, at first glance, obvious that rural pressure would result in migration into the working class. In fact, we could conceive that rural people might simply become more impoverished and marginal, dividing up ever smaller properties, while outsiders filled the mine jobs. Therefore it is necessary to look for a specific mechanism by which rural pressures were translated into working-class formation. We will return to this subject shortly.

Attraction by wages instead of coercion seems to have been important in northern Sonora. Besserer, Novelo, and Sariego write that mines in northern Mexico entered into a fierce wage competition (1983:21–22). They were competing not only with other Mexican mines but also with the insatiable North American labor demand. Ruíz reports that from the 1890s on, high wages were generalized throughout the north of Sonora, not only in the giant operations but even in small mines (he also justly points out that prices were equally high; 1988:102–103).

Flores, Velasco, and Ramírez (1985:Cuadro 92) report statewide wage figures for the daily pay of mine operatives (that is, not white-collar employees); these numbers serve for general trends only, for their nature is limited: They are not true average mine wages but unweighted statewide averages of maximum and minimum numbers reported for each mineral product. The average minimum daily wage, presumably reflecting pay of unskilled laborers in numerous smaller mines, increased from .84 peso a day in 1902 to 1.75 pesos a day in 1907. This can be judged against customary Mexican rural daily wages of 50 centavos (.5 peso).

The high wages offered in advanced industrial mines is illustrated by Esteban Baca Calderón's testimonial about Cananea in 1906, the year of the great strike: The lowest pay (for helpers and carters) was three pesos a day; for drillers, four pesos; for carpenters, five pesos; for smelters' helpers, six pesos; and for smelters, eight pesos (two pesos to the dollar). The company paid American workers twice as much for the same work (cited in Meyer et al., 1980:70).

Even when a labor market offers cash wages, one cannot assume that this will attract a work force. People must need money for something. Not only must consumer goods be available, but obtaining them must require some form of extended participation in the wage economy, whether because the goods are sold on the American side of the border, or because their price favors time payment and thus persistent work.

The Role of Consumption

Border consumption acquired its fundamental outline between 1890 and 1910. Virtually all consumer goods—down to the bags of flour sold in American-owned mine towns—were obtained, in one way or another, from the United States. Working families depended indirectly on the United States because mine company stores were heavily stocked from north of the border (this is repeatedly stated in oral histories and is corroborated in Ruíz, 1988:103). Immigrant workers and even whole families bought large items such as sewing machines in the United States with money earned there and later brought them to Mexico, sometimes reselling them. Soon a thriving group of peddlers known as *fayuqueros* specialized in selling American goods in the villages of Sonora. In contrast with recent times in Mexico, shopping trips to the United States were uncommon, but people could ride a self-propelled railcar on the Nacozari-Douglas railroad. Each of these patterns, with the exception of village peddling, connected consumer desires with the sale of labor in either a temporary or a permanent manner.

The payroll credit system in corporate mines encouraged relative permanence of work.[7] Miners bought appliances and furniture, as well as daily groceries, from company stores or local agents for Singer sewing machines and the like. Company store purchases were automatically deducted from the paycheck at the end of the week, and what small portion remained was paid in cash. The sums deducted included both petty shopping and installments on large purchases. The company was more than happy to extend credit, the limit for which was set according to the earnings of the worker, so as not to lose much if he left. This careful balancing of credit influenced miners to live close to the edge, neither threatening to save too much money nor to get away with too much.

Installment purchases in particular bound workers to continued effort. A workingman would have to make quite a number of weekly installments on an expensive, but essential, item—a cast-iron cooking stove, say—before he would own the item, and could quit work with it in his possession. It should be noted that this was not debt peonage, in which the laborer was obligated to work until all his debt was discharged; in this system workers were not legally bound, but they were motivated to continue laboring because they wanted to keep the goods rolling in. This should be understood in the context that it was hard to keep people still, and that companies actively sought to discourage turnover (at least the kind workers initiated).

Consumer needs could motivate sporadic outbursts of work. Trips to the United States were the most important form of this. Frequently the results of a voyage were brought home through material goods not readily obtainable in Mexico. A chain in which consumption flowed in the opposite direction from labor linked Mexico and the United States. Temporary construction work and labor in the numerous smaller Sonoran mines outside farm villages added to the intermittent consumer–earner pattern.

Circulating cash had an important role in the creation of a population available for hire and ready to move where jobs were offered. Hard specie was certainly known to the Sonoran frontier; Officer recounts how villagers in the Santa Cruz valley (of Sonora and, later, Arizona) would sell supplies to passing Anglo Americans for silver only—Mexico's currency—not gold (1987:222, 225). However, paid labor brought a qualitative change in the currency passing through the hands of the common people.

The era of early industrialization was marked by the shift from silver to paper currency. Inflation was hidden within rapidly increasing amounts of currency in circulation. Pay in paper was sufficiently novel that my oldest informant, Jesús Ramírez, recalled the Bank of Sonora notes with which he was paid when he worked at the Lampazos mine before 1907 (interview, Douglas, Arizona, April 22, 1985). The use of U.S. currency was also widespread, especially at the border; several of my informants spoke of dollars, quarters, and dimes.

The large mines generally paid their workers in cash, although the payroll deduction system limited the amounts in the hands of individual workers. Company scrip, spendable only at company stores, was banned by state law in 1899 (it had been used at Trinidad in the 1880s and Nacozari in the 1890s; Ruíz, 1988:76). Proximity to the United States and the general climate of wage competition made difficult the corporate monopoly over earning and spending in which scrip would be used.

Pay in freely circulated cash instead of scarce silver and recompense through the favors of the patron meant that the individual worker could leave and take his accumulated earnings with him. He was free to move within the labor markets of two nations to compare the relative values of different employments. This not only made for a market society, it made for a working people who knew a diversity of treatments, who talked and compared experiences, and whose field of vision was wider than a powerful family and a few fellow villagers.

It also meant, with respect to consumption, that purchases were not made conservatively. Wage workers earned cash repeatedly, payday after payday, and spent their cash without hesitation, as opposed to the peasant who carefully restricted his limited cash to bounds of certain items that must be purchased. The mold for future border life, craftily switching among the currencies of two nations, was set early.

Kinship and the Social Organization of Working-Class Formation

The Porfirian assault on resources of country folk, a powerful event in history, and the more intimate cycles of farm work and inheritance, interlocked to produce both permanent and temporary wage labor, alternatives we first identified when we asked how humans convert themselves into an economic phenomenon, a supply of labor.

Unfortunately, little is known about peasant life in northeastern Sonora during the early industrial period. I have placed greatest reliance on the life history of Dolores Duarte (a pseudonym), born in 1902, and his recollections of his relationship with his father, Francisco Javier Duarte. I also draw on two published ethnographies of interior rural Sonora from later periods: Owen's study of Marobavi (1959) and Sheridan's work on Cucurpe (1988).[8]

In theory, inheritance in Sonora is partible among all children, male and female. I suspect, but cannot prove, that sons tend to get land, while daughters receive animals, appliances, and such. The date of partition is the breakup of the parental household. Single sons work for their fathers, as do a few married ones; but most married sons have their own economy, whether their own land, or sharecropping, or wage work. Siblings, once they have inherited, each have their own economy and work their own land; cooperative labor is obtained through wage hiring. Owen found that even brothers deal with each other in monetary terms.

Migratory wage labor may exist within the limits of the established father–son relationship for two reasons. First, single sons may travel in search of work to bring home money for their fathers, in expectation of a share of the inheritance. Or they may accumulate cash in anticipation of setting up their own household, possibly buying a parcel of land or sharecropping. Second, married men may seek outside work in a situation of marriage with no or insufficient inheritance, or while awaiting an inheritance.

In a life course structured around the relationships described above, it is likely that key junctures will come at life cycle events, such as marriage and establishment of a neolocal household, or the death of a father and the division of land among siblings. At these junctures, the alternative chosen by a young man who may have been working the majority of time in the wage economy will be to return to rural production (and, therefore, temporary tenure in the working class) or to remain at work (and, therefore, permanent entry into the working class).

Permanent wage labor was also caused by inheritance partition, specifically in a tight situation caused by outside pressures on rural resources. This was the case in Sonora when the industrial working class was forming prior to 1910. Sheridan (1988:37–38) found that although partible inheritance was the ideal for rural Sonorans, in reality many siblings did not claim their shares. Often the inheritance share was too small to be worth claiming. If the person was already working or living outside the community, he or she might not return. The Duarte history indicates that if they remained in the community, partible inheritance was often accompanied by disputes between siblings; the siblings who triumphed could retain most of the inheritance and stay, while the siblings who lost, left.

Permanent exodus involved both male and female co-inheritors (in contrast with male temporary wage labor). Sheridan found that 38 percent of all the children of Cucurpe families were residing elsewhere, either at work or in school (the more educated urban labor market context of the 1980s is admittedly different from the turn of the century). The Cucurpe out-migrants were nearly equal in numbers of sons and daughters (slightly more females; Sheridan, 1983:107–109). In genealogies I collected corroborating evidence: brothers working as miners and sisters married to miners, spread across both nations.

We may model this by situating bilateral kinship in two alternative types of resource control. In the rural setting, siblings (brothers and sisters, including their spouses; that is, siblings-in-law) are potential rivals for a limited set of resources, the inheritance. It is possible to resolve such disputes when a labor market opens up and all but one sibling leave. This should be visible in genealogies when descendants of only one sibling retain rural residence and land rights—the "rural root"—and all the descendants of the other siblings are found in waged, urban locations. Informants from the latter group forget or never possess the detailed knowledge of plots of land and names of cousins needed for inheritance politics.

A labor market, in contrast with landed resources, is not the possession of the workers; they do not control it, but they may have some influence on the allocation of jobs. In the context of corporate employment, there is no harm in bringing one's relatives onto the payroll, and perhaps some future advantages. In the partible inheritance situation, there is always the potential for conflict among siblings/siblings-in-law. In the labor market, siblings/siblings-in-law have no structural rivalry, and because they are more or less of the same age group, they are often in a good position to offer aid.

I call the phenomenon "leverage" where kin help one another within institutions they do not control, whether wage labor markets described here, or immigration to the United States. It is charac-

teristic of proletarianized people who do not own resources themselves, but who are deeply involved within institutional powers.
This model goes beyond the by-now simplistic observations that
kinship continues even when people move from the countryside to
the urban working class, and specifies how that kinship operates and
what most likely will be observed.

Kin who lever one another do not necessarily have to be close
personally on a day-to-day basis, though they may be. It takes only
one strategic favor at one time—getting a job, or helping a person
settle in the border city—to structure their life thereafter. Thus the
analyst can discern this process especially well in genealogies that
show the long-term results of leverage in the form of parallel or related occupations and locations among siblings and their descendants. Precisely such genealogical data will appear in the family history that follows, the Aguirre-Peralta history.

Cross-Border Kinship and the Border Working Class in the Formative Era

The working class produced by these kinship processes was in constant motion across a network of neighborhoods in mine and smelter districts on both sides of the international boundary. Employment grew before 1910, subject, as the historian Ruíz has stressed, to
rapid ups and downs, the opening and closing of individual operations, and the short but severe metal-mining depression of 1907–
1908 that hit both Arizona and Sonora (1988:46–49).

If we contemplate the diversity of major and minor employers in
this epoch and the ironic situation of unpredictable but expansive
wage employment, we can draw an implication readily tested in the
histories: Families had to move among several bases. Men who lost
or quit their jobs in industrial sites could easily switch to sharecropping, working on parental lands, or in rural wage labor or crafts such
as carpentry; and later, when the labor market improved, they could
be fairly confident of their chances of return. In this context my
distinction between permanent and temporary labor is more an analytical than a practical division; only later, during the 1910s and
1920s, with the tightening of the labor market, would men be forced
to make a permanent commitment to mine work. Even when people
remained inside the wage sector, families were prepared to move
among work sites ranging from isolated labor camps to crowded
mine cities. When leaving and when returning to the countryside,

and when moving between mines, families often crossed the international border.

We recall that in the era before 1929 immigration to the United States was easy and essentially unrestricted. There was little or no differentiation by legal citizenship among North American labor markets. We also recall that the labor demand, masses of unskilled male workers for industrial mining and construction, was very similar on both sides of the border.

It was therefore possible for families to reside in both nations. This was "cross-border" kinship. Its principal form was the network of bilaterally related households scattered between similar industrial neighborhoods on both sides of the border. The individual household shuttled between locations within this network, including frequent crossing of the international boundary (for parallels in Baja California, see Alvarez, 1987). In some cases there were also arrangements between rural and urban siblings that allowed for movements in and out of the urban economy. Kin living in the two nations were not clearly differentiated by official citizenship status in their fates, their working opportunities, and their personal security, as they would be after the repatriation and visa tightening of 1929.

Neighborhoods located directly beside mine entrances or smelters were the nodes in the network of cross-border kinship. When people entered the working class, they did not simply migrate to one industrial center; rather, they entered a circulation among these neighborhoods in both nations. Key nodes included Cananea Viejo, Buenavista, and other sections of Cananea (see Peña and Chávez, 1985:239–242); Pilares de Nacozari, which was the actual mine site of Nacozari; Zacatecas Canyon in Bisbee; the mine center of Morenci, Arizona, and the smelter area within Clifton; the old barrio in Douglas; the small, unincorporated settlement of Pirtleville, north of the Douglas smelters; and its twin south of the smelters and the border fence, the Barrio Ferrocarril of Agua Prieta. One company, Phelps Dodge, spanned Clifton–Morenci, Bisbee, Douglas–Pirtleville, and Nacozari, and workers could find work on each side of the border with the recommendations of Phelps Dodge supervisors.

Pirtleville played a particularly crucial role in linking different segments of cross-border kin groups. It was right at the border, and an important stop for immigrants to Arizona. Men could walk directly to work. Pirtleville, known locally in Spanish as Pueblo

Nuevo, attracted Hispanic workers from both sides of the border because lots were sold more cheaply than in Douglas and it lacked municipal restrictions on worker-constructed housing. It sustained a vibrant sense of Hispanic community around the annual Fiestas Patrias (Mexican Independence Day) celebrations. Though an international boundary marked by a low cattle fence lay between Pirtleville and Barrio Ferrocarril, in fact they were, as one elderly resident put it, simply like two neighborhoods.

It is the constant movement of persons between the nodes of this cross-border network that made the copper-based, Hispanic population of Arizona and Sonora one working class prior to the Great Depression. This is to be seen in the international arrays of siblings, the final result of levered exits from the countryside. The cross-border working class can also be seen in the prerevolutionary activities, aimed at Cananea, of the Partido Liberal Mexicano in Douglas, Pirtleville, and smaller mining camps (Cockcroft, 1968: 146–147), and, early in the revolution, the recruitment of Maderista rebel bands in mining towns north as well as south of the border (Aguilar Camín, 1977:133).

THE AGUIRRE HISTORY: LIFE IN A MINE TOWN

My wife and I visited Luis and Angelita Aguirre in the simple but comfortable living room of their solid brick house in Agua Prieta. It had been more than forty years since they had been pushed out of the mines by unemployment. In that time Luis had worked hard in far-flung American fields while Angelita carefully saved and planned their new home on the border. Still, their memories turned back to those years when they were newly married, living in a two-room house made of wooden boards, when for chairs they used empty dynamite crates. For, young and poor though they were, it had been a happy time: They settled in the same neighborhood where they had grown up and met each other; all around them were Luis's older married siblings, his mother, his father (still at work in the mine), and Angelita's widowed mother with her half brothers and sisters at home. The neighborhood, named El Molino ("the mill"), was overshadowed by a giant ore concentrator; the men of the neighborhood, including Luis, worked there.

El Tigre was a mine company town, dense with the ties of family, neighborhood, and labor union. Called into being through a basic economic relationship, this nevertheless was a working class in the full, human sense. Because I am interested in how the economic situation gave rise to a distinctive way of life, I will look at it as a process that takes time, a sequence of events stretching from Luis's father's employment in 1903 to the epoch Luis and Angelita recalled for me, the 1930s.

Luis Aguirre: Family Origins

Luis knew little about the background of his father, Santiago, in distant Zacatecas. He was told years later by his father that at the turn of the century he worked in the United States as an agricultural laborer and on railroad track crews, typical of Mexican immigrant labor of that era. We can surmise, however, that he had relatively good education for that period, because when Santiago came to work at the El Tigre mine in Sonora in 1903, his occupation was paymaster. His duties included recording the quotas and piecework of men working the mine faces on contract. As his son said, it was a "high" job, one requiring writing, not hard work, and at times he was even called to fill in at the office for Americans on vacation (one has to keep in mind how segregated these mines were). Santiago conforms to the pattern of origins described above, in which skilled men came from outside the region, while his laboring Peralta in-laws represent the other characteristic source, the rural valleys of northern Sonora. Their home was the village of Bacerac, strung along the Bavispe River beneath the ridge to which El Tigre clung.

Santiago Aguirre married Antonia Peralta in 1903. The marriage location was reported by Luis as Bacerac. Santiago and Antonia had nine children, beginning in 1903. The birthplaces of their children indicate frequent visiting between the mine center of El Tigre and the peasant town of Bacerac. The first three were born in Bacerac, up to the year 1906, and the remaining ones, including Luis, born in 1912, were born in El Tigre. It seems likely that Antonia went to Bacerac at childbirth to stay with her mother, because her husband certainly worked in El Tigre during these years.

The link between Santiago Aguirre and the Peraltas of Bacerac was expressed in another way—leverage into the labor market. The Peraltas were peasants with small landholdings (*agricultor con tierra propia pequeña*). Antonia's oldest brother, José María (by estimate born in 1880) kept the family land and passed it to his youngest son, Trinidad. Antonia's three sisters and her other brother all ended up in El Tigre. Her brother, an electrician, later went to Cananea when El Tigre closed. One sister married a miner in El Tigre; two others supported themselves after separating from husbands, one with a small restaurant and another as a domestic. Two nephews, sons of the peasant Peralta brother, also became miners in El Tigre, and a niece worked as a domestic (Figure 3.3).

The Peralta family consisted of a peasant core, descendants of one

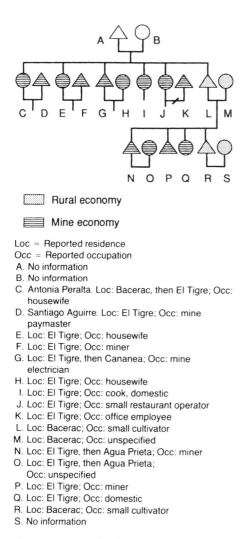

Rural economy

Mine economy

Loc = Reported residence
Occ = Reported occupation
A. No information
B. No information
C. Antonia Peralta. Loc: Bacerac, then El Tigre; Occ: housewife
D. Santiago Aguirre. Loc: El Tigre; Occ: mine paymaster
E. Loc: El Tigre; Occ: housewife
F. Loc: El Tigre; Occ: miner
G. Loc: El Tigre, then Cananea; Occ: mine electrician
H. Loc: El Tigre; Occ: housewife
 I. Loc: El Tigre; Occ: cook, domestic
J. Loc: El Tigre; Occ: small restaurant operator
K. Loc: El Tigre; Occ: office employee
L. Loc: Bacerac; Occ: small cultivator
M. Loc: Bacerac; Occ: unspecified
N. Loc: El Tigre, then Agua Prieta; Occ: miner
O. Loc: El Tigre, then Agua Prieta; Occ: unspecified
P. Loc: El Tigre; Occ: miner
Q. Loc: El Tigre; Occ: domestic
R. Loc: Bacerac; Occ: small cultivator
S. No information

Figure 3.3. Peralta family: labor market leverage and rural roots

sibling who kept the small property, while the alternate inheritors, both siblings and nephews (siblings in the next generation), joined the mine economy either by work or by marriage. Luis's partial knowledge of his own kin is of some significance. Luis clearly remembered every cousin who came into his world, the world of the mines, long after they had dispersed from El Tigre. In striking contrast, he lost track of the line that kept the plot of land in Bacerac. In a personal sense, he knew his peasant cousins. They left their mules in a corral to the side of his mother's house when they came to sell beans and chilies in town. But when we spoke of genealogy, it became apparent that he did not know who inherited the land in Bacerac: the key information needed to link kin with resources. To put it simply, because of permanent working-class formation, the mine cousins no longer had an interest in the inheritance of land. None of them went back even when the mine closed in the 1930s.

It appears likely that Santiago Aguirre, who started at El Tigre in its first year, brought the Peralta siblings into the mine economy. I base this on the genealogical evidence about the distribution of the Peraltas, and from Santiago's position at the mine. Paymaster was the top rung in the mine hierarchy that was filled by working-class Mexicans. Although employment was controlled by the American company, recommendations among Mexican workers would lever access to El Tigre. The result was bunching of kin around mine jobs.

Angelita León: Family Origins

Luis Aguirre's future wife, Angelita León, grew up in a series of mine towns, finally settling in El Tigre. Angelita reported that her mother, María Martínez, was born in 1897 in Dolores, Chihuahua, a small mine town in close communication with Sonora, but she did not know her grandparents on either side. Angelita's father was a miner from Parral, center of the southern Chihuahua mine district. Angelita was born in 1916 in Dolores. Her father died of the Spanish influenza in 1920, while in Nacozari.

In 1921, at Pilares de Nacozari, María married another miner, Arturo Fierros, who within the year went to work in El Tigre (Pilares was closed during the 1921–1922 depression while El Tigre operated, albeit with pay cuts). María's brother and sister also lived in El Tigre when Angelita knew them. The exact chronological relationship is unclear, but a coordination of residence is evident. María's second husband, Arturo (born about 1896), had two brothers who farmed their own land in the village of San Juan in the *municipio* of Villa Hidalgo, south of Nacozari and El Tigre. Arturo died in 1936 of silicosis, at the age of forty. María, twice widowed, with three younger children by Arturo, was supported by her oldest daughter, Angelita, by then married to Luis.

Luis and Angelita

Luis Aguirre went to school for three years; only four years were offered in the company-funded school of El Tigre. In fact, Luis's youth prepared him for little but walking through the mine's gates. He was, as he told me, an indifferent student (though I knew him to be an intelligent and perceptive person), but he avidly played baseball: "After I left school, this is what I most enjoyed. There was a flat mesa to the side of El Tigre filled with stones. We cleared the stones, and played there." He would later work alongside many of the boys with whom he had played. Indeed, it is characteristic of the Mexican life cycle, as among many working peoples, for boys to form their personal relationships in the play of youth, and then plunge into the heaviest and bitterest of adult labor.

Luis started work in 1928. He told me, "My father got me the job. The American manager of the mine's machine shop spoke very good Spanish, and had very good relations with my father. At that time I was, I think, sixteen, but he put down my age as eighteen so they would take me into the company." Luis started out as a machinist's helper, earning the day wage of 2.50 pesos. Much of his work consisted in cleaning up and observing, but among his duties was inserting and removing red-hot iron bars as they were being tempered in the furnace to make drill bits. In this he was under the instruction of senior machinists, all of them Mexicans. Although an American engineer visited the shop to give orders to the Mexican foreman, Luis recalled that the men used to laugh and say, "We don't need the American to tell us how to do our work." Both in this instance and in his father's role in securing him his position, Luis as a young worker was enveloped by more senior Mexican workers from the distant authority of the Americans.

However, Luis's stories show that this pattern was not entirely consistent. In 1930, Luis was switched from the mine to the concentrating mill.[9] There he earned 3.60 pesos a day, working the evening shift. At first Luis operated an ore grinder, but he thought the clouds of dust were damaging his lungs. He went directly to the American manager, in the manner of a personal request, to ask for a transfer out of the mill. " 'You're fine here,' he said to me," Luis recalled, " 'but I'll tell you what I'll do for you, I'll move you upstairs.' " There Luis dumped ore cars into the flotation tank.

By this time, conditions in the mine were worsening. There were popular protests in 1930 against 10 to 25 percent wage cuts by the Lucky Tiger Mining Company, and in 1931 the secretary of industry had to intervene with the company to prevent the closing of the mine. Considering their collective importance, it is striking how little Luis recalled of these events. After 1931 El Tigre was unionized. The local was a branch of the Cananea union local. Luis mainly recalled the union in connection with a later period when it ran the mine as a cooperative. He was young and not active in working-class politics, yet even his loosely shaped attitudes toward socially separated American managers and experienced Mexican workers tell us how the miners' union found its strength.

Meanwhile, Angelita León, an oldest daughter, grew up taking care of her three younger half siblings. She apprenticed household skills at the side of her mother, for Mexican girls early learn to labor within the set of family and kin relationships. She learned to sew, for example, on her mother's American-made pedal sewing machine, the machine she bought from her mother at the time of her marriage to Luis. Angelita said, "I made plenty of clothes, I spent enough time sewing on it [to learn]." Sewing was a skill important to a young housewife in a mine town, and it would prove yet more important to the family's survival in later years.

When she was a young woman, Angelita took a job as housekeeper for the mine manager. She stopped working when she married, for a young woman might work when she was still a "daughter," but she would cease at marriage. El Tigre, like other Sonoran mines, employed almost entirely adult males and no women (Ruíz, 1988:103). The Aguirres told me that boys and old men, not women, were occupied in picking ore from tailings.

Luis and Angelita could hardly recall how they first met, because, they said, they grew up together in the neighborhood. They saw each other at dances, such as the ones sponsored by "Club Violeta," a social club that collected admissions from the mine town youth. Luis recalled attending with a pack of brothers and male cousins.

Angelita told me that after she started seeing Luis, she made friends with his sisters.

Luis and Angelita married in 1936. Their choices about how to set up their new family life were shaped by the policies of the American corporation. These were directed toward an ideal model in which male wages sustained neolocal households inside an occupationally hierarchical and racially segregated company town. This unified and overarching system was applied by assigning houses to new couples, the form of the city, the company store and payroll deduction system, and the workplace itself.

When they married, for example, Luis and Angelita were placed in a house by the company. In fact, they had no choice. Angelita would draw a contrast with later experience in the border city: "In those days, we were unaccustomed to the business of [house] lots, as it was all company land." As a junior employee, Luis merited a small house, one of three in a row of "apartments." It had one room, with a tin roof, wood walls, electricity, a cold water faucet (they heated water and bathed in a large bucket), and an outhouse. There was no room for a garden. The rent, deducted directly from the paycheck, was 10 pesos a month including utilities, which was less than three days' wages for Luis.

This house is significant in two senses. First, the company established neolocal kinship by assigning newly married couples their own houses, rather than leaving them to reside with their parents on one side or the other (this is not to say that Sonorans would not have resided neolocally anyway—all but perhaps one child would have— but in this situation neolocality became entangled with reinforcing corporate policies). As Luis phrased it, when the Aguirre sons reached working age, they went to the mine "to help my father" and "we all cooperated for the family"; but when the sons married, they worked for "their [new] house," though they always gave a "little help to their mother." Second, Luis and Angelita's one-room apartment was smaller than Luis's father's house, the difference corresponding to the difference in their occupational rank and pay; that is, residence corresponded to the hierarchy of the workplace.

The company-town form was true not only for individual houses but also for the pattern of the town itself. The neighborhoods of Mexican workers were aligned with their places of work. The Aguirres lived in El Molino, within walking distance of Luis's job at the concentrator. It was the smaller and more insular of the two

Mexican neighborhoods; the larger one, called La Gran China, contained the mine head, company offices, and the main company store.

Set apart and, it should not surprise us, above the main Mexican neighborhood were the fancy houses of the American engineers and managers. A telling detail of inequality was the bathrooms. "There were outhouses, but no bathrooms inside," Luis explained. "My father put in a little room, and then he put in one of these basins. We put in water and bathed ourselves, but the company didn't have anything like this. The company had it for themselves, for the highest people in the offices, but for the workers they never had anything like that." The built form of the town corresponded to, and reinforced, the social–racial ranks of the corporation.

Luis and Angelita had two children in El Tigre (1938 and 1941) and two later on. Luis's salary, Angelita remembers, was sufficient—but barely—to buy them food and clothing (medical coverage was free). The mark of a decent life was meat, and they could afford one piece of meat a week. Angelita did the shopping. "The company store had everything," Angelita remarked, "there was clothing, all the food that was needed—American, pure American." For the Aguirres this began a lasting preference for American goods, Angelita noted.

Each worker had a yellow slip on which purchases for the week were recorded, and the total was deducted from the weekly paycheck. "Yes, they gave us credit," Angelita told me, "each week you went with your order book and bought what you were going to need, and they would mark it down. On Saturday, payday, they would deduct this, and give you what was left over, if some was left over, and if not, well they didn't even pay you a cent." I asked if they were frequently short, and she replied, "Well, a little was left since we didn't have a very big family, but people with big families never saw money—pure credit." Luis told me that he did not roll up persistent debts to the company, but he did keep up steady effort, rarely missing work (as he noted), in order to keep slightly ahead of his weekly quota.

There were a few small private stores, butchers, bakeries, and such; these, too, were on lots rented from the company. Peasants brought meat, cheese, fruit, corn, beans, and chilies to sell. The Peralta kin from Bacerac stayed with Luis's family when they came to sell corn and chilies. But there was no marketplace (there are none in northeastern Sonora). When Luis and Angelita moved to a house with more room, Angelita fed chickens and pigs with corn bought from farmers from San Miguelito de Bavispe, and this made it unnecessary to buy meat and eggs. All in all, however, there was little competition for the company store.

The remainder of their material culture was quite simple. The Aguirres bought a cast-iron wood stove (the company sold firewood from mine lands) from an aunt of Luis's. They saved some money and bought a bed and a mattress from an agent of a Nacozari furniture store who came to El Tigre to take orders; they paid cash (others made time payments). They used wooden dynamite crates because, at first, they didn't have money for chairs. Angelita had the sewing machine she bought from her mother. She sewed most of the clothes, and this saved cash. Unfortunately for Luis and Angelita, they started off within a few years of the collapse of the El Tigre mine; they were to endure years of scarcity in the 1940s, before the great change in their lives.

THE SOCIAL ORGANIZATION OF THE MINE WORKING CLASS

In a company town every aspect of life—residence and consumption, as well as work—was as one, a "unitary structure" of power between miners and the corporation (Epstein, 1958; see also Nash, 1979). This basic social fact informs two major historical events of the 1930s: the rise of mine labor unionism, and collective vulnerability to layoffs and mass exodus. It is beyond the scope of this book to explain those dimensions of labor union history which evolved at the organization, state, and national levels. My purpose here is to establish the settings of community and workplace without which these dramatic events of history could not have taken place.

The first generation had seen at first hand the effects of industrialization and had sporadically protested abuses, such as American–Mexican discrimination. Still, as the Hernández story showed, their ideas for a better life were diversified by the circulation of laborers between the peasantry and small and large mining. In the 1920s and 1930s employment, and thus human communities, consolidated around a few mines. Overlapping experiences of nationality, kinship, locality, and labor did not spread an even layer of class consciousness among all workers, as Luis shows. But Luis's words, especially his basic assumptions, demonstrate how this setting did bind people within a dense web of expectations about each other in contrast with an external corporation, in particular equating being a miner with being Mexican (as opposed to American managers).

The consolidation of this understanding was made possible because families tended to conserve mine jobs within themselves. Mine companies deliberately hired sons of miners, and though I have no certain evidence about a policy concerning other male kin— brothers, nephews, cousins—it appears that personal favoritism and possibly company policy also brought them in. This is seen in the distribution of Luis's siblings. His oldest sister (born 1903, married 1930) married a miner/machinist in El Tigre. His oldest brother (born 1905, married 1930) and next oldest brother (born 1906, married 1933) both were miners who married in El Tigre. The third brother (born 1910, no date of marriage recalled) worked in El Tigre but married in Cananea, probably after El Tigre closed in 1938. Luis was the fourth brother. The next two sisters (born 1915 and 1919) both married miners in Cananea. The last two brothers (born 1920 and 1922) were too young to enter the mine at El Tigre and instead went with their parents when they moved to Esqueda after the mine closed; they married in that town and neither became a miner. As I reconstruct the residential history, all the marriages were neolocal except that a divorced daughter later returned to the parental house in Esqueda (Figure 3.4).

Despite the very solid appearance of these kin blocs, they could not together control their fate as a kin group. In contrast with the case of inheritance in the countryside, the strong relationships between senior and junior males did not regulate the flow of resources or production. That was in the hands of the company. Each related household was an independent economy relying on the same corporate provider of livelihoods. They did not pool wages or consume jointly, although there was much passing of small material aid. When mine employment came to an end, there was little they could share except mutual help in flight. This explains the terrible vulnerability of the mine communities to the Great Depression, and the finality of the mass exoduses that emptied El Tigre and Pilares de Nacozari.

The nearly complete overlap between work site and residence was the strength of the mine community. We saw much of this in the intertwined stories of Luis and Angelita: growing up to become a miner and a miner's wife; family members and friends, the older

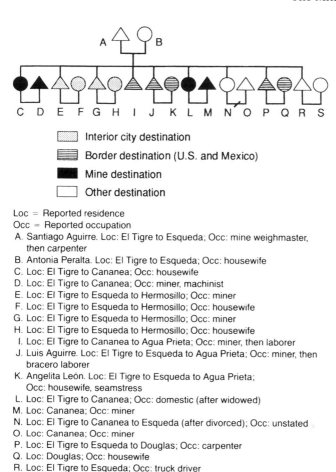

Interior city destination

Border destination (U.S. and Mexico)

Mine destination

Other destination

Loc = Reported residence
Occ = Reported occupation

A. Santiago Aguirre. Loc: El Tigre to Esqueda; Occ: mine weighmaster, then carpenter
B. Antonia Peralta. Loc: El Tigre to Esqueda; Occ: housewife
C. Loc: El Tigre to Cananea; Occ: housewife
D. Loc: El Tigre to Cananea; Occ: miner, machinist
E. Loc: El Tigre to Esqueda to Hermosillo; Occ: miner
F. Loc: El Tigre to Esqueda to Hermosillo; Occ: housewife
G. Loc: El Tigre to Esqueda to Hermosillo; Occ: miner
H. Loc: El Tigre to Esqueda to Hermosillo; Occ: housewife
 I. Loc: El Tigre to Cananea to Agua Prieta; Occ: miner, then laborer
J. Luis Aguirre. Loc: El Tigre to Esqueda to Agua Prieta; Occ: miner, then bracero laborer
K. Angelita León. Loc: El Tigre to Esqueda to Agua Prieta; Occ: housewife, seamstress
L. Loc: El Tigre to Cananea; Occ: domestic (after widowed)
M. Loc: Cananea; Occ: miner
N. Loc: El Tigre to Cananea to Esqueda (after divorced); Occ: unstated
O. Loc: Cananea; Occ: miner
P. Loc: El Tigre to Esqueda to Douglas; Occ: carpenter
Q. Loc: Douglas; Occ: housewife
R. Loc: El Tigre to Esqueda; Occ: truck driver
S. Loc: Esqueda; Occ: housewife

Figure 3.4. Aguirre family history: mine employment and paths out

ones demanding work and respect and the younger ones providing companionship; the almost total monopoly of the company store and the implementation of the credit system that bound each family to the payroll; the Mexican neighborhoods where men walked to mills and mine heads, while Americans lived distant lives in the heights above. Although abstract, perhaps the most profound element of community form was the correspondence (allowing for a little diversity) between hierarchical roles in the productive system and hierarchical roles in daily social life away from the job. The Mexican laboring community, internally divided as it was, nevertheless formed a whole with respect to the foreign corporation, as Epstein learned in his study of the Copperbelt in Zambia (1958).

The patron saint of the Sonoran mines was the Holy Cross; a simple, perhaps incomplete, but still effective way of looking at the ritual for the Holy Cross is to see it as the collective representation of lines of social solidarity. Angelita mentioned the celebration for the cross, and Francisca López, who also grew up in a mine town, provided a beautiful remembrance from her childhood:

> The miners worshipped the Holy Cross, they danced the *matachines* to it each May Third. The festivals they made were very beautiful. Each level of the mine had its own Holy Cross, and a few days before the Third, they would take it out—five or six people would share the cost of dressing it.[10] On the day of the Holy Cross they would give it a mass at the church, then take it out of the church and put it back on each level of the mine. But first they would dance to it, and make a celebration in the tunnel, in the shaft as they call it, before they put it back down in the mine.
>
> [Question: Could you tell me about the matachines?]
>
> Well, it was a little song that they played, and I danced to it numerous times, four or five years as an older child I danced to it. A man who took care of the church organized the people, he taught us how to do the dance before the day of the Holy Cross arrived. We bought our costumes, each of us. . . . There was the *malinche* and a deer and the coyote, and at the end of the festival, they killed the deer, only in appearance, though.

Of course, there is more we want to know that a child would not remember, such as the sponsors and the costs, but it is possible to draw out a few basic points. The fact that the cross was removed from the mine, taken to the church, and then returned, symbolically unified workplace and residence as a sacred collectivity. It is important that these two informants were women (I also collected Holy Cross stories from men), since it shows the involvement of the larger community in the male domain of the mine. The dance in the mine shaft was, several informants noted, one of the rare times when women and children were allowed to enter the mine.

The mine complex consisted of three main parts—the mine, the concentrator (the mill), and the smelter—as well as subsidiary operations such as machine shops, power plants, and maintenance buildings. Inside the mine, crews drilled and blasted the ore faces, "mucked" (shoveled ore), and placed timbers. These men were paid on a piecework basis through the contract system. There were also specialists in plumbing, pumping, hoists, electrical lines, ventilation, and other areas, paid by the day. In the concentrator, rock was separated by the size of pieces and ground up, and the ore isolated by flotation. The concentrator was organized by a hierarchy of skill and responsibility that workers ascended by seniority. Workers in the mill made a daily minimum and extra pay by the metal content of the ore. Smelters had a similar hierarchy of posts by seniority, the base being the men who loaded and charged the hot reverberatory furnaces (Ingersoll, 1924; Leland, 1930; Catron, 1930; Peña and Chávez, 1985:242–244).

Mine organization in Mexico was simple in relation to the giant size of the operations. At Cananea, there were a general mine superintendent, four or five general foremen over major operations, and shift bosses who ran sections that included several mine levels. These positions were filled by Americans. The American shift boss had one to five Mexican foremen (*mayordomos* or, as Americans called them, "jigger bosses") who were directly in charge of the men. Each Mexican foreman had two to three stopes (areas where mining actually takes place) with an average of twenty-five men in the crew (Catron, 1930:37). Because the Americans were spread so widely, they relied on blunt, vertical authority phrased in "racial" (American–Mexican) terms (see Burawoy, 1979:260).[11]

The American boss dealt only with the contractor, not the mass workers (this was explicit policy at Pilares, stated in Leland, 1930). The contractor, not the company, hired men. This reinforced kin leverage. One miner I interviewed about contract membership worked at Pilares with the same contractor as his father had, and he was related to two other crew members—one was his half brother and the other was the husband of a niece. He also worked for a brother-in-law who had a timber cutting contract. The men who were hired as contractors—and the ones who attracted men by paying well—were experienced, skillful senior workers. Contractors usually worked alongside their crews. The Mexican foreman—who stood between American engineer and Mexican worker—had an enormous amount of control over the workplace, especially if the Americans did not speak Spanish.

At the Pilares mine, in 1929, 79 percent of the men underground were on the contract system (Leland, 1930:28–29). At Cananea, 50 to 60 percent of the underground labor force worked on contract (Catron, 1930:37). Elaborate piecework rates were constructed for various tasks—the number of feet advanced at a face, the number of ore cars loaded, or the amount of timber placed, for instance. The engineers made weekly measurements that determined the amount of payment. Each crew member was guaranteed a daily minimum, credited to his ticket at the company store. This amount was deducted from the contractor's payment on settlement day, and the contractor was responsible for dividing the extra earnings, which included his profit (Leland, 1930).

The daily dealings of American engineer and Mexican contract miner formed the key synapse in the hierarchy of nationality and power. Ralph McA.Ingersoll, a novice engineer from Yale, was introduced to the Pilares de Nacozari mine in 1921. His somewhat naive reminiscences provide numerous examples of the tensions in this relationship. In one incident he offended the pride and injured the material interests of a contractor by mistakenly failing to count half of his crew's work. The contractor said to Ingersoll, in great anger, that he thought the American was his friend; told of the woe caused his family; and asked what grudge the American held against him. When Ingersoll refused to budge, the contractor retreated to sudden silence and then stated in a sickly sweet tone that the engineer was really his friend, could have the two hundred dollars, and so forth (Ingersoll, 1924:66). One could hardly illustrate any better a combination of anger and dependence in the context of social race (I learned from the extended analysis of an African mine by Gordon, 1977).

Ingersoll also writes of measurement day, when engineers determined the extra pay of each crew. Contractors would charge in, apparently enraged, and yell at the engineers that they deserved more. The American engineers would try to baffle the contractors with technical jargon, or turn the dispute over to the foreman. In particular, since he was the rookie engineer, three or four contractors at once would try to pressure Ingersoll: "It took me some time . . . to realize that the performance was a well-established custom, almost a religious rite" (1924:78–80). Carlos Córdoba, a miner who worked on a geological drilling crew under the contract system at Pilares in 1940–1944, told me, "Well, as always, they try to take more away from you, everything they can, but at any rate one has to fight over that. When I wasn't satisfied with something, well, it was fought over." After I asked whom he fought with, Carlos said, "With the engineer, he had first responsibility, he had to ascertain in his office why they paid me in that way. If they went and lowered the price of something on me, I would complain to him in his office."

We can obtain considerable insight, I think, into the strength of labor unions in Sonoran mines from this portrayal of the mine as a workplace. There was a visibly unfair separation of American management and Mexican workers, yet there was surprisingly great self-reliance and direction among the workers, conveyed in part by the contract system. The union had to replace the power of individual contractors to assert its own strength; union contractors set the amounts each worker earned on contract piece rates, eliminating the contractor's personal cut, and rationalized hiring on the principle of seniority, not personal networks. One former Pilares de Nacozari laborer told me that the greatest accomplishment of the union was eliminating the ability of contractors to abuse their crews. The lines of mutuality and authority, a general quality that added strength to both contracting and unionism, also came from the interwoven fibers of age, kinship, and respect for work knowledge.

The miners' union started in the social–racial separation of Mexican workers from Anglo American bosses in on-the-job relations. Because the mine workplace and residential institutions overlapped completely—the "unitary structure"—the union evolved into the representative of the entire mine community. It dealt with the North American corporation about issues beyond the work site, such as the conversion of company stores into union-owned cooperatives in the late 1930s (Peña and Chávez, 1985, describe this process for Cananea). The mine union and community drew on the legacy of Mexican nationalism in Sonora dating to the period of mid-nineteenth-century border conflicts, reinforced by resentment of armed intervention in the 1906 Cananea strike and many smaller incidents of racial discrimination (Ruíz, 1988, catalogs many cases). The structural importance of social race in the organization of company mines and cities dovetailed with the cultural strength of nationalism to explain the particular militancy of Sonoran miners against American-owned copper corporations.

4. Alternative Forms in the Mine Period, 1886–1949

The portrait of the working class thus far has concentrated on the mine towns, specifically on the male miners. I began to notice that this was a limited selection of the facts when widows began to crop up in the mine genealogies. In fact, the changes brought about as women tried to cope with their widowhood seemed unusually important to the life histories of their children.

These women and their children, as much as their other kin, were characteristic parts of the working class. The mine system was programmed to produce and utilize a male-wage-based family. However, men's dangerous work and poor health frequently resulted in women's widowhood and children's orphanhood. To survive, they had to use the tools not of miners but of manufactured material culture that the mines and the money had brought. For this reason I call them alternative forms of the same historical transformation. The study of their lives will present us with more challenging and general ideas about the nature of working classes, ideas not tied as closely to the classic industrial workplace.

INSECURITY IN THE MINE TOWNS

Conditions of security had an enormous power to determine the patterns of life courses. These include work safety and occupational health, and also the compensation or lack thereof for illness and death of wage earners, layoffs, and indemnities. Underground mining is the most dangerous industrial occupation in the world. Although hard-rock mining is not as dangerous as coal mining, accidents and silicosis from the copper mines made widows of many miners' wives. Widows and orphans were left with no security because they did not receive indemnities or pensions prior to the mid-1930s. Security is important anywhere, of course, but it is particularly important in mine towns, where women and children depend on one major male wage earner.

Before the 1910 revolution, safety regulation was nonexistent in Mexico; the fifty-peso compensation paid for fatal accidents was cheaper than implementing safety measures (Bernstein, 1964:88). In 1909, for instance, the Cananea Consolidated Copper Company reported 18 deaths and 769 accidents, 47 of them "serious" (Ruíz, 1988: 91). Ruíz points out that everyday damage to health was not even reported.

The first safety laws for mines were promulgated in 1912 but not enforced until the late 1920s. At that time the first effective mine inspections were made, timbering was required, first aid training was instituted, and, most important, arbitration boards and government inspectors held corporations responsible for accidents, thus making safety cheaper than lives. Phelps Dodge instituted model safety measures at Nacozari that not only were the best in Mexico but also withstood comparison with those in the United States (summarized from Bernstein, 1964:95, 155–156).

Water drilling to dampen dust was mandated in December 1928, an important though incomplete measure to reduce silicosis. Leland (1930) states that all drilling except sampling used wet drills at Pilares de Nacozari; Peña and Chávez (1985) report that Cananea lagged until 1932. Compensation for silicosis was the concern of the Cárdenas administration (1934–1940). Mine companies were required to examine prospective employees for silicosis, and either reject them or accept all responsibility for compensation at 75 percent of wages for occupational loss of lung function or life. The law had the contradictory effect of giving more security for the employed worker should he become ill while producing a large group of rejected miners who made do with prospecting and firewood gathering at the edges of mine cities. The strong national and local mine unions and the Cárdenas government with its labor constituency brought a great variety of safety and health laws to reality during the 1930s. Nationally, there were 27,163 mining accidents in 1925, leading to 378 deaths; in 1931, 10,315 accidents and 125 deaths; and in 1936, 72 deaths (Bernstein, 1964:156, 193).

There was no indemnity for the loss of a wage earner prior to the 1930s, and therefore no security for the families who depended on the wages. After the 1930s, Sonoran state laws guaranteed a miner's widow a pension (no amounts are cited), and federal regulations supplemented by union contracts mandated compensation for various accidents amounting up to 914 days' wages. For fatal accidents, companies had to pay 612 days' wages and 30 days for the funeral expenses (Bernstein, 1964:194). The law required three months' pay plus twenty days per year of seniority for unemployment compensation, but in reality these amounts were not forthcoming. Instead, negotiation and power plays by mine companies, labor unions, federal work inspectors, and Sonoran state governors resulted in diverse payouts.

Safety, disability compensation, protection of widows, and employment security increased for employed miners with union contracts (e.g., at Cananea) beginning in the mid-1930s. However, the majority of miners lost their jobs during the Great Depression (e.g., El Tigre and Nacozari before 1937). Some of them worked as prospectors inside extremely dangerous abandoned mines and tunnels, or in small, marginal mines with no effective protection. Thus a large population was as insecure as before.

Life was dangerous for wives even after the reforms of the 1930s; before then, it was terrifying. Not only did men die in mine accidents and from silicosis, they also died during the 1919 Spanish flu epidemic, from malaria, tuberculosis, and other endemic diseases in the countryside, fighting in the revolution, or as civilian casualties. Women also were abandoned by their husbands. In the new life of cities and stores a source of cash was an absolute necessity. When a money-earning husband died, the family had to discover a new range of activities to survive.[1]

TWO WORKING WIDOWS

Two women, now in their sixties, recalled their lives, holding their mothers at their very heart. The point of view is that of an older daughter, helping with child care and chores, and learning, with great respect, the daily labors of the home. The closeness of feeling and learning is important, I think, because it brings to light the hidden story of women's housework. The timing is also important, for these women described what was passed to them from their mothers, now long dead, who were the first in the family to use imported, manufactured kitchen tools and household appliances—working-class formation from the women's point of view.

Amalia Galaz

In 1932, Amalia Galaz, a widow with three small children, was running a tiny restaurant in one room of her adult daughter and son-in-law's house. Her second husband had died of a lung ailment a few months before. Her daughter Francisca López, seven years old that year, remembered a childhood of serving in the restaurant. "There was a firewood stove," she said, "and a table with benches so people could eat. Sometimes as many as twenty or twenty-five came there, sitting on both sides of the big table. We served food at midday, when the most people poured in; then those who worked the second shift [three P.M.] would begin arriving—they woke up and came in to eat."

Amalia came from the small riverside village of Tres Alamos in the municipality of Aconchi, located along the upper valley of the Río Sonora, and married there for the first time in 1916. She had one daughter before her first husband died or left her. Amalia later married Ildefonso López, who worked in Las Chispas ("the flecks of gold"), a mine employing 150 men in the municipality of Arizpe, just up the valley from Amalia's home in Tres Alamos (Gracida, 1985:84; Radding, 1985:334). Francisca, their first child, was born in 1925; and her younger sister and brother, in 1927 and 1929, respectively.

Ildefonso, who was originally from the state of Sinaloa, had worked in several Sonoran mines. He had to quit mining when Francisca was very young. He may have suffered from silicosis or tuberculosis, because "he was sick in the lungs."[2] Ildefonso was reduced to peddling lunches in Cananea, and finally succumbed to his illness in 1932. His daughter estimated that he was about thirty when he died.

This time, however, Amalia did not remarry; her daughter from the first marriage was old enough to help her survive on her own. Luisa, who was sixteen in 1932, had married and was expecting her first child. Her husband, Ricardo Rodríguez, had been managing a mine company store at Las Palmas near Hermosillo; when they married, he hired on to run the company store at Santo Domingo in the municipality of Nacozari. Luisa sent for her newly bereaved mother to help her with the birth. Thus Amalia and her three young children moved to Santo Domingo.

Santo Domingo was a substantial copper mine, though not on the scale of Pilares de Nacozari. The mine was owned by Susano Montaño, who also owned the company store that was managed by Ricardo Rodríguez; Montaño contracted a succession of Americans to operate the mine. In terms of production the mine was an annex of the Phelps Dodge complex, since the milled ore from Santo Domingo was sent to Nacozari de García to be concentrated and then on to Douglas to be smelted.

While living with her daughter's family, Amalia began to serve food to the bachelor miners and peddlers who came through Santo Domingo. The restaurant was successful enough that Amalia decided to build her own house—a four-room house with two bedrooms, a kitchen, and a front room for the restaurant—on a lot rented from the mine owner. The restaurant was supplied on credit extended by the Santo Domingo company store, managed by Amalia's son-in-law (Figure 4.1).

Working at home and in the restaurant, the young Francisca learned cooking skills that utilized new technologies rather than traditional hand tools. She learned to grind the *masa* dough in a cast-iron hand-cranked corn mill. She told me that she did not know how to use the metate and *mano* (the massive Mexican stone equivalent of a mortar and pestle) with which her mother made the masa finer. Mother and daughter still made tortillas by hand, and likewise mashed beans (the blender was yet to come). They cooked meals on a cast-iron kitchen stove rather than over a clay oven typical of rural Sonoran women; Francisca did not learn to reshape the caved-in walls of the clay oven each day.

Cooking was now done in an indoor kitchen instead of an outdoor shelter leaning against the back of the house. The stove used purchased firewood as fuel; this was a mine town where cash was available and wood was sold by the company. This relieved women and children of the exhausting chores of gathering and splitting firewood. They ate from purchased enamel dishes (Francisca recalled buying a set when she married), which supplemented the use of tortillas as utensils. Some of the other items of food technology were still traditional—for example, they kept vegetables and cheese cool in wet, clean sand, and cooled water in new porous pottery urns covered with wet cloth—both operated on the principle of heat loss

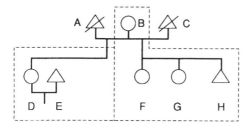

::::: Household unit

Loc = Reported residence
Occ = Reported occupation
A. No information
B. Amalia Galaz. Loc: Aconchi to Las Chispas to
   Cananea to Santo Domingo; Occ: small restaurant
   operator, Santo Domingo
C. Ildefonso López. Died 1932. Loc: Las Chispas to
   Cananea; Occ: miner
D. Luisa Galaz. Born 1916, Aconchi. Loc: Santo
   Domingo; Occ: housewife
E. Ricardo Rodríguez. Loc: Santo Domingo;
   Occ: mine store franchise holder
F. Francisca López. Born 1925, Las Chispas.
   Loc: Santo Domingo
G. Born 1927, Cananea. Loc: Santo Domingo
H. Born 1929, Cananea. Loc: Santo Domingo

Figure 4.1. Amalia Galaz, widow: work and household arrangements as of
1940

by evaporation. Meat was still preserved by drying and sun-curing,
since in Santo Domingo there was no ice for iceboxes.

We learn three important lessons from Francisca's detailed recol-
lection of food technologies. The changes in material culture were
associated with Amalia's moves from rural Aconchi to mines at Las
Chispas and Santo Domingo. Not only did peddlers and the company store provide access to new tools such as the stove, but the
payroll of the mine provided, through her restaurant, the cash
needed to sustain technologies such as buying the firewood for the
stove. Amalia, though not a wage earner, was fully part of the wage
economy.

Second, Amalia Galaz was familiar with the older alternatives,
but her daughter Francisca was completely enculturated to the new,
commoditized technologies and knew no other option. Third, Francisca learned these skills working side by side with her mother in
the manner of an informal apprenticeship centered on the use of a
specific set of material items. Because Francisca was the oldest

daughter still living at home, she had great responsibility for household chores while her mother was in the restaurant, and thus she was intensively exposed to this training.

After spending her childhood waiting tables, it is not surprising that Francisca met her husband, Carlos Córdoba, a somewhat older bachelor miner, at the restaurant. "It was there I met the man who today is my husband," Francisca explained, "and there we married." They married in 1940, and moved neolocally to their own wood frame house rented from the mine company. With Francisca leaving her childhood behind, we will leave her story for a later chapter.

Margarita Encinas de Acosta

Enriqueta Bojorquez was undoubtedly the most skillful housewife my wife and I knew in Douglas and Agua Prieta, where women take great pride in their rich tamales and fine sewing. It is not altogether surprising that she had such ability, for she had grown up in a handsome house in the center of Nacozari de García that was filled with women who had lost their husbands: her grandmother, her mother, and her aunt. Out of the wealth of detail Enriqueta was able to supply on all aspects of women's work, I have highlighted sewing because her mother spent time as a seamstress; her story allows me to represent an emphasis on sewing machines that occurred in family histories with surprising and important frequency.

The family origins of Enriqueta's parents, Margarita Encinas and Trinidad Acosta, are of particular interest for the discussion about the routes that culturally European mestizos took into the formative working population. There are three processes at work: industrial mining replaced prior silver mining traditions; cash and consumer goods attracted family members; and the new mine cities appealed to persons who ultimately derived from the Spanish urban tradition.

Margarita Encinas was born in 1906 in Mulatos, Sonora, where, at the turn of the twentieth century, non-Indian ranchers and miners were aggressively pushing into the lands of the Lower Pima Indians (Dunnigan, 1969:43–44, 49–52). Trinidad Acosta was born not far to the south, in Nuri, Sonora, another area originally settled by Piman peoples. It lay on the north edge of the district of Alamos, the heartland of colonial mining and European settlement in Sonora.

Following Trinidad Acosta's side of the family, we find that his father (Enriqueta's FaFa) was described in passed-down, not direct, remembrance as a *gambusino*, a prospector who had "mine fever." Enriqueta indicated the scale of his mining by saying that he had *compañeros*. This means equal partners in work, rather than employees. He prospected about the Trinidad area in the district of Sahuaripa, but since the silver-based mining of that region was failing at the turn of the century (Ruíz, 1988:36–38), he ended up at the northern copper center of Pilares de Nacozari. There, Enriqueta's grandmother (FaMo) worked as a midwife. She delivered Enriqueta.

As young men, Trinidad Acosta and his brother went from Pilares to Douglas to work in the smelter. They also worked in the copper mine of Miami, Arizona. Trinidad's brother worked in the United States until he retired to Santa Ana, Sonora, where he bought a store and a ranch. Trinidad returned from the Douglas smelter to work as a plumber in Pilares de Nacozari. In the course of two generations the men of the Acosta family had gone from small, independent miners to industrial employees.

Enriqueta's mother's side of the family was well off. Margarita Encinas's father, Federico, was originally from Madera, Chihuahua, but he married and raised his family in nearby Mulatos, Sonora. He owned cattle, agricultural lands, and a mine in partnership with some Americans. He bought cattle in Sahuaripa and Chihuahua, and assembled large parties to drive them to the railhead at Nacozari. To keep the cattle there while they were sold, her father rented a ranch in a nearby village, Los Hoyos, and built his city house (with "five of these big rooms") in Nacozari de García.

Federico Encinas died in 1921. The family businesses were split in half. The ranches in Mulatos were retained by the two oldest daughters, whose husbands were ranchers in the area. Federico's widow kept the house in Nacozari and the cattle in Los Hoyos. With her went three daughters and the two young sons, at that time all single. She placed the cattle in *partido* (calf sharecropping) arrangements with local ranchers. Enriqueta, who had grown up in this household, explained that the exciting life of the city appealed to her grandmother, with its American style and active commerce, and they lived off the income from the cattle. As adults, all but one of the siblings who came to Nacozari ended up living in urban locations in U.S. or Sonoran border cities.

Margarita Encinas married Trinidad Acosta at Nacozari de García in 1921. They had four children, Enriqueta and three sons. Enriqueta was born in 1926. Trinidad, who worked underground as a plumber, died in 1931 of "double pneumonia," leaving Margarita widowed at the age of twenty-five. A sister of Margarita's also was widowed and left with two small daughters at roughly the same time. Now there were three widows: Margarita, her sister, and her mother.

After Trinidad Acosta died, Margarita received an indemnity—a lump sum, not a pension—from the mine company. Enriqueta was unsure of the amount. "My mother had not worked [outside the house] before my father died," Enriqueta explained, "but then she had to, because what she had gotten was not sufficient, with three children and one more on the way. So she waited till after the birth, and then she began to work." She worked as a seamstress in a shop where they cleaned and fixed formal clothes. "Well, it was very hard," Enriqueta continued, "and they worked long hours to get a little bit more, even into the evening they worked, because the pay was so small they had to work overtime. And then after that, they closed the shop, and my mother continued working on her own, whatever she could do—the same things, sewing and cooking to sell, she combined these jobs to help herself." During this era, the mine was not operating and the town of Nacozari was badly depressed.

Margarita had been taught to sew on a sewing machine by her mother. This was Enriqueta's mother's mother, a simple genealogical fact that dates the introduction of knowledge about the sewing machine to the female generation which was adult before 1910 (Margarita was born in 1906). Margarita had had her own sewing machine since she married, but while her husband was alive, she could afford to buy clothes. When she was widowed, she not only sewed for others, she also made the clothes for herself and the children. Only a special dress would be bought.

Margarita and her mother copied clothes from Sears and other catalogs. "They copied from catalogs, they were always copying and copying," Enriqueta remarked. "My grandmother was very modern, she wasn't one of these old ladies dragging their skirts. She was very modern—a shorter skirt with her stockings and high heels. Even more so my mother, she wasn't one of these little old women all wrapped up." As she noted elsewhere, the lengths of skirts varied according to the rhythm of fashion that came from the U.S. side of the border.

The cycles of dress fashion were one case among many in which Sonorans were attuned to the temporal cycles of the American marketplace. Enriqueta's family celebrated Christmas with a Christmas tree, Santa Claus, dolls, toy soldiers, and little dishes. They kept the *posada*, the tradition of visiting on Christmas Eve, but they abandoned the traditional giving of gifts on January 6, the day of the Three Wise Men (it was still important "for the church," Enriqueta said). The change in Christmas is significant, in particular the date; since Christmas is a time for gift-giving, the new date placed the shopping season of urban Sonorans in proper sequence with the commercial imperatives of the United States. The timing of shopping can be seen even today at Christmas along the border.

Enriqueta summarized the state of affairs when she said, "There was everything, traditional and modern. In Nacozari the people had a very American style. They nicknamed Nacozari 'little Douglas' [Douglas *chico*]; there was a lot of Americanized style in all the system of life and people." Nacozari was, of course, directly connected to Douglas by railroad.

Margarita Encinas continued to be attracted by the American border.[3] When the seamstress shop closed, she tried to move to Agua Prieta with the help of her husband's brother, who worked in the Douglas smelter. Margarita returned to Nacozari in 1934. She had gone north to see if there were more opportunities for business there, but commerce was low with Depression-era Douglas, and it was hard to get U.S. immigrant visas. In addition, she was removed from her supportive network of female kin: She could find restaurant work, but there was no one in Agua Prieta to care for her children while she was at work (Amalia Galaz had had her restaurant inside her home). It is worth noting that the next time Margarita attempted to move to Agua Prieta, her sister already lived there.

Back in Nacozari, Margarita moved into her mother's house. She could sew, and sell food and clothes she ordered from a factory in Mexico City, while her mother took care of Enriqueta and her siblings. Meanwhile, Margarita's sister Manuela, also widowed, opened a tiny store. After several years, Margarita saved enough from her little businesses to do the same: "We worked for ourselves, because my mother opened up a grocery store that they called a *changarro* because it was small, not a big store, a large commercial operation; it was more or less a little store, stocked with everything. There we worked with my mother. My older brother began to work very young, he went to a print shop. Running errands in a print shop, that's how he got started." Margarita and Manuela were able to exchange help and stock between the two stores, and both depended on their mother's help with child care (Figure 4.2).

In the late 1930s, Manuela moved from Nacozari to Agua Prieta, and then a few years later to Douglas. Her oldest daughter had married in Douglas, and she brought her mother to the border, and later to the United States. Manuela helped her sister Margarita return to Agua Prieta in 1942 or 1943 (when Enriqueta was sixteen or seventeen), and gave her a small house. Enriqueta's oldest brother opened up a print shop that supported the family. In 1950, Enriqueta married Julio Bojorquez, a furnace fireman at the smelter, and she went to live neolocally in Douglas. Her mother later stayed with relatives on her late husband's side until her death in 1974.

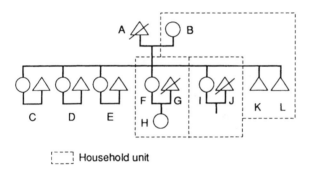

⌐ ¬
⌐_⌐ Household unit

Loc = Reported residence
Occ = Reported occupation
A. Federico Encinas. Died 1921
B. Loc: Nacozari de García (after widowed); Occ: housewife
C. Loc and Occ: ranches near Mulatos, Sonora
D. Loc and Occ: ranches near Mulatos, Sonora
E. Loc and Occ: store at Magdalena, Sonora
F. Margarita Encinas. Loc: Nacozari: Occ: seamstress, small store owner
G. Trinidad Acosta. Died 1931. Loc: Pilares de Nacozari; Occ: miner
H. Enriqueta Bojorquez
 I. Manuela Encinas. Loc: Nacozari de García; Occ: small store owner
J. Died 1935. Loc: Nacozari de García; Occ: bookkeeper.
K. Loc: Nacozari; Occ: laborer
L. Loc: Nacozari; Occ: laborer

Figure 4.2. Margarita Encinas, widow: work and household arrangements as of 1935

WIDOW'S WORK AND KIN RELATIONSHIPS OF WOMEN

Death of a spouse had far different implications for women than for men. Of course, many wives died—of disease, in childbirth—and left men widowers with families. But men whose wives died might remarry or leave children with female kin, and they would not necessarily change their work; for a housewife, widowhood meant a profound change for her and her children. If we think of widowhood as a key juncture, we ask what patterns are seen in subsequent alternatives among locations and activities.

Widows with young children sometimes looked for jobs, but frequently they tried to set up businesses that operated out of their houses. Widows with teenage and older children would not work for money because their children would; and widows with married children, especially married daughters, might offer help with child care while living with or near them. The two cases examined above were women with access to very good resources among their families: Margarita Acosta came from a prosperous family, and her mother's house was important to her survival; Amalia Galaz's son-in-law gave her credit at the Santo Domingo company store for her restaurant, with tacit company approval. In each case these resources enabled the widow's business to thrive. I want to emphasize, however, that the process of widowhood and subsequent activities is general, while access to supportive resources determines the degree of prosperity or misery in particular cases.

Seamstress, selling clothes, running small stores, cooking food for sale, and restaurants appear in the two family histories above. To this list we should add paid domestic labor. The key items of technology include the sewing machine, the cast-iron stove, and the hand-turned corn mill. The knowledge of contemporary, U.S.-derived fashion was important. Women's work for money (jobs, businesses) sometimes appears to be an extension of "customary" household tasks. Florence Babb (1986) and Judith-Maria Buechler (1986) point out that this is not an adequate explanation. People are capable of great alterations, especially in life crisis situations. Widows in Sonora undertook these occupations because these were the gender-specific skills and technology available in the early twentieth century; they were not traditional female technologies but new ones that came from the United States at the same time as the industrial mines. Margarita and

Amalia did choose types of production that could be conducted in the house with minimal interference with household tasks; in this sense they were "extensions."

Margarita moved to Agua Prieta three times and tried to immigrate to Douglas twice; Amalia Galaz's losses of husbands resulted in two moves, from a rural location to a mine town, then to another mine. In their locational choices widows pushed closer and closer to the cash and consumption economy found near the mines, in the cities, and especially at the border. The markets for women's work and business were better in larger and more commercialized places. Restaurants sell to miners and travelers, there is more cash to spend on dresses and suits, and so forth. In turn, because young widows bring unmarried children with them, their residential changes have ramifying effects on family histories. Widowhood was a major force in sliding people down the long-run slope toward the U.S. border.[4]

When Amalia Galaz was widowed, she moved in with her oldest daughter; her son-in-law helped her supply the restaurant; and her daughter Francisca worked in the restaurant. The interrelationships among Margarita Acosta, her mother, and her sister are too manifold to repeat. The relationships among women went beyond the daily exchange of mutual favors, however. There was an informal, but fundamental, arrangement by which the older generation of women apprenticed their daughters in the crucial skills of the new repertory of purchased appliances: the stoves, hand mills, and sewing machines.

The passage of appliance skills corresponded to an actual passage of goods between the generations. In the material culture histories, appliances were passed from mothers to daughters, particularly when the new household was being equipped at marriage, a dowry-like transmission. For example, at the time of her marriage Angelita Aguirre bought her mother's sewing machine, a tool that was to prove vital in the future survival of her family. I propose that women invested in appliances as insurance for their daughters because of their own experiences with the insecurity of relying on male breadwinners.

Women's relationships with their daughters differed from those of men with sons. Most women's work (except certain jobs for unmarried daughters) was still not paid, though it might have involved a business that brought in cash. Daughters worked for mothers in expectation of an inheritance. The female life course resembled the way sons worked for fathers on the land, but not the young men seeking their own work careers in the labor market. The strong kinship ties among women, particularly mothers and daughters, made good sense.

These stories of widowhood have implications that go beyond the trials and tribulations of individuals. The tools and trades of widows suggest that industrial males were not the only people to undergo working-class formation. Women's residential moves toward wage and consumption centers also suggest that purchased material culture imparted a direction to long-term movements of people.

TWO U.S. WORK HISTORIES OF WIDOWS' SONS

The stories of widows' sons differ from those of widows' daughters. Though loyal to their mothers, the sons showed more interest in youthful adventure than in chores at home. This is no surprise. They largely supported their mothers by departing to work and remitting the money they made and goods they could buy. For this reason, the two histories here provide insight into an important period of U.S. immigration history, the hiring of huge numbers of persons from Mexico during the boom years of the 1920s. They also turn our attention from women's skills to men's, a broadly mechanical environment of tools, trucks, and metal. Last, but not least, Pedro and Carlos retell their stories of youthful adventure in an exciting style.

Carlos Córdoba

Consuela Hoyos de Córdoba was widowed in January 1918 when her husband, Ramón Córdoba, a Mexican horseback customs patrolman, was killed by American soldiers in a tragic incident near the border crossing at San Bernardino, east of Agua Prieta. The soldiers had crossed onto the Mexican side intending to hunt at the San Bernardino marshes, and when they were challenged by the Mexican horse patrol, they shot and killed three men, including Ramón (this story from Ramón's son Carlos is corroborated in Sandomingo, 1951:200).

When Ramón Córdoba was killed, his wife Consuela received a small and irregular pension from the government. She moved in with her husband's sister and brother-in-law (Figure 4.3). He was a blacksmith/mechanic who had businesses first at Cananea and then

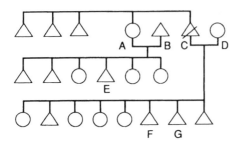

Loc = Reported residence
Occ = Reported occupation
A. Loc: Agua Prieta; Occ: housewife
B. Loc: Agua Prieta; Occ: blacksmith.
   Apprenticed Carlos in his shop
C. Ramón Córdoba. Died 1918
D. Consuelo Hoyos. Loc: Agua Prieta;
   Occ: housewife. After widowed, resided
   in house attached to A and B
E. Apprenticed with Carlos in workshop of B
F. Worked and traveled in United States with
   Carlos
G. Carlos Córdoba. Born 1909. Apprenticed in
   workshop of B

Figure 4.3. Carlos Córdoba, orphan: family relationships

in Agua Prieta. His family and the family of Ramón and Consuela had always been close; indeed, the two families moved from Cananea to Agua Prieta at roughly the same time (1914).

As Carlos grew up, he apprenticed in an informal manner in his uncle's workshop.[5] "Well, I began first with blacksmithing," he told me. "There, where my aunt lived, my uncle had a workshop, repaired carriages there, made tools, and all those things. Well, then, my cousin and I grew up there, we were learning, and then later came along the business of cars, of automobiles, so we began on the automobiles." Agua Prieta, lying along the border, was among the earlier areas to see automobiles; and this city, along with Cananea, was one of the centers for the importation of North American mechanical technology into Sonora. In his uncle's shop Carlos learned the properties of steel and iron, forging and tempering, types of tools, and so forth. Though Carlos and his cousin acquired traditional skills such as hot and cold forging of iron, they also learned to use American measurements and parts, and to do simple drilling and machining.

After a year in Hermosillo, where he attended the Cruz Galvez School, a vocational school for orphans, Carlos in 1924 launched the first of a six-year series of job trips to the U.S. side of the border. He was fifteen years old, and had reached an age when periods in the U.S. labor market were part of the normal sequence of events in a Mexican man's life. The patterning of life courses was set within larger historical processes, however, for the economic disparity between Mexico and the United States in the 1920s brought about the full consolidation of Mexican male life-cycle migration (Cardoso, 1980:82, estimates that 65 to 70 percent of the entrants in the 1920s were young men).

I asked Carlos why he went to the United States rather than seeking work, for example, in the mines of Cananea or Nacozari. "Well, here in Mexico it was more difficult," he replied. "They paid less, you had to look for work in other places, and jobs were scarcer, there wasn't much." Carlos's recollections accurately reflect his time: Manuel Gamio (cited in Peterson, 1975:10) found that corn, the basic measurement of the cost of living in Mexico, was more expensive there than in the United States.

Carlos went to Nogales, Arizona; brought his "birth certificate and all the papers in good order"; paid eighteen dollars; and obtained a visa for permanent immigration to the United States. He then went to Douglas, where he joined a Mexican American friend (not a kinsman) who was to be his partner (*compañero*) while wandering about. They first worked at the Paul Lime quarry, located halfway between Douglas and Bisbee, which supplied metallurgical limestone to the Douglas smelter.

Today, the Paul Lime plant is a twenty-minute drive from Douglas, but in 1924 it was a separate little company town, with houses for married workers and dormitories for bachelors such as Carlos and his companion. Carlos loaded and emptied the "charge" of limestone as it went into the furnaces to be roasted and purified; the work was hot and heavy, and, from his description, did not seem to utilize or develop his mechanical skills. He made $2.50 a day, and he brought the portion that he was paid in cash, after room and board had been deducted, to his mother in Agua Prieta when he visited on weekends. He worked at Paul Lime for three years.

During 1927–1928, Carlos worked in Phelps Dodge's Copper Queen mine in Bisbee. He worked above ground, in the maintenance department, keeping track of tools given out to workers. Carlos also journeyed with his older brother to California. On this trip, Carlos told me, "In California I transplanted tomatoes; then came the tomato harvest, picking tomatoes. I also worked on the construction of a bridge with the Santa Fe Railroad . . . to one side of San Juan Capistrano. . . . One had to search for the work, solicit it, but in other places, Los Angeles, for instance, there were employment offices, and they would send you where they needed to."

The last job Carlos had in the United States was in a small mine in Cochise County, Arizona (the county in which Douglas and Bisbee are located). He worked there for just over a year, from 1928 to 1929. Workers were paid by the amount of ore and its metal content; he left with one hundred dollars in savings. The way Carlos describes it, he was not repatriated (in the sense of being "sent"). He left the United States because the mine closed after the great crisis of 1929, and there was no work to be found. He left, like many Mexican immigrants, without notifying U.S. immigration, so that he lost his visa and could not return.

Looking back on his time in the United States, Carlos realized that he had not saved much money from all that work; it was too irregular. At Bisbee, Carlos did work at a large, relatively stable industrial site; but he soon moved on, and did not seem to have a commitment to occupational permanence. This was a logical consequence of Carlos's age and family relationships. He was not married, and his major relationships remained in Mexico; Carlos and his brother, as the sons of a widow, were flexible money earners for a household in Agua Prieta organized around his mother and older sisters (one of whom was working as a seamstress).

In the United States, Carlos and his brother bought wood for floors and tarpaper for the roof of their mother's house and installed them. Carlos bought his mother a sewing machine, a stove, and a hand mill. In addition to their household contributions, Carlos and his brother bought a car while in California. "Yes, I had a car that we bought in Santa Ana, California. There we bought a little Ford car. Are you familiar with it? First you floored the clutch and then yanked the gas—it was a Model T. We came back in this, got back here very well, passing all the way through the desert." This was a brief adventure but, seen in the context of Carlos's prior mechanical training and his future work, it was also a key item of material culture.

After Carlos returned from the United States, he went to Churunibabi, a middle-sized mine center just north of Nacozari. He then bounced between several small mines and a sawmill in the Los Ajos mountains between Cananea and Fronteras. Work was getting more and more scarce, and Carlos was competing with a flood of men laid off from the giant mine at Nacozari. He continued to return periodically to his mother's house in Agua Prieta. In 1936 his mother died. Carlos said that the siblings took their own paths (*rumbos*) in life, meaning that their widowed mother had held them together in bonds of obligation to her. When she died, so did this family as a unit.

In 1936 Carlos found a job at Santo Domingo in the mine tool shop. His sister's husband was a manager of a small mine near Santo Domingo, and he helped Carlos to get the Santo Domingo job despite the difficulties of the Great Depression. Carlos had various above-ground mine jobs as a machinist and power plant mechanic, using and expanding his training in industrial skills. In a small restaurant in Santo Domingo, as we have learned, Carlos met his wife, Francisca López.

Pedro Durazo

Before we get to Pedro Durazo's tale of years spent working in the United States, we will look at his widowed mother, María, and her deceased husband. Her story is valuable because after she was widowed, she abandoned a farm for life in a mine town. This was an important change at a critical juncture, and we can try to understand the reasons why she moved. The details of kinship splitting demonstrate the alternatives she faced in the urban and the rural economies.

There were four Durazo brothers in San Pedro de la Cueva, Sonora, born in the (estimated) period 1866–1875. According to Pedro Durazo, his father, Francisco Durazo, and his three brothers were small landowners (*propietarios pequeños*). This is a term of some complexity, since today it is a euphemism for large landlords. Pedro's description of his father's farm in the period 1910–1917 makes it clear that they were prosperous farmers who worked the land themselves and did not employ others.

His father's land was his own. He did not sharecrop or employ sharecroppers. He raised wheat, corn, beans, and chilies to feed the family, and sold small, sweet peanuts as a cash crop. He produced three to four, sometimes five, loads to join the burro trains of peanuts shipped from San Pedro de la Cueva to Hermosillo. His father had a burro and pigs, but not cattle or a horse. The family lived in a house at the center of town, in front of the city hall, a clear sign of prosperity in rural Mexico.

Pedro's mother, María, was born in 1884. She had three sisters and two brothers. Her oldest brother, Andrés, rode on horseback to California in 1875, one of the many Sonorans who populated this state (Camarillo, 1979:25; Romo, 1983:33). Years later, when Pedro visited Andrés, he lived on a small parcel of land in the northerly part of the Central Valley, where he and his sons hired themselves out cutting roses and pruning grapes. María's other brother, like her husband, was a propietario pequeño in San Pedro. A sister left San Pedro de la Cueva for Nacozari when she married; María's other sister married one of Francisco's brothers. Between Pedro's mother's and father's sides of the family, then, there were four lines that kept land in San Pedro (as of 1920), two that had left before 1917, and Pedro's family.

In Pedro's spotty kin knowledge we again see that once a family leaves behind a bloc of rural kin, they lose track of the connection between persons and lands (Figure 4.4). Pedro was able to recite the landholdings of the generation of his father and uncles on both sides. Names were given to particular plots of land; for instance, one uncle, Raymundo, had a plot called *mundito* ("little world," a pun on his name). However, Pedro was not involved in the inheritance of land in his own generation, for his mother had removed Pedro and his brother to the urban economy in Nacozari. After about 1920 he lost track of the four lines of landholding first cousins. The only lines about which he was knowledgeable were the family of his mother's brother in California prior to 1929—that is, as long as he worked there—and his mother's sister's children in Nacozari, with whom he was very familiar. Of the six lines of descendants of mother's and father's siblings, Pedro lost track of four. This kinship evidence tells us that María's widowhood led to Pedro's permanent disconnection from a base in landed resources, and his lifelong involvement with resources stemming from North American technologies.

It should be noted that temporary, migratory wage labor would not in itself have caused this splitting of resource bases and kinship if in the long run the young man were to return to the original village. For example, Pedro reported that as a young man his father had worked in mining, possibly at Las Prietas, before returning to share his land inheritance with his siblings.

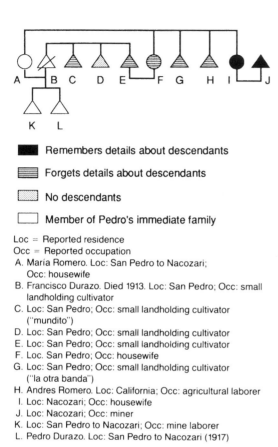

■ Remembers details about descendants

▤ Forgets details about descendants

▦ No descendants

☐ Member of Pedro's immediate family

Loc = Reported residence
Occ = Reported occupation
A. María Romero. Loc: San Pedro to Nacozari;
   Occ: housewife
B. Francisco Durazo. Died 1913. Loc: San Pedro; Occ: small
   landholding cultivator
C. Loc: San Pedro; Occ: small landholding cultivator
   ("mundito")
D. Loc: San Pedro; Occ: small landholding cultivator
E. Loc: San Pedro; Occ: small landholding cultivator
F. Loc: San Pedro; Occ: housewife
G. Loc: San Pedro; Occ: small landholding cultivator
   ("la otra banda")
H. Andres Romero. Loc: California; Occ: agricultural laborer
 I. Loc: Nacozari; Occ: housewife
J. Loc: Nacozari; Occ: miner
K. Loc: San Pedro to Nacozari; Occ: mine laborer
L. Pedro Durazo. Loc: San Pedro to Nacozari (1917)

Figure 4.4. Pedro Durazo: patterns of remembering kin

Why did María leave for Nacozari? Francisco Durazo died in 1913 of "natural causes." He left his farm to his widow, who was twenty-nine, and two sons, aged thirteen and six. María farmed for three years and then sold the land, for, as Pedro commented, she did not like farming and did not attend to it. Spicer suggests that in this region of northwest Mexico "the division of labor in agricultural activity was not sharp until the introduction of livestock when men became the herders" (1969:788). Prior to the changes the Spanish brought, such as livestock, Johnson reports that among the Opata the "women assisted the men in the labor of cultivation, but unlike the Pima, the women did not have to do all the work" (1950:11). The gender-based division of labor was profoundly influenced by the European model, whether via cattle ranching or mission instruction. It established a pattern in which women's work was centered on the house site and men worked in fields and pastures.

In my interviews I found that men did most of the grain field labor[6] (see Owen, 1959:29) while women planted household vegetable plots; men herded cattle while women milked and made cheese; women worked with cloth and men did not. There were exceptions; people mentioned some women who rode horses and ran cattle by themselves, often noted with vigor as interesting and unusual cases. Though peasant women are capable of meeting many challenges, European divisions of labor made it more likely for widows to abandon farming.

Still, María's decision might have been different except for the terrible consequences of the Mexican Revolution for the small town of San Pedro de la Cueva. In 1912, the "Colorados" (Pascual Orozco's rebels) sacked the town. In December 1915 the retreating army of Pancho Villa encountered resistance upon entering San Pedro. Many residents hid, but those unfortunate males who did not hide were rounded up and executed by the angered Villa. "Pancho Villa entered, and he was very angry, he ordered that the town be burned. I remember it," said Pedro, who was eight at that time. "I saw from my house, which was in front of the municipal hall, which they tried to burn but they couldn't because it was so tall, but they did burn many houses, many houses. They did many atrocities, stole everything they could; they took something like eight or nine women from there—they took them, abducted them. They departed firing rounds in the street." As if the terror of 1915 was not bad enough, 1916 brought drought, hunger, and epidemic disease to the central highlands of Sonora.

In 1917 María Durazo sold her house and land to a nephew and moved her family to Nacozari de García, where she had a sister. Pedro's older brother was seventeen, and he went to work as an apprentice carpenter with the mine company. Pedro, who was ten, went to school for four years. "My mother couldn't stay there," Pedro explained, "there were many calamities and all. In Nacozari, there were many people working, and my older brother, he got work bit by bit."

This move was strategic: When María left the countryside for the American-owned mine town, her line of descent shifted its fate toward the border. Pedro married in 1931, and his older brother in

1934; María lived with Pedro after 1934 until she died in 1947. Pedro and his family came to live in Agua Prieta after several intermediate stops. Over half of his children now live in the United States. His brother joined his wife's father in construction labor, and together they moved from Nacozari to Agua Prieta and then Tijuana. That family ultimately arrived in southern California.

Pedro finished six years of elementary school in Nacozari at the age of fourteen. He began the next stage of his life with a trip to the United States. I asked him what motivated him to go there. "For two reasons," he replied. "The first was the spirit of adventure, and the second was to improve myself, to earn more money than I earned in Nacozari. I earned at the most 1.50 pesos in Mexican currency, and in the U.S. I made three, four, five dollars [each worth two pesos]—in the U.S. they paid fifty cents an hour!" Pedro's clear explanation shows that the idiom of adventure in the male life cycle is inextricably linked to the relative inequality of the two nations when, and only when, men need to earn money wages.

Pedro's first journey in 1921 was indeed an adventure. Let us hear it in his own words:

> When I left Mexico, I was very curious. I brought the money to buy a ticket to Madera, California, where I was going to meet my uncle. When I went to Douglas to buy the ticket, I met up with two friends. "What's up? What are you doing?" And I replied, "Nothing. I'm going to buy a ticket to California." "Why do you want a ticket? Come on with us." And after more or less an hour, a train came. In those days it was one of those steam trains, not diesel, and it moved very slowly, very slow. "If you want to, come with us, and we'll grab one of the cattle cars, and get inside in it." And I said, "That's good," and grabbed a blanket. It was three in the afternoon, and we climbed in the cattle car. It was empty, full of hay and trash, and we laid [sic] down there.
>
> The train went along with us until midnight, even later, and we slept, until—I don't remember what that little town is called, maybe Maricopa, I don't remember—the point is that at like three in the morning I woke up and I got scared, the car was stopped, it was alone, the train had left, it left us there in the car and we didn't even feel it. So I said to them, "Get up, the train left us here." So we took off, and soon we began to hear some roosters crowing and a cow mooing. "Somewhere there's a ranch," so we walked and walked. We were on a Japanese ranch. I said hello and . . . "What are you doing here?" "Well," we told him, "we slept, and the train left us, and . . . " "You don't have any work. What do you know how to do?" There was a Japanese there milking cows, and I also know how to milk, so he said, "Good," to me, "grab a

bucket there, wash your hands." And I washed my hands and began to milk. And . . . [the other boys] "We don't know anything." Well, there were pigs, many huge pigs, and he said, "We're going to wash them." Well, we lasted eight days. I lasted eight days, the others . . . after three days they said, "Pay us, we're going," and got the train. They left me there. I stayed eight days and they paid me, paid me very well, a lot of food, the Japanese ate a lot of pork. . . .

It was April, and I arrived in Madera the eighth of May. Again I tramped, I didn't pay, I liked to . . . Well, I finally arrived at my uncle's in Madera, and he said, "Hey, kid, what are you doing?" And I said, "I came from Nacozari, from Mexico." He said, "But what are you doing?" And I said, "Well, nothing, I just came to meet you." What a kid I was, my body so small and thin, I didn't even look like I was as old as I said (I was fourteen). My aunt Emilia asked me when I was born—I was born on May 10—and she said, "We're going to give you a little party." So they sent down to San Francisco for some cousins, and to Fresno for some other ones, and had a very good party, they slaughtered chickens, turkeys. So I turned fifteen there. After two days I wrote a letter to my mother telling her I was in Madera, and I stayed there from May until I returned to Mexico in December.

Pedro traveled to the United States each year until 1931; in 1927, when he was twenty, he took out a visa and immigrated legally for the first time. Prior to that, there was little enforcement to keep him from crossing without a visa. Pedro made two trips each year, in the spring and in the late summer and fall. The timing of his trips provides interesting social insights. In the spring months Pedro worked in planting, including transplanting and pruning roses with his uncle and cousins. He returned to Mexico in June. On June 13 there was the festival of San Antonio in Tepupa; on June 20, the horse races in San Pedro de la Cueva; and on June 24, riverside picnics in celebration of water amidst the Sonoran desert, in honor of San Juan Bautista.

Pedro went back to the United States in July to begin the long harvest season: plums, figs, apricots, and especially grapes. At three cents a carton for table grapes, Pedro could make upwards of six dollars a day; he made four or five dollars for raisin grapes. There was the cotton harvest in November and December, but Pedro preferred to return to Mexico, for cotton paid only 3 dollars for an exhausting 14 hours picking 200 pounds. Except for the work with his uncle, Pedro was sent to jobs by labor contractors, and lived in tents at outdoor work camps. He would return to his mother's house for

Christmas. He estimated that he saved one hundred to two hundred dollars a season, which he brought to his mother; as a son, his form of support was remitting money rather than working alongside his mother, as a daughter might.

On his second trip Pedro began the practice of buying a car in California and returning with it to Nacozari, where he would sell it to get the money for the return to California. He had learned to drive while in Nacozari. In 1931, when his years of work in the United States came to an end, he kept one truck. With this truck, Pedro began the business he would have for the rest of his life: operating a truck for hire and small retailing. His many seasons of American work had left him not only with a small investment but, more important, with a specialization in the automotive material culture of the U.S.–Mexican border.

Although Pedro spent most of ten years in the United States and had immigrated legally, he ended up living in Mexico. As the pattern of his annual cycle shows, he kept his frame of social reference in Mexico though his economic being was in the United States. For example, he met Juanita Yáñez, his future wife, while in Sonora attending the festival of San Juan Bautista. Pedro stopped going to the United States when he married in 1931, the change in his life cycle coinciding with the advent of the Great Depression.

As they drifted from village to village from 1931 to 1947, Juanita ran a series of small stores, bartering coffee, shoes, and such for eggs, cheese, and flour, while Pedro hauled the bulk rural produce to Nacozari and Agua Prieta in his truck. Rather than continuing to sell their labor power, Juanita and Pedro were able to fill a small commercial niche created in 1931 when Chinese immigrants, who had been the chief rural intermediaries, were expelled from Sonora. In 1947 the Durazo family moved to Agua Prieta, where we will rejoin them.

INDUSTRIAL SKILLS OF MEN AND WOMEN

The four histories revolve around the use of two technologies, sewing machines and automotive transportation. These goods were not only manufactured in America, they were bought with money made from American employers, whether in the United States or in Mexican mines. They were part of the process of the industrialization of the border. However, these technologies came under the control of the Sonoran working people themselves, unlike the tools used in mines and other industrial workplaces owned by corporate employers.

Sewing Machines and Women's Work

Johnson reports that the Opata used a stationary ground loom to weave cotton and, after the Spanish introduced sheep, wool; they also cured and dyed skins. Women did the work of weaving and spinning. Men had worn cotton breechcloths, and other garments of skins, and women wore cotton cloaks (1950:15–16; Hrdlička also describes women's skirts made from scraped cottonwood bark, 1904:73). By 1902, however, Hrdlička described the male residents of Tuape as wearing white cotton (*manta*) pants and shirts, and women as wearing loose shirts, jackets, and long, full skirts of calico or manta, with a few serapes. What he described was typical rural Mexican mestizo clothing. Similarly, Officer reports that among the Hispanic residents of southern Arizona during the 1830s, women wore blouses and long skirts of unbleached cotton cloth, as well as shawls and scarves, while men's clothing, he says, was extremely simple (1987:147).

The first transformation was that rural Sonorans no longer wove their own cloth, but used purchased cotton fabrics. Officer remarks that in Hispanic Arizona some of the cotton cloth may have been made in the local settlement, but most of it came from Hermosillo, the state capital of Sonora (1987:366, n. 39). The sources of some fabrics may have reached to the powerful early textile industries in the United States, Britain, and France. Juan Domingo Vidargas del Moral (1982) reports an interesting case of the contraband sale of fabric by an American ship docked in the port of Guaymas in 1808, attracting buyers of the lower classes from throughout Sonora. He comments that such contraband forged a connection between consumers in isolated provinces of the Mexican frontier and foreign commercial capital.

In keeping with the European gender division of labor, Mexican women did the commonplace sewing. Officer, summarizing journals of 1849 visitors to Tucson, reports that "'Mexican women and Indians' visited the camp, eager to trade. Needles and thread were among the items most sought after" (1987:226). Sonorans participated in external commercial relationships, but the work process, and women's lives, had not yet started to change.

The sewing machine came so early to northeastern Sonora that even my oldest informants' mothers, women reaching young adulthood in the 1880–1910 period, used sewing machines. Angelita Aguirre reported, when tracing the history of her mother's and later her own sewing machine, that Nacozari de García had a Singer agency which sold machines to wives of miners on time payment. It is striking that the dates of this change in women's unpaid work coincides so closely with an industrialization which overwhelmingly concentrated on males.

The sewing machine made sewing much faster and permitted women to take advantage of commercial fabric supplies. Women reported sewing virtually all their children's and their own clothing, including the expensive dresses for rituals like confirmations, and also some men's clothes. The remainder of men's work clothes, such as tougher jeans and overalls, was purchased readymade with cash in company stores or during work trips to the American side of the border.

Copying dresses from Sears and other catalogs accompanied machine sewing. Roger Owen reported that even in the small rural village of Marobavi in the 1950s, sewing was done by machine (virtually every house had one, though many were broken), and that men dressed like southwestern Americans and women's dresses were fashions copied from catalogs (1959:30–31). Sewing from patterns on a machine was essentially an entirely new skill. Angelita Aguirre specifically recalled that her mother taught her this as a child. The use of fashion patterns was one of the first and strongest influences on Sonorans to make them eager consumers of American goods; I suggest that perception of differences in visible style, accompanied by the opportunity for money needed to fulfill newly created desires, drew people from mines and farms toward the border, or other cash and consumption locations.

While sewing had long been a woman's task in Mexican Sonora, the sewing machine—truly an item of material *culture*—changed the way women dealt with each other and with the wider economy. The sewing machine became the tool most important to women's informal apprenticeships and marital inheritance patterns. Through the sewing machine women entered into relations of need for purchases and cash earnings, at first perhaps swamped within the larger mine economy, but nonetheless compulsions that had a determining effect over the longer run.

Cars, Trucks, and Male Mechanical Skills

The internal-combustion engine transformed mechanical work while it continued the Mexican male domain of transportation knowledge. This domain began with the Spanish cattle and horse complex. As Spicer (1969) comments, the technology and orientations associated with the horse and cow were one of the deepest transformations Spanish culture wrought among the indigenous peoples of northwestern Mexico. Before mechanical transportation in northeastern Sonora, and of course away from roads and railroads even today, men rode horses for personal transportation when possible. Owning a horse is an expensive sign of prestige, it is associated with non-Indian status (Pennington, 1979:240–241), and riding skills are a basic symbol of manliness (Owen, 1959:26; Sheridan, 1988:89).

The railroad constituted the first displacement of animal power dating to 1900, but only in the areas served by the lines to Cananea and Nacozari. Cars and trucks were introduced in very small numbers and only in the larger towns; by the late 1920s there were *diligencias* (town-to-town taxis) between Agua Prieta and Cananea and Nacozari. In the 1930s and 1940s, Pedro Durazo drove truck routes between Nacozari, Cumpas, Moctezuma, and several smaller outlying villages. Truck transportation began to spread to the small, more isolated lumber mills and small mines after the repatriates returned in the 1930s, and through the 1950s; good paved highways were built through the region in the late 1970s and the 1980s. Recently, as cattle trucks displace cattle drives, the dominance of mechanical transportation has spread beyond industrial and border zones to rural areas.

Not only did the internal-combustion engine change transportation, it also served as a repository and training activity for more general metalworking and mechanical skills salable on the industrial labor market. An older generation of men—Carlos Córdoba, Pedro Durazo, and Antonio Hernández—learned mechanical and driving skills at lumber mills in the United States or near the border. Skills at mechanical work or ownership of a cattle truck served to raise those three men a notch above common manual laborers, to give them a trade that did not decline rapidly with age, and to facilitate their work arrangements with important local patrons.

Today automotive skills are thoroughly internalized in Mexican communities; they are passed down from father to son or along other lines of male relationship. I asked men and women how they learned to drive. Older women rarely know how to drive, while most younger women do drive. But my informants reported that car repair is an exclusively male domain. For young men in Agua Prieta, learning mechanical skills by working on cars—putting in rebored engines or heavy-duty suspensions for bad roads, welding cracked chassis, expanding truck beds—is both an occupation and a fascination, even at the expense of further schooling. The continuity in northeastern Sonora from horsemanship to pickup trucks is very impressive, both as a body of technical knowledge passed along male lines and as simultaneous idealizations about cattle and wealth, physical and social power, and manliness.

CONCLUSION: MATERIAL CULTURE AND THE BORDER WORKING CLASS

Manufactured goods emanating from the United States transformed the simple material culture of the Sonoran frontier, and in so doing altered the texture of men's and women's lives. Some changes can be understood at the simplest level as the replacement of items made by people for their own use by purchased goods. This has been termed "commoditization." However, Sonora had been linked to European commerce since the eighteenth-century expansion of mines and secular Spanish settlement. But it was only a distant and sparsely supplied frontier. Turn-of-the-century material culture change not only brought commodities where once none had been, but also redirected the regional network of material goods away from trade south to Mexico or by sea to Europe, in favor of a much more intense and nearby influx from the U.S. border. The direct linkage of consumer purchasing systems with paid work provided a strong channel.

But why did Sonorans change the intimate practices of their daily lives? If we look at the stories of the persons who actually changed the material culture, we see that these people were uprooted and closed off from contexts where they had used rural technologies.

The kinship evidence shows that families split apart, with only one portion retaining access to the highly restricted rural resource base. Without this base, those remaining persons had to change their daily material activities to utilize a new set of resources. Pedro Durazo, for example, had broken with the kin lines that held land and burros in San Pedro; in trucks brought back from the United States he found a new basis for his work life. Likewise, widowhood forced women to search for a new manner of earning a livelihood (whether replacing a husband's farm or his wages). They found this in the creative application of powerful new technologies—stoves and sewing machines—that would have been impossible with the older versions of hand sewing and cooking.

During working-class formation, people not only went to work for a daily wage and consumer goods. They also came to involve the new consumer goods in crucial roles in their lives, as part of the knowledge needed to be a woman or a man (their gender roles), as part of the teaching and learning relationships between generations (even inheritance at marriage for women), and thus as part of their life cycles. Appliances of American origin, such as cars and sewing machines, were now fundamental to what it meant to be a man or a woman.

We add the history of the commercial changes (in which the network of regional material culture was redirected under the powerful pull of the United States on northern Mexico) to the repatterning of maleness and femaleness to reach the conclusion that use of these items locked the fate of individuals to the U.S.–Mexican border. In pursuit of buying such goods or selling those skills involved in this material culture, people had to move closer and closer to the source of it, the United States. This is to be seen at the superficial level in the Americanization of border Mexicans as shoppers and consumers; at a more profound level, speaking of lasting effects on the courses of lives, it is to be seen at life junctures when persons redirect their choices of alternatives toward the border. There has come into being a distinct people and culture of the U.S.–Mexican border.

We have learned from the stories of Amalia Galaz and Margarita Acosta, widows, and Carlos Córdoba and Pedro Durazo, orphans—persons we might have bypassed in a structural picture of the Sonoran working class, heavy with miners—to think more inclusively concerning what is "working class" about people's lives.

We have come to look not only at explicit forms of industrial labor but also at a range of new activities rooted in manufactured goods, even when they are tools owned by the immediate producers. We have seen how appliance skills were built into learning and the life cycle, into relations between generations, and into the roles of male and female. We have seen that when people were faced with key junctures such as widowhood, they moved closer and closer to wage centers, consumer suppliers, and the U.S. border, with an accumulated result being the reinforcement or repetition of a working-class experience among later generations, even as employers come and go. I propose that this more general perspective, one not dependent on a single era or industry, can help us when we face the ethnographic complications of working classes with diverse members, interests, and experiences.

These patterns, seen during the mine period among widows and orphans, became widespread coping responses after 1929, when mass firings of working men meant that whole families suffered the conditions of insecurity that once afflicted widows. What we have learned about the tools and skills of women, and the reasons why widows tended toward the border, will enable us to understand the family stories to come.

5. Uprooting and Transformations at the Border, 1929–1967

UPROOTING

Seven thousand people left Pilares de Nacozari and Nacozari de García in three months beginning September 21, 1931. Inez Horton, the American wife of the mine's general manager, portrays caravans of mules loaded with massive stoves, kitchen pans, trunks, sewing machines, chairs, tables, bureaus, and iron beds, wobbling and banging as they descended the mountainside. When people see their home come to an end in such a sudden manner, they will, of course, feel tremendous emotions. Horton reproduces a departure party invitation:

> The baseball team, the Tigers, have the high honor of inviting you and your esteemed family to a little dance to be given in farewell of our beloved Nacozari, at the home of Sr. Jesus Ochoa, Saturday. . . . Don't fail to come and be with your friends for the last time. Forget your troubles and come and dance; for very soon we will not be seeing one another. Nacozari will be no more! So why not come to pass the last hours with your friends? Come, come and have a good time, to make merry just once more before the unknown future overtakes us.
> (1968:200)

And on July 1, 1949, when the Pilares de Nacozari mine was closed definitively, Sandomingo reports very similar sentiments: "Young people danced and cried out 'Goodbye, Pilares!' and others said 'Never will there be another Pilares!'" (1951:56; present author's translation). Yet another enactment of this scene could be found during the repatriation of the early 1930s, when nearly half a million

American residents of Mexican origin were coerced into fleeing to uncertain fates across the border (Hoffman, 1974).

Such images are not just sentimental. They point out that these people had been uprooted from one way of life without being offered any immediate alternatives. "Uprooting" means the uncontrollable loss of accumulated work experience and job security, special knowledge, social ties and community life, and housing. Cut off from the old, people begin their search for new lives. At first both unemployed miners and repatriates fell back on kin connections in the Sonoran countryside. There families stayed for the course of the 1930s, as long as the labor market was puny. But their stay was unhappy, and serious family disputes broke out. As paid employment reappeared after 1940, these people left their rural refuges, frequently heading north to border cities such as Agua Prieta, close by the powerful U.S. labor market.

I argue that the repatriation and the mass exoduses of unemployed copper miners can, and should, be analyzed together, although the events took place in two different countries. They involved the same key juncture—expulsion from the wage economy—and similar sets of residential alternatives; both groups merged when they came to the border after 1940. In brief, these people, though once uprooted from wages and consumption, returned again to paid work and consumer goods. What in the prior construction of their lives explains this renewal?

REPATRIATION HISTORIES

Rural Retreat and Border Rebound

While some repatriates went to the half-closed Sonoran mines or state agricultural colonies on the coast of Sonora, and a few remained near the border crossings, the bulk of repatriates went to villages in the Sonoran countryside. This was the "rural retreat." I collected seven family histories in Agua Prieta and Douglas that involved a repatriation on either the male or the female informant's side. In five of the seven cases, when they left the United States, they came to live with kin in rural Sonora; at least initially they tried to support themselves with small-town trades such as carpentry, farming a share of family land, or sharecropping. The other two cases were bachelor sons who returned to established residences of widowed mothers.

Kinship on either the male or the female side was used to renew access to both individually held farmlands and communally restricted access to shared lands. Of the five repatriate cases of rural retreat, three retreated to kin on the male side (husband's siblings or father and siblings), one on the female side (wife's father and siblings), and in one case both sides came from the same Sonoran village. In fact, retracing the alternative landholding situations on each side indicates that the choice of kin was not systematic but depended on which side had the most resources available to share.

The rural retreat lasted through the 1930s. It ended in a "border rebound" after 1940. The World War II economy in the United States stimulated neighboring Mexican cities. War industries that had lost employees to the military were given priority for immigration petitions. The Douglas smelter hired immigrants quite actively during the war years. The bracero contract labor program started as a war measure in 1942. Since many workers found only impermanent employment in the United States, they resided in a Mexican city from which they could shop for used or cheap goods on the U.S. side.

All five families that had gone into a rural retreat had left for the border, at the latest, by 1947; six of the seven cases overall were in border cities by the same date. From the initial border rebound, family members spread into the rapidly expanding postwar U.S. Southwest. U.S.-born children of repatriate families found that they could reclaim their citizenship north of the border. The lasting presence of the repatriation therefore can be found both in the modern population of the Mexican-side border cities, and in the Mexican American population of large U.S. cities.

Family Disputes, Material Culture, and Waged Life Patterns

Repeated mention of bitter family disputes was a striking feature of the repatriation oral histories. They usually pitted sons against fathers, but both generations of women joined with the younger men. This group complained about the lack of accustomed consumer goods and entertainment in the countryside, and insisted on a return to the United States, where they supposed they could use their skills and find jobs. I propose that these were arguments over two incompatible designs for the life course.

The fathers expected their sons to follow a generational succession in which the younger generation worked, either directly on the farm or in temporary wage labor work, to contribute to the father's household in anticipation of land inheritance. This required the sons to subordinate their own choices of jobs, work skills, and work location to the obligations owed the father. Following this life course during the repatriation meant staying with the father in the rural retreat. However, sons chafed under this regime. They insisted on moving back to the U.S. border, the location of potential employment and mechanical technology. The young men had launched a new life course, in which they were more responsible to the market for the sale of their work skills than they were to generational obligations. I call this the "waged life."

Five of the seven repatriation histories reported such disputes. Once again, the two exceptions, Pedro Durazo and Carlos Córdoba, were single men who returned to widowed mothers residing in Sonora, and therefore were not involved in such father–son conflicts. The oral histories about conflicts between generations are confirmed by a contemporary observer of the repatriation, James Gilbert (1934), a North American sociology student who wandered about Mexico during 1933, conversing with repatriates. He found that repatriates who had left Mexico as children or had been born in the United States (that is, the younger generation) were much more dissatisfied with rural life than those who emigrated as adults.

I have proposed that new commodity skills were worked into the upbringing of men and women, and that they had come to expect to obtain and use such goods, at home or to make money. The technological activities were, in fact, basic to their sense of self. In the repatriation, and in particular in the rural retreat, families were removed from the sources of these goods, of the money used to buy them, and the necessary infrastructure to utilize them. Stresses and strains during crises often expose what is hidden in normal times: The repatriation shows in vivid form just how completely the younger generation, the generation reared in the United States, was imbued with the new commodity way of life.

The pioneering Mexican anthropologist Manuel Gamio compiled data on possessions of immigrants returning from the United States that they were allowed to bring duty free through Mexican border ports in 1927 (1930:Appendix V). Although these data precede the repatriation by a few years, they give us a valuable indication of the transformation in material culture that work and residence in the United States had wrought. The figures for Naco (thirty-five entrants) and Agua Prieta (sixty entrants) can be taken to represent northeastern Sonoran emigrants, since there is virtually no other place to go to from these ports. The ninety-five entrants brought forty-one cars and trucks, roughly one for every two entrants. Other male-associated items were fifteen agricultural implements, eighteen mechanical and carpentry tools, and four guns. In the domain of women's production, we note especially the forty-five sewing machines imported among ninety-five entrants, as well as thirty stoves and fourteen refrigerators (iceboxes), two washing machines, and sixteen washtubs. Among general household furnishings were 4 clocks, 86 beds, 69 mattresses, 99 tables, 21 dressers, 58 bathtubs, 192 records, and 4 pianos.

However, the goods, skills, and activities to which repatriates were accustomed were not viable in the Depression-era Sonoran countryside. Mechanical technologies required infrastructure: Cars and trucks took gasoline, which was supplied from Nogales, Sonora, and was rare in rural towns. Automotive equipment, parts, and supplies came from the United States, and trucks required a steady cash income for maintenance. The businesses associated with cars and trucks found their best markets in bigger towns and cities, not villages. In Guanajuato, Gilbert (1934) saw that such occupations as taxi driver were largely the invention of returnees. But the rural market could not sustain many of these new occupations: Gilbert estimated that only one-quarter used skills from the United States in jobs in Mexico. Likewise, there was very little in the way of a cash economy in rural northeastern Sonora in the 1930s.

If young men were to use these tools and skills to make a living, as they had been brought up to do, the only place they could do this was at or across the U.S. border, particularly as the economy began to revive there after 1940. As straightforward a response to the market as this seems, however, it meant breaking with the young men's expected obligations to their fathers. Social obligations and responsiveness to the market proved to be incompatible.

During the repatriation decade, women's interests as a whole were opposed to the withdrawal from the cash-consumption economy. Just as with sons versus fathers, this conflict was expressed in stories of disagreement over family location and expressions of longing for the North American material culture and fashions. The rural retreat threatened more work and worse conditions for women. The numbers of household amenities are notable in the list of material culture that repatriates brought from their U.S. sojourn. But these appliances broke down or lacked electricity. Rural houses made of adobe, with dirt floors and cane and mud roofs, required added effort. Firewood was gathered by women and children, not bought; water was hauled by women and children, not piped. Above all, access to new consumer goods—supplies of fabric, let us say—was difficult both for lack of cash income and because of physical isolation from the commercial, U.S. sources on which people had grown dependent.

These privations were suffered by mothers as well as daughters. The older generation of women had launched into the commodity way of life as unequivocally as the younger ones; mothers had taught their daughters the new household technologies, not the older ones. Women relied on such appliances for their security and small businesses. They showed a clear preference for commercial centers and the border. Thus there was no basis for a generational split among women.

In summary, families had begun to restructure their lives around earning cash and purchasing goods while residing in the United States. The repertory of material culture is evidence of the new activities repatriates had taken up. Many of these items were entirely novel, and others replaced older skills. While the older generation of male immigrants could leave behind those objects and occupations to which they had been exposed as adults, the generation that had grown up in the United States had been thoroughly socialized to wage work and purchased ownership of items, and could not go back. The new generation was identified by—indeed, had built its life around—a new set of activities. Many of these were work activities that had been in demand in the U.S. labor market. But they were not salable in depressed rural Mexico, where the cash economy was minimal; nor was there much money to buy manufactured consumer goods. Therefore the pursuit of these activities—indeed, this entire new way of life—stood in tension with the retreat to older relations.

I propose that the family rifts exposed a change between two male life courses. One was a life encased in an understood social form, a sequence running in place from one generation to the next. The new life course was one in which the individual assumed responsibility for locating himself in a place where the market existed for his work capacity, and over time he pursued the relocations of that market. I call the new life course pattern the "waged life," since it refers not just to wage labor at one particular time (in fact, quite compatible with the older generational sequences) but to a life course that repeatedly, predictably drew the individual wherever wages might beckon. That the waged life course continued even when the formal characteristics of an employed working class were removed during the 1930s suggests that it is basic.

Hernández History: Repatriation and Return

Mercedes Romero de Hernández is the wife of José Hernández, whom we left in 1937, tiring of farming and ready to try the border. But let us take up Mercedes's story in her own right.[1] Curiously, though Mercedes met José at a village dance in the Sonoran countryside, she had grown up on the American side of the border. As we step back in time, we find that Mercedes, her parents, her brothers, and her sisters were a "cross-border family," a way of life that combined Arizona and Sonora, rural and urban, American Hispanic and Mexican Hispanic. They suffered the repatriation, fought among themselves, moved back to the border and beyond, and finally—now looking at the combined roles of Mercedes and José— made a life by balancing on the tightrope of the international line. Mercedes's life is truly the remaking of a border people.

I suggested previously that the flux of kin between neighborhoods associated with industrial sites, as well as rural hometowns, was crucial to the social unity of a transborder working people before 1929. In 1910, for example, Mercedes's parents combined through marriage two different sources of Hispanic population, one "immigrant" from Sonora and the other from territory inside the United States after 1848 (Figure 5.1).

Isidro Romero, a common laborer in the Copper Queen smelter (as well as a part-time dance orchestra musician and store clerk), had come to Pirtleville, a scatter of small houses lying just north of the two Douglas smelters and the international boundary, from the rural village of San Pedro de la Cueva, some hundred miles south in Sonora. The family of his wife, Carmela, had come to Pirtleville from the north, from the town of Solomonville, Arizona. Carmela's father and uncle were attracted by hiring for smelter construction in 1901. They bought some of the earliest house lots sold by Elmo Pirtle, from whom Pirtleville took its name.

Their previous residence, Solomonville, was in the upper Gila Valley, a relatively new zone of Hispanic and Mormon farms settled in

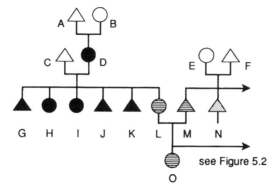

Group that remained in the U.S. during repatriation

Group that was repatriated

Group that had remained in Mexico before repatriation

Not living at time of repatriation

Loc = Reported residence
Occ = Reported occupation
A. Loc: La Mesilla, New Mexico
B. Loc: La Mesilla to Pirtleville
C. Loc: El Paso to Solomonville to Pirtleville; Occ: construction laborer
D. Loc: La Mesilla to Pirtleville (see husband); Occ: midwife
E. Loc: San Pedro de la Cueva, Sonora; Occ: small landholding cultivator
F. Loc: San Pedro de la Cueva; Occ: made religious images
G.–K. Loc: Various urban locations in Arizona and California, including Pirtleville; Occ: diverse wage worker and small business operator
L. Carmela Varela. Born 1892, El Paso; married 1910, Pirtleville; 1910–1930 alternating between San Pedro, Sonora, and Pirtleville, Arizona; 1931–1939 San Pedro; 1940–1968 (death) Agua Prieta. Occ: housewife
M. Isidro Romero. Born 1880? San Pedro; married 1910, Pirtleville; died 1963, Agua Prieta. Intervening locs, see wife. Occ: small cultivator, laborer
N. Loc: San Pedro; Occ: small cultivator
O. Mercedes Romero. Born 1914, San Pedro; married 1937, Pivipa; 1940– resides in Agua Prieta. Occ: housewife

Figure 5.1. Romero family: cross-border ties and repatriation

the last decades of the nineteenth century in proximity to the Clifton–Morenci mines (Meinig, 1971). However, I was told that Carmela had been born in 1892 in El Paso, Texas. From speaking to two of Carmela's surviving younger brothers in Pirtleville, it seems that their father and uncle were masons who moved from one booming construction zone to the next during this turn-of-the-century era

of labor flux. The family claim is that Carmela's mother's side ultimately came from La Mesilla, an older New Mexican settlement in
the valley of the Rio Grande directly north of El Paso.

Mercedes's parents frequently moved back and forth between
Mexico and the United States. This is shown in the list of birthplaces of the children: Pirtleville (Arizona), 1913; San Pedro de la
Cueva (Sonora), 1914; Pirtleville, 1916; San Pedro de la Cueva, 1919;
Pirtleville, 1922; San Pedro de la Cueva, 1924; Pirtleville, 1928.
Since Carmela's mother and female relatives were in Pirtleville, this
sequence of residential moves cannot be explained by the pattern of
women returning to be with mothers for childbirth. It may instead
indicate a male strategy of holding two bases at once, farming and
paid labor. The daughter of Isidro's younger brother, who remained
in San Pedro all his life, recalled that each of five brothers inherited
a share of land, and that Isidro had left his share to her father on a
sharecropping arrangement.

Pirtleville served as a central location for the network of households extending on both sides of the border. It linked the group of
relatively permanent households on Carmela's side of the family,
through the more mobile household of Isidro, with the interior of
Sonora.[2] During this era, kinship could proceed without any impedi-
ment placed by immigration and legal residence policies.

Isidro lost his job at the old Copper Queen smelter in 1931, the
year the Douglas smelters were merged and the old Copper Queen
closed. When Phelps Dodge offered laid-off workers paid transportation to Mexico for their families and their household goods, Isidro
decided to leave behind life in the United States for his natal home
and his portion of farmland in Sonora. In the analysis of this turning
point, I take up two issues. When Isidro abandoned Pirtleville, he
separated Carmela from her brothers and sisters, so I will examine
the impact of repatriation and immigration restriction on former
"cross-border" families. I then turn to the Romero household's own
attempts to revert to the rustic life as a case study of rural retreat,
family conflict, and border rebound.

Carmela's brothers' and sisters' descendants stayed on the U.S.
side. They now reside in Pirtleville, Phoenix, and California. When I
spoke to one of them (Carmela's brother's son) about his cousin Mercedes and her family, he referred (speaking in English) to Mexico
"over there" as strange and dangerous. That, in fact, was Agua Prieta, a mile or so away. The closing of the border split unrepatriated

kin branches from the repatriated. Nationality, which had previously been of lesser importance, now accounted for divided fates among related persons.

As we shall see below, the family of Isidro and Carmela Romero returned to the border at the end of the Great Depression. When they came back, citizenship status had become more important than when they left. Four of their children were born and registered in the United States (Pirtleville), and during World War II and afterward, they reclaimed their right to live and work there. Three had been registered in San Pedro; after 1940 they and their descendants remained Mexican citizens (a few would immigrate much later to the United States). Birth location, which had meant so little at the time, would determine national status, and therefore the entire course of life after 1940.

Knowledge of kin reflected the various split paths. I obtained outstandingly detailed information on siblings and their descendants (down to birthdays of nephews) from Mercedes, even though most live hundreds of miles away in Los Angeles. This group—the repatriate bloc—was vital to her husband's work in the United States, and the families had remained close. Information on the descendants of the siblings of her father, Isidro, was provided by a first cousin of Mercedes's who had grown up in San Pedro de la Cueva and much later came to Agua Prieta. This group had remained on the land in San Pedro after Isidro's household left in 1941. Last, I went to a younger brother of Carmela's to learn the descendants of Carmela's siblings because Carmela's daughter Mercedes had lost track of this branch of the family. This was the portion that had stayed in the United States during the 1930s, and split from Carmela's own children (see Figure 5.1).

The post–1929 repatriation brought an end to the open-border family. It was no longer possible to make the flexible movements between the two countries that had formed the links among cross-border kin. Repatriation to Mexico failed to recognize that the Mexican people of Sonora and Arizona were one, and that New Mexico and California were also linked with Sonora. The subsequent control of legal immigration and punishment of illegal immigration hastened their differentiation. One portion of these families remained in the United States or was able to reimmigrate legally. These family branches obtained jobs at American wages substantially above the Mexican ones. They sent their children to English-speaking, often socially segregated schools. The groups of kin who ended the decade in Mexican border cities faced a poorer job market and had fewer years of schooling, but had a very different experience in schools, where everyone was of Mexican nationality. Elements critical to a complex sense of identity began to diverge.

The U.S. Southwest recovered, and indeed increased, its voracious demand for Mexican manual labor, but this was structured in a new context of immigration controls and temporary contracts. When kin cross the border today, they do so as bearers of two very distinct legal positions: one with full citizenship privileges and the other as temporary and often extralegal laborers. The result was that kin networks spread on both sides of the border before 1929 became differentiated into distinct branches, Mexican and Mexican American. This does not mean that they no longer see each other, or do not send money across the border, or forget their kinship, or cease to immigrate from Mexico to the United States. But as state control of immigration and citizenship rights grew, the international boundary increasingly defined two different populations—"Sonora" and "Arizona"—in a form that had not existed before.

In San Pedro de la Cueva, Isidro reclaimed the land he had sharecropped to his brother. He bought a house in San Pedro with some savings from the United States (they left the house in Pirtleville to one of Carmela's nieces). Isidro planted corn, wheat, sugarcane, and beans, with advances for cash and seeds from one Carlos Maldonado, and at harvest he sold the crop to Maldonado. He also worked for Maldonado, herding his cattle, and in turn he hired day laborers at 1.50 pesos a day to plant and harvest wheat. From this we can surmise that the Romero family did not ultimately leave San Pedro because their farm was inviable.

The move from Pirtleville to San Pedro de la Cueva brought cultural juxtapositions and family conflicts. Mercedes recounted a story that when she told her playmates about movies, they called her a crazy *pocha* (an insulting term for Americanized Mexicans). When I asked her to describe life in San Pedro, she did it in the narrative form of repeated contrasts between the rustic and the modern, the former having *mucha calamidad*. The denotative meaning of calamidad is "calamity," but Sonorans use it figuratively to refer to rural backwardness, poverty, and suffering. Mercedes implies a general rejection of things rustic, though she also nostalgically imagines that the country life was pure and clean.

Many of the changes in the Romeros' lives involved domestic labor and the loss of access to purchased goods. They brought with them a bed, a mattress, a set of box springs, a clock, and a pedal sewing machine, but they left behind a truck, a stove, a phonograph, and furniture. Mercedes mentioned many of the chores—gathering firewood, hauling water, rebuilding clay oven walls—that typically burdened women and children in the countryside. One story in particular epitomized the changes. In the United States cheap sneakers cost only ten cents, so making one's own shoes was hardly worth the effort. In San Pedro, Carmela, the mother, made canvas shoes by hand, cutting the form and sewing the uppers. When the family returned to the border, Carmela's kin were horrified at their poorly shod state and immediately went out to buy shoes for them. In Mexico, shoes are a particularly potent sign of the gap between the indigenous rural poor and European-oriented townspeople (indeed, Carmela made shoes, and not the moccasin-like *teguas* which are indigenous to backcountry Sonora).

The Romero family was riven by a power struggle between Isidro and his oldest son, Ernesto (born 1913). None of the children was happy in Sonora, but Ernesto was the most irritated by rural life. Mercedes recalled his saying, "I am going to die if I don't get out of here." Ernesto tried to recruit the support of his younger siblings. Mercedes witnessed a conversation in which he asked the next younger brother if he were going to say anything, and then said to him, "Well, you are more guarded." In 1931, when the Romero family was repatriated, Ernesto was eighteen and, as the oldest son, bore the greatest burden of farm work under his father.

Ernesto left San Pedro, first to finish school in Douglas (staying with his mother's relatives) and then to join the Civilian Conservation Corps (CCC) at Fort Huachuca, west of Douglas. He married in 1937 at Pirtleville, and by this act set up permanent residence on the U.S. side of the border (he was a U.S. citizen by birth). Ernesto sent money to help two younger brothers come to Douglas to complete their schooling. He had begun to contest with his father the location, and thus the control, of the family. By 1939 two brothers and two sisters had joined Ernesto in Pirtleville.

The last break with rural Sonora came in 1940, when Carmela Romero came to the boundary to be near her sons: The younger ones had also entered the CCC and Carmela, misunderstanding the situation, feared they had been drafted. Her husband reluctantly came to the border with her. His commitment to rural Mexico was reflected in the fact that at first he did not sell the farm or house, but left them with his cousin. Isidro and Carmela, along with their youngest child, a school-age boy, remained on the Mexican side of the border, setting up house in Agua Prieta. Isidro worked by the day as a construction laborer, and Carmela earned money taking in sewing and knitting.

Mercedes did not immediately join them, for she had married José Hernández in 1937 at the village of Pivipa. She had her first two children in Pivipa in 1937 and 1939. When she was pregnant with her third child, in 1941, she felt she needed the help of her mother. "I'm going to have a baby," she said to her husband, "and neither my mother or yours is here." After Mercedes had the child, she began outside work to help her mother. "I saw that my mother was falling behind," Mercedes explained, "so I went to work and left the kids with her. . . . We went to work in Pirtleville, sometimes on foot, to wash, to iron, to help my parents with the approval of my husband, because he worked." Mercedes made a dollar or two a week, mostly working for relatives.

José joined Mercedes twenty-two days after she left because his crop was hit by a severe frost just after he had put it in the ground. José's personal disaster touched off a more general discontent, as he emphatically stated, with the low return to his days on the farm contrasted against the higher wages he knew he could make along the American border.

José first worked inside Mexico as a carpenter. Soon, however, he immigrated legally to the United States. An Arizona rancher of a prominent family, for whom José had worked without documents, recommended his immigration to the INS officer. It was 1942, a war year when working immigrants had unusual priority; Phelps Dodge hired heavily among new arrivals from Mexico. Mercedes's brother Ernesto was hired at the smelter in 1942 (he worked there until 1979); another brother and two brothers-in-law (Mercedes's sisters' husbands) also worked there. José, with the help of his brother-in-law (WiSiHu), was hired at the smelter in 1943.

A group of Mercedes's kin moved to Los Angeles in 1946, at a time when a prolonged strike had closed the smelter. José soon followed. This group formed an important set of relationships for the Hernández family, so it is worth examining the kinship involved. Mercedes's brother Ricardo and sister Aurelia married a sister and brother from Pirtleville, and their first cousin married Mercedes's sister Concepción. In Los Angeles, Ricardo worked in a Ford factory, as did one brother-in-law; the other brother-in-law became a foreman at a crushed rock firm. The latter got José his first job in Los Angeles. Mercedes's family was distributed thus: her parents with their youngest son in Agua Prieta, living with Mercedes and her children; three married siblings in California, hosting Mercedes's husband while he worked there; and one brother living and working in Pirtleville (Figure 5.2).

With the rock quarry job in 1946, José started three decades of irregular and diverse jobs, usually involving extremely heavy effort, that took him throughout California and Arizona. Examples of José's

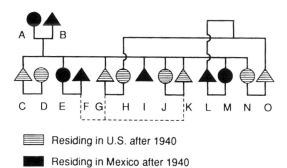

▦ Residing in U.S. after 1940

■ Residing in Mexico after 1940

⌐___ Line of Assistance to José Hernández

Loc = Reported residence
Occ = Reported occupation
A. Isidro Romero
B. Carmela Romero
C. Ernesto Romero. Loc: Pirtleville; Occ: smelter worker
D. Loc: Pirtleville; Occ: housewife
E. Mercedes Romero. Loc: Agua Prieta; Occ: housewife
F. José Hernández. Loc: Agua Prieta and various U.S. sites;
   Occ: diverse laborer
G. Loc: Pirtleville to Los Angeles (1947); Occ: auto plant worker
   (Los Angeles)
H. Loc: Pirtleville to Los Angeles; Occ: bank teller
 I. Loc: Agua Prieta; Occ: construction laborer
J. Loc: Pirtleville to Los Angeles; Occ: housewife
K. Loc: Pirtleville to Los Angeles (1946); Occ: construction
   foreman (Los Angeles)
L. Loc: Agua Prieta; Occ: bookkeeper, store owner
M. Loc: Agua Prieta; Occ: housewife
N. Loc: Pirtleville to Los Angeles; Occ: cafeteria worker
O. Loc: Pirtleville to Los Angeles; Occ: auto plant worker

Figure 5.2. Romero family: border rebound; José Hernández: leverage into U.S. labor markets

work history[3] illustrate the life of the "secondary labor market" that most Mexicans encounter in the United States (Portes and Bach, 1985). In 1951, José worked for St. Anthony Mining in Arizona, living in the company barracks and sending to Agua Prieta money and goods bought from the company store at subsidized prices. One pay stub showed that José earned forty dollars for the week, after deductions of six dollars for shoes and six for board. From 1953 to 1957 he worked in another Arizona mine, the Johnson Camp of the Coronado Copper and Zinc Company, which he left after a steel fragment from a drill embedded itself in the pupil of his left eye. José was compensated for the loss of 57 percent of the vision in that eye (he received $121.67 a month for fourteen and a half months), and the doctor's report read: "Mr. Hernández could return to any type of work not requiring real good vision."

In 1959, José was back in California, cleaning ships in a shipyard and sharing an apartment in San Pedro with three other Mexican men, all of them away from their families. At that time, he recalled, he was sending fifty to eighty dollars a week home. In 1961, José received another eye injury, this time losing 63.6 percent of vision in the right eye, while working for the Fisher Contracting Company in Tucson. Again he was compensated. In 1968, José worked in the Pima Mine outside Tucson. There he received $2,426 for one-quarter loss of the use of his left arm when a high-pressure water hose knocked him to the ground. The list of jobs goes on until 1981. In the spaces between these jobs, José would scrounge up agricultural field labor by word of mouth—anything to keep working. We have a sense of the personal sacrifices José was willing to make on behalf of his life back home.

While José voyaged, Mercedes remained in Agua Prieta with their children (ten in all, born 1937–1958), as well as the separate household of her parents and her youngest brother. She was responsible for using the money sent by José to support the two households. "When he was paid there, he would send money to me," Mercedes explained. "I would cash it over on the U.S. side and buy groceries, and then I would bring over here the money left over to pay the water, the electric bill, the taxes on the house, and so forth."

With a steady income in dollars, José and Mercedes's children were able to stay in school, especially the two sons, who obtained preparatory and commercial education; three of the eight daughters went past secondary school. Though the sons and several daughters worked in stores and one daughter in an early maquiladora, their income was not vital to the family; it could be saved by the children for their marriages.

The two-part workings of the Hernández family economy are particularly well illustrated by their houses, which were both major investments and a clear sign of the family's social commitment to the Mexican border city. In 1945, with money from José, Mercedes bought three lots on Sixth Street, one each in the name of her father, her brother, and herself. Her father, her brother, and José (when he was home) built two small adobe houses, one for her family and one for her father's family. The money for materials for her father's house came from her married sisters in California, and money for her house came from José. Later one lot was sold, and another went to Mercedes's brother; her parents lived on the third one, with some rental apartments for income, until they died; then the houses there went to two of Mercedes's daughters. Meanwhile, Mercedes and José bought a small house on Seventh Street for five thousand pesos obtained by changing José's dollars. This house had to be expanded to fit their family. José did not do the work. Mercedes explained, "He put the masons to work. He didn't work, he was working in the mine, so he came every week and left orders to do this and that."

What accounts for the two-legged form of the Hernández household? There was José's green card, his status as a permanent resident of the United States, which permitted him to work there without fear of expulsion. (After 1962, he was also a member of an American union, the Laborers International Union, which sent him to jobs from a hiring hall in Tucson.) On the other side of the border were the houses, children's education, and José's circle of friends at the Carne Asada restaurant, where he liked to talk politics—all made possible, ironically, by the buying power of his dollars.

This arrangement, which I call the "border balance family," is defined as a household that receives its income from the U.S. side of the border but maintains its residence, its reproduction, and its social life in the Mexican border town. Balanced families are important to border life. In 1970, for example, before the full presence of the maquiladora industry was felt, the second largest employment sector in Agua Prieta was agricultural labor in adjacent areas of Arizona; it was surpassed only by miscellaneous urban services (Gildersleeve, 1978:174–176, 183). Balance on the border also demonstrates the reshaping of the designs of Mexican lives because of the structuring power of U.S. immigration policies and economic demands.

U.S. BORDER POLICY AND MEXICAN LIVES

After 1940 the United States tried, with incomplete success, to channel and control Mexican immigration among several legal and, by implication, extralegal statuses. Status with respect to legal immigration determined the relative fates of various persons. Richard Mines's powerful model of Mexican immigration describes this differentiation (1981). There was a relatively small number of Mexican immigrants who gained permanent resident status, which conveyed full, secure, and lifelong entrance to the United States. The returning repatriates who were U.S. citizens by birth and had the good fortune to hold documents to prove it should be included in the secure group. This portion of the population could live in the same country they worked in.

On the other hand, the bracero contract labor system and the subsequent, smaller commuting worker program operated to keep Mexican residence separated from U.S. work sites. Though commuting status permitted regular renewal, the bracero system cut employment into discrete periods without any certain long-run tenure. Most insecure of all, and of course removed from home, was undocumented border crossing in search of work.

Legal status relates closely to the life path of immigrants. One group of workers starts in the United States as young men, gains some form of permanent legal (green-card) access, enters the higher rungs of the U.S. secondary labor market, and continues wage work there until retirement, often with land or houses bought in the home village with savings. The other life cycle also starts with youthful work, but employment is either contractually temporary (such as the braceros of the 1942–1965 era) or extralegal. That is, there is no legal permanence in the U.S. labor market. This group has a descending work career, enters the more irregular ends of U.S. labor, loses work, and leaves for Mexico—thus exiting the U.S. labor market sooner—and finishes up with sharecropping or employment, such as it is, in Mexico.

Mines (1981) adds to the legal and life sequence frameworks a broader historical model of Mexican migration in which expulsions, such as the repatriation, break off older waves of migration. After the immigration restrictions ease, as in the 1940s, the young men who are able to gain legal immigration status act as a beachhead, channeling increasing numbers of hometown arrivals seeking temporary employment. But this cycle of expansion stops upon the succeeding expulsion (such as the end of the bracero program in 1965). The followers—contract workers or undocumented migrants—abandon the U.S. wage labor market, while the leaders with residential rights retain their commitment to permanent employment in the United States.

In summary, Mines delineates two groups: One can sustain a presence in U.S. labor markets in spite of occasional retrenchment, and the other cannot withstand aging or U.S. border expulsions. Balancing one's household at the border is an attempt to emulate a degree of access to the United States held by the former group, despite an immigration situation of limited or insecure entry resembling the latter group. Furthermore, as Mines makes clear (and as other scholars, such as Kearney [1986], also emphasize), the several immigration positions are linked when cross-border kinship is utilized to leverage migration resources, though they represent unequal locations and fates as specific households. This characterizes the post–1940 controlled border in contrast with the relatively equal networks found during the open border period.

After the repatriation had swept away the earlier wave of Romero family immigration, Ernesto Romero began a new beachhead, drawing his siblings in his wake. They in turn married into a kin group who remained in the United States. Ernesto could pioneer this beachhead in part because of a very favorable status—U.S. citizen by birth—in the newly discriminating American system. The Romero beachhead started in Pirtleville, but it soon shifted to southern California, in response to the manual labor demand in boom areas of the U.S. Sunbelt. Yet the Romeros never entirely left behind their channel to the Mexican border at Pirtleville and Agua Prieta. José Hernández ebbed and flowed within this channel in his lifelong commute between marginal American jobs and secure Mexican border residence.

José, a secondary kinsman who followed pioneer immigrants, would be expected to have a descending work career and rapidly to exit the U.S. labor market during some subsequent wave of expulsion were it not for his surprisingly secure legal resident status. Why did José, who had the legal right to reside permanently in the United States, instead form a border-balance family? (A more typical border-balance family, based on bracero or commuting status, has no such residential option but follows similar social patterns.)

The secondary labor market in the United States is harsh and unpredictable. Erratic jobs, like the ones José had, might be dangerous to the survival of the household economy were it placed in an American city. In Agua Prieta, dollars could be used to buy the security of homeownership. Employment that would provide for a marginal existence in the United States supplies enough dollars for an unusually prosperous working-class existence in border Mexico: new furniture bought on time payment, well-educated children, the dresses and dinners for weddings, and all the other things that Mercedes told me she bought.

Perhaps even more important to life choices is the deeply felt level of daily social relations. Mexican immigrants, especially those in the more insecure of the paths outlined by Mines, are pushed to the bottom of the hierarchy in southwestern U.S. life. On the border José had prosperity and social standing. As Piore suggests (1979), the immigrant will take work of low standing to enable a social life of higher standing than is usually possible at home. The border-balance family exists within the legal barriers and openings provided by the American economy and government, but it also represents an attempt to build a decent and satisfying social life by the Mexican people themselves.

THE BORDER SETTLEMENT PROCESS

Introduction

Although the Hernández family history concentrated on immigration, their story includes arrival at Agua Prieta, the initial scramble for survival, and their proud achievement of education and housing, accomplished in substantial part by the women of the family. Such was the process of settling the modern border city in the post–1940 period. Since the dying mines at El Tigre and Pilares de Nacozari were so intimately tied to Agua Prieta by an umbilical railroad, it should hardly surprise us that displaced miners poured into this city. We have already noted the reflux of repatriate families.

Though it is not possible to count retroactively the immigrants who arrived in this era, an approximation can be made using James Greenberg's (1981–1982) census of 104 male and female heads of households in Barrio Ferrocarril (a neighborhood that received much of the inflow at the time). For those who were not born in Agua Prieta, the average year of arrival was 1958. I use locations of birth as an approximation for place of origin. I found a distribution not surprising for Agua Prieta: seventy-one from northeastern Sonora, five from coastal Sonora, twenty-two born in other states (predominantly the northwestern corner of Chihuahua), and one born in the United States (Pirtleville). Of those born in Sonora, twenty were born in Agua Prieta, twenty-one in identifiably mine communities, and thirty in other towns (ranging from purely peasant localities such as Bavispe to mixed rural, railroad, and mining centers such as Esqueda). Besides Agua Prieta, the single most common municipality of origin was Nacozari (Nacozari de García, Pilares de Nacozari, and Churunibabi), totaling thirteen persons.

Agua Prieta of the late 1940s, the 1950s, and the 1960s lacks the dramatic presence possessed by the great working class of the mines, and the new border maquiladora industry was still to come. Yet to study these working people only in negatives would be unsatisfactory. In the subtleties of change at this time we can realize the factors that came to compose Mexican border life for decades to come.

There was no longer one principal source for money earning, nor did money come predominantly through men. Males pieced together complicated sources of work. Migratory labor in the United States was important, but it frequently was limited to contract periods or risky covert trips. Laboring men sought jobs inside Mexico from the powerful businessmen who were profiting from the border boom, in the process rediscovering the idioms of personalized work and thereby retreating from the institutions of labor unions and impersonal markets. The change in work patterns, however, was yet more profound: Women came to the fore, responding to unpredictable male employment by elaborating those business skills and roles first identified among widows. Each household, torn from the payroll pattern fixed by the company town, renegotiated the interests of wife and husband in its own way.

Consumption of American manufactures continued, but through very different channels; the monopoly presented by the company store was replaced by an elaborate network of transactions in two currencies and two nations. Unlike the mines, where the workplace was central, at the border consumption became an important organizing principle in its own right. Likewise, these families left behind corporate housing for a heterogeneous city where each family was responsible for acquiring its own lot and building its own house. In the process of maneuvering through such complexities of consumption, housing, and work, families accorded more public activity to women as the managers of household interests and developed new relations with the wider social order. The institutions of the mine centers, the union and the company hierarchy, were no longer relevant. Families focused on narrow concerns of starting a new and prosperous life. Yet by seeking house lots from the municipal government, and other simple acts, they inevitably took steps into the social power structure characteristic of the border city.

People's understandings of their own histories reflect the undulations of this time and, on the whole, give it a markedly optimistic cast. I get at these understandings through the narrative order of oral histories, in which people select certain events or accomplishments to represent a direction or order in their lives. This was especially visible in the largely uninterrupted narrative life summary with which many persons began their recorded interviews. Mine closings or repatriation appeared in the stories as a cataclysmic separation from the past.[4] The narratives frequently began at this point, even though it was not the start of the person's history. After this time, they presented their lives (with much reason) as a gradual series of accomplishments, the most important of all being obtaining a city lot and building a house. They also emphasized their investments in their children's education; some men told how they progressed from irregular paid labor to ownership of their own workshop. Family goals are notable, frequently lineal investments passing from the older to the younger generation, rather than individual careers or larger class goals. All in all, they recalled these three or four decades very positively, repeatedly contrasting them with the visible economic erosion at the time of the interviews (1984–1986).

The optimism of Agua Prieta informants resembles the "generational optimism" that Balán, Browning, and Jelin (1973) found in Monterrey during the same period. They found that there was relatively little upward mobility within generations but that fathers could feel optimistic about the education and occupations of their sons relative to their own lives. It is worth noting that Balán et al. predicted optimism would be frustrated by increasing social closure within Mexico's highly unequal form of economic growth (1973: 316, 330).

Luis and Angelita Aguirre told such a story of death and rebirth.

When we left them, Luis was still employed in the mine at El Tigre. The mine closed, and Luis attempted a futile retreat to an older prospecting technology. Eventually he and his wife left El Tigre for Agua Prieta. In this sense the Aguirres are typical of displaced mine families who fled to the border, yet their story of carefully reorganizing each piece of their life once they were in Agua Prieta remains extraordinary.

Aguirre History

On July 18, 1938, while Luis was at his usual station above the ore hamper of the concentrating mill, the electric power at El Tigre was suddenly shut off. Other men were trapped inside the mine. One of them, a friend of Luis, told me his story:

> It was very sudden. We weren't expecting anything. Picture it: they caught us inside, they caught us closed up inside without any hoist cage. We climbed the ladders, many people in the lower levels went all the way by ladder . . . because suddenly there was no power, nothing could be seen, and we had to exit by the ladder.

Though the men at first did not realize what was going on, the Lucky Tiger Mining Company of Cincinnati had abandoned the mine.

In lieu of the proper indemnities owed to laid-off employees, the mine was transferred by the Mexican government to the miners' union (Section 65, based in Cananea), to be run as a cooperative. The American company, despite its avoidance of liabilities, was compensated for plant facilities from the cooperative's funds; for this reason, the El Tigre cooperative was never fully viable. Born without hope, it gradually failed, left to former employees and hungry outsiders digging inside the mine for scraps of gold and silver ore (Ramírez, León, and Conde, 1985:61, 127; Bernstein, 1964, discusses the legal aspects).

Although I spoke to four former employees of El Tigre, the oral history of the cooperative period—involving complicated maneuvers between company, federal labor inspector, state governor, and miners' union leaders—remains difficult to reconstruct. Apparently the union at first tried to run the mine as the company had done, with the same managers and foremen. During this period Luis worked in the mill, testing metal content in the ore. Workers were supposed to be paid their day's wage and a share of the metal value; in reality, Luis reported, miners took their pay in goods at the former company store, now leased to a private businessman.

One day a union officer told Luis, "No, it's not worth it to you to keep on working, we already owe you so much you are never going to see the money."

"So what am I going to do?" Luis asked.

The officer replied, "Look, we'll give you an order for the merchant . . . so that you can liquidate what we owe you."

> He was going to pay me with merchandise. I took it to the businessman, and sure enough, he paid me everything—I bought clothes and many things, it was something like eight hundred pesos [two hundred days of work] they owed me. . . . So I didn't continue working there; the union ended and prospecting started, people came from all over, and there were agencies there that bought the metal.

Luis expressed a sense of bewilderment at the decline of El Tigre, for as he knew by experience, and as had been proven by many years of unusually high dividends, it contained ores rich in gold and silver. His sharp sense of betrayal by the Lucky Tiger Company was diffused, however, by the added confusion of the cooperative, which seemed to start so well but gradually fell to pieces. In fact, as Bernstein (1964) makes clear, the mine cooperatives were failing mines with little access to capital; they were encouraged by the federal government in order to limit outright unemployment, and for Luis it served this purpose.

Luis stayed at El Tigre until 1943, subsisting as a prospector. The skills of the gambusino (a term that covers everything from well-organized small mining to scavenging old tunnels and dumps) was one of the major bodies of knowledge brought in the Spanish period and retained in the rural mestizo culture of Sonora (a valuable ethnography of this tradition is contained in Peña and Chávez, 1985: 244–247). Throughout the colonial period and the nineteenth century, Sonoran mines alternated between periods of organized development and individual mining. Although in the twentieth century industrial mine organization appeared to supersede the gambusino, when massive unemployment came in the 1930s and 1950s, small mining and prospecting resurfaced, the recourse of Sonorans in need.

Luis, like many gambusinos, worked in an equal partnership with a man who had come from Jalisco to El Tigre after the mine had closed. They were looking for selected ores that, to their experienced eyes, revealed relatively high contents of gold and silver, and could be sold. Their objective differed from the bulk extractive techniques of industrial mining. Selective mining was a result of the lack of capital inputs: They did not have power drills, so they drilled by hammer and bar; they restricted the use of expensive dynamite, replacing it with powder or muscle. They had to do their own timbering and development work, with no one to pay them for it, and of course there was no safety organization or compensation for accidents. Luis's wife laboriously ground the ore by hand (substituting for the mine's mill) and added mercury—inside their house—so that dross could be floated off the amalgam of gold particles and silver ore.

Luis and Angelita Aguirre wanted to stay in El Tigre. It was, after all, the only home they had known. Every prospector, Luis reflected, dreams of finding a bonanza. Unfortunately, the gold of El Tigre never made Luis wealthy. Luis and his partner sold ore to one of the several ore merchants in El Tigre. I was permitted to study Luis's collected ore sales slips (a detailed analysis is provided in Heyman, 1988:246–248). There was no evidence of advances or indebtedness. The return to Luis was less than half his former wage, and much less than the high value of the assayed gold and silver ore he brought in. Ore finds were unpredictable, and therefore weekly income was extremely variable. Some weeks they had no money for food. Not only that, the slips showed that earnings declined over time. With multitudes of prospectors "high-grading" ores, and no geological development work being done, returns fell steadily. With two young daughters and another child coming, Luis and Angelita regretfully left El Tigre early in 1944.

ALTERNATIVE PATHS OUT OF THE MINES

When employers closed shop, the principles of seniority and solidarity, whether of kin or of union, could not give the miners much help. Each household, snapped off the corporate wage provider, sought its own future among available exits. Alternatives included nearby rural towns and small mining and prospecting, the Mexican border cities, and the cities growing amid the mass agriculture of the Sonoran coastal region. The Aguirre and León kindreds show a variety of paths leading away from this junction.

By the time Luis gave up on El Tigre, his father, Santiago, had already departed. He had obtained a job as a carpenter for a government agency, making cattle pens and watering tanks in the nearby town of Esqueda. He got Luis a job as a construction helper for 2.50 pesos a day. This work halted after a little over a year. Angelita began to find scattered jobs in Esqueda, washing and repairing clothes for friends of her mother-in-law. Luis and Angelita rented a house separately from the house of Luis's father, mother, and sister.

After a brief stay in Nacozari, Luis and his wife moved to Agua Prieta in 1947, leaving his parents behind. In one statement Angelita listed all of the interests applying to herself, her husband, and her children for going to the border:

> When we left El Tigre, we arrived in Esqueda and lived there for two years, but there wasn't much future. Not for me, since I couldn't work at what I was able to do, sewing. And then there wasn't much work [male employment]—well, he did work on some irrigation wells, but very little. Finally they finished the wells and left, so we departed and came here. At that time they were hiring people here to work in Arizona, and also there was the meat-packing plant where he worked. There was more work here—not much, but always more than in Esqueda—and I also thought about my daughters, that they might go to the secondary school, that they should study some more, because we never were schooled, nothing more than the primary grades. So that I thought that if we were lucky, my daughters could study.

The emerging border economy underlay Angelita's reasoning. Obviously there was the bracero hiring. Angelita's sewing business found its market strength through the flux of dollars translated into local currency characteristic of the border. Even her investment in the children's future reflected the context of growth. Both the sale of male labor and women's work activities drew Luis and Angelita toward the field of North American attraction.

Luis and Angelita's siblings split along their own paths. The Aguirre family had already branched out when three daughters married miners who went to Cananea; as El Tigre declined, another son went there. Though this shifted location, it reproduced Aguirres within the mine working class into the second generation. However, in the third generation (the children of Luis's siblings) there were only two miners/wives of miners.

Although the farm–railroad town of Esqueda offered a temporary refuge for Luis's kin after El Tigre's collapse, like the rest of interior northeastern Sonora it did not offer enough work or pay to sustain most of the Aguirre siblings. Luis's parents lived in Esqueda with a divorced daughter and a son who worked as a truck driver until the parents died in 1955 and 1956. In the third generation, only two of twenty-seven descendants lived there.

All that was left the Aguirre siblings, then, were two basic options—the border or the coastal region—both of them urban and tied either directly or indirectly to the American economy. One brother and one group of children of a deceased brother went to Hermosillo, the state capital and agroindustrial center; one brother, Luis, went to Agua Prieta; and one brother immigrated to Douglas through marriage. In the third generation, ten of twenty-seven were in Hermosillo, spanning a diverse range of education and occupations available in a large city. Eleven of twenty-seven were near the border: five in Agua Prieta, two in the United States (Tucson), and four in the massive border urbanization of Baja California. Such was the fate of the people from the Sonoran mines.

Like Angelita, most of her half siblings ended up in Agua Prieta. They took a very different path to the border city, however, and finished in a much less advantageous position. Her widowed mother, María, and three younger children accompanied Angelita to Esqueda, though the two families lived separately. María's oldest son found work in various small mines, first near Esqueda and later in the Magdalena area; and as he wandered about, María went with him. He worked as a gambusino from the early 1940s until he died in 1981, and his family still lives in Magdalena. The two younger sisters married small miners in Esqueda. From the 1940s to the 1960s, they moved from prospect to isolated prospect. Only in the 1970s did the sisters settle along the fringe of the city, in the more or less poor Colonia Ejidal, a neighborhood where the majority of their children live.

In contrast with Angelita's well-educated and prosperous children, her half siblings' children include nine maquiladora workers, three domestics, two day laborers, and two daughters married to *ejidatarios* (possessors of land rights on agrarian-reform farms). Why such different fates at the border? Angelita and Luis went almost directly to the border in the late 1940s, Luis worked in the United States and earned dollars, Angelita herself worked and invested in businesses, they built a home in a mixed but generally prosperous area of the city, and they kept their children in school. The other group went through a long transition of irregular work in small places and did not arrive at the border until the 1970s, with fragmentary education, mine skills of little use, and few resources to sell except their labor. The difference in neighborhoods where the families reside is symptomatic.

Lateral connections weakened when the need to establish a new residence emphasized the investment within the immediate family line. Mutual assistance did play a role in the exiting process. Angelita boarded two nephews in her home while they found work in maquiladoras in Agua Prieta; after working for a while, they bought a house and brought the rest of the family to the border. Nevertheless, the specific path leading out and subsequent lineal investment had profound, lasting effects on the relative fate of different kin branches.

The material on alternative kin paths demonstrates an important generalization about the transitional phase of the Sonoran working class. Although the wage complex of the mines was shattered, virtually all paths led toward other sources of wage earnings and purchased consumer goods. This was true whether the end point was the U.S.–Mexican border or the cities of the Sonoran coast. It can be contrasted with a counterfactual hypothesis that the breakup of the mine working class ended in a rural retreat. This suggests yet again that, whether particular industries come or go, waged life continues.

BRACERO WORK

Luis spent several months without work when he arrived at Agua Prieta in 1947. Angelita sustained the family by taking in washing and sewing. In the summer of 1947, Luis signed his first contract to work in the fields of the United States as a bracero. Bracero contracting was announced on the radio and by word of mouth; preference went to residents of Agua Prieta or those with "local passports" (a limited permit to visit the local U.S. side of the border). Until 1951 Luis contracted at the U.S. port of entry at Douglas, where workers were given their job assignments by U.S. authorities.

Luis was initially sent to Elfrida, north of Douglas, where he weeded chilies. Having been a miner all his life, he didn't know how to weed:

> When I began, I wasn't familiar with the hoe. I didn't know agricultural work, but my friends showed me how it was held, how it was swung down, until I got it. It was easy work, they didn't push us, only that when I began, two or three days, no more, the foreman would inspect the furrows, and when somebody like me had dug out a [chile] plant, he would say [in English] "Oh, boy, one dollar"—that the plant was worth a dollar. Since I had dug it up, I lost a dollar, so I was more careful. But still, since I didn't know the work, after a while I would knock down another plant, and he would come over and look at me, and say, "Oh, boy, one dollar more." I got more and more careful until I got the hang of things.

On this job, Luis made three dollars a day. At 8.65 pesos per dollar, this was roughly six times as much as he earned in day labor in Agua Prieta. Aware of the comparison, Luis regarded his earnings in the United States very favorably.

After the first three-month contract was over, Luis returned to Agua Prieta. In the late summer he obtained another contract to work in the chile harvest, cutting and loading trailers that went to packing plants in Elfrida. Luis continued to contract in Arizona until 1952, harvesting onions, radishes, squashes, and most frequently picking cotton, 250 pounds a day for $6.25. Each harvest was short, but with a three- or six-month contract, Luis could do several harvests and send home between twenty-five and one hundred dollars a month. He did have to pay for his food, at $1.50 a day, and he also liked to buy work pants and boots in the United States.

In 1952, contracting was removed from the border and centralized in recruitment centers. Luis went to one in Empalme, Sonora. At such centers, American doctors gave a "medical inspection" that ranged from listening to the lungs to checking for callouses that showed who was an experienced agricultural laborer. When Luis had contracted at Douglas, there was little waiting and investment of savings before he obtained work. But when Luis contracted at Empalme, he had to have bus fare to the coast and money to live until he was assigned a contract, after which he was given transportation to the United States. To get bracero work required savings, and involved the risk of making the trip and not getting a contract. Luis told me that he shared food with other workers from Agua Prieta who did not have enough money.

The investment in trips to the recruiting center fit well with Luis and Angelita's strategy: He could seek longer trips that paid off in bigger earnings because he was working not for the daily bread of the family (Angelita provided for this) but for large lump sums to invest. The alternative Luis avoided was riskier undocumented crossing.

From Empalme, Luis was sent to California, where he was assigned to various farmers. He worked in numerous and diverse jobs in agriculture, ranging from exhausting stoop labor picking cotton to an avocado orchard where, Luis remembered, they enjoyed working in the shade of the trees. The pay was generally higher in California than in Arizona—a minimum of seven dollars a day harvesting melons and up to twenty-two dollars a day culling peaches   thus returning the investment in recruiting trips. Except for six months' work in the Agua Prieta meat-packing plant in 1949, Luis worked consistently in the United States from 1947 until 1960, when the bracero program was winding down and contracts were getting scarcer. After a few years of sporadic, poorly paid construction labor in Agua Prieta, he retired.

Luis generally regarded his time as a bracero well, largely because of the money:

> I was tying up onions, then radishes. At that time they paid ten cents for the bunch of onions, and the same for radishes—radishes were very hard work because they struck you with a very strong odor. It didn't go very well—very hard work. Then when we were done tying up the onions and radishes, the American came over and he told each one of us what we had made, and it went very well. In place of three dollars, there were times that one could make as much as eight dollars. It was good because of that. When the American had extra tasks, he would ask us if we would work on contract. We made a good day's pay there.

María Herrera-Sobek (1979) insightfully observes that the braceros had little contact with general U.S. society (Luis worked alongside undocumented Mexicans, he saw black Americans in the fields occasionally, and some of the foremen were Mexican American, but that was the limit of his experience), and thus they were unconscious of discrimination to which they were subjected. She goes on to suggest that because their work in the United States was a means to a goal back in Mexico—Luis's houses and his children's education, for example—braceros judged their work not according to the hard labor and primitive living conditions, but according to the positive results their income brought at home.

One grievance Luis stressed was that the official contract allowed only one thousand dollars insurance for loss of life, and five hundred dollars for loss of a hand or an eye. As he showed me the documents he had saved, he said:

> Here it is in the contract, what they paid for a death, for a finger, for the eyes. The thing is, they paid very little, for a death I think it was a thousand dollars. . . . It was in the general contract, you couldn't ask for more—if you asked for more, they would tell you it was in the contract.

While Luis was aware of many incidents of workers being let go without back pay, he affirmed that he was always fully paid. If he had had any problem, he suggested, he would have gone to the Mexican consulate. It is notable that he would take grievances to the representative of his home government, for Luis did not recall having any contact with a union or even a mutual aid society. There was little enforcement of formal contract provisions in the bracero program before the 1960s, and pay rates and conditions were set unilaterally by employers (Galarza, 1964). As Galarza emphasizes, the bracero program was an attempt to provide as insulated and purified a supply of labor (with the exception of the home government connection) as possible.

WOMEN'S PAID AND UNPAID WORK

From 1944, when they left El Tigre, until 1947, when they arrived in Agua Prieta, Angelita coped with Luis's unemployment by taking in sewing and laundry; what is interesting is that even after Luis started sending back dollars from the United States, Angelita continued to sew—indeed, she expanded her effort. Rather than subsisting on the money earned by Luis, she allocated the money from her sewing to daily expenses and left the American money, as much as possible, to long-term savings and investments.

When they left Esqueda, Luis's mother had referred Angelita to a *comadre* (the godmother of one's child) who lived in Agua Prieta, and Angelita formed a lasting friendship with her. She helped Luis and Angelita find an apartment to rent, introduced Angelita to subtleties of border life, such as shopping in Douglas and pricing items in dollars, and introduced Angelita to women in Agua Prieta and Douglas who became her sewing customers.

Copying from catalogs and store displays, Angelita became extraordinarily capable at translating observations into patterns and measurements. She used a pedal-driven sewing machine as old as she was, the one bought from her mother when she was a newlywed; much later she would buy an electric one. As Angelita's skill as a seamstress became known, she ensured herself a steady stream of work: dresses for weddings, confirmations, and *quinceañeras* (girls' fifteenth birthday celebrations); yarn work; and items given to her on special order from millinery shops. (She was not doing true putting-out labor for garment manufacturers.) She charged about one dollar a day for labor, and the customer paid for materials.

Angelita's work as a seamstress took anywhere from two to six days a week. It was quite unpredictable, and at times she was forced to meet customers' deadlines. In addition there were her house chores. My interviews with Angelita and the material culture history of her household indicate that certain appliances she owned by the late 1940s helped reduce her drudgery and thus facilitated her new work role. She herself emphasized the importance of a washing machine in facilitating her sewing. When she lived in El Tigre, she had done her wash by hand. Washing took two days a week, working until late at night, and waking the next day with stiff and sore forearms. When she moved to Agua Prieta, one of her first acquisitions (1949) was a roller-type washer, electrically driven.

She used a hand mill to grind corn (which took fifteen minutes, compared with an hour by metate) or bought milled masa, and she took about an hour a day making the tortillas. In cooking beans, Angelita did not begin to save time until about 1968, when she bought her first refrigerator, and the mid-1970s, when she bought a blender and a pressure cooker. Before the refrigerator, she made refried beans every day; with the refrigerator, she could make them once a week and freeze them. Using a regular pot, cooking beans took three hours, while a pressure cooker took an hour; to mash them by hand takes ten minutes of hard work, while the blender does them easily. The refrigerator also meant less frequent shopping, and meat could be stored raw, rather than dried in the sun.

Angelita bought a gas stove in 1960; this saved the effort of bringing firewood into the house and stoking the fire, but getting butane fuel tanks is a notorious struggle in Agua Prieta, so much so that most families keep a wood stove in reserve. The cast-iron wood stove, which dated to her mother's time, had already brought a considerable reduction in effort.

There were, however, contrary developments. When Angelita lived in El Tigre, a small company store was nearby, and neighboring ranchers brought fruit, cheese, and beef to sell. At the border Angelita did most of her shopping, for food and sewing supplies, on the American side until the 1976 devaluation. While shopping in Douglas was enjoyable—Angelita often went with her friend—it could be a long trip when loaded down with bags, especially if the shopper was on foot. In addition, as Simonelli (1985) points out, when children stayed in school longer, their labor was forgone. Angelita's oldest daughter graduated from secondary school about 1953, and went to work as a store clerk to help her family. The other three children stayed in school until they married, and Angelita made the effort to keep them there throughout the 1950s and 1960s. Finally, Angelita had to make up for tasks that her husband might have done had he been in Agua Prieta: Specifically, several times she was responsible for the paperwork required to purchase a house.

It is not possible, using this retrospective data, to make a precise calculation of the change in labor time, but it appears that there were several key points when women saved exhausting effort, if not hours: stoves and other appliances acquired when women shifted from rural to mine-town patterns; the washing machine that Angelita acquired when she came to the border; and, in the seamstress craft, the sewing machine that increased business productivity while leaving time for housework. Other appliances arrived in later decades, after Angelita's greatest need was past.

WOMEN'S MANAGERIAL ROLES ON THE BORDER

In the Aguirre family, the wife invested money earned and remitted by the husband. She therefore managed the household's long-run trajectory (prosperity versus poverty) and social position (houses, education, and children's marriages) in their residential base. "We've never had to spend everything," remarked Angelita on their lifetime of saving, "always we've left aside a little bit."

> It's true, my daughters suffered privations, they didn't go to dances where they charged, didn't go to the movies, we never went to eat in restaurants. But not food, nor clothes—we always had the basics. And then times changed, more people here had jobs, and I was able to charge more for my work. And he [Luis] always had his good runs of luck on the other side [the United States]. When he would bring his dollars, we would save them to see what else we could do to give us more. . . . Something more, like I told you about those lots—we made houses so that we could rent them, for very little but something.

Angelita bought a two-room house for two thousand pesos in 1951, and through the 1950s added four rooms with hired construction labor. Around 1960, Angelita and her oldest daughter, Ana, started a small grocery store (on a rented lot) that was capitalized from savings. They kept the store until Ana married in 1972.

The family invested in the education of the two younger daughters and their son: Their second daughter attended secondary school and normal school from 1953 to 1960, and she worked as a teacher for two years before marrying in 1962; their third daughter had secondary school and three years of nurse's training before she married in 1965; and they supported their youngest son through a master's degree in chemical engineering. He now teaches in Guaymas. While their daughters did not use their professions, their social background permitted them to marry prosperously: one to a schoolteacher, and the other to a co-owner of several tortilla factories.

Around 1965 Angelita bought another small house with two rooms that she rented out. She obtained a commercial bank loan in Agua Prieta and used the money (ten thousand pesos, about eight hundred dollars) to build two three-room apartments to rent. Her access to formal credit, very unusual among Agua Prieta working people, came because her son-in-law with the tortilla stores cosigned the loan. The construction labor was done by her other son-in-law, the schoolteacher. In 1970 the Aguirres bought two large lots for thirty thousand pesos; the same son-in-law built two houses, one for his wife, containing a grocery store, and the other a handsome house for his mother- and father-in-law, using materials they supplied. The current property is registered in Angelita's name, rather than her husband's, indicating her formal control over family capital.

With these investments, Angelita provided for the retirement of herself and Luis, along with her divorced daughter and granddaughter. Women in their forties, fifties, and sixties can develop businesses if they can find some manner of access to starting capital, even as the work career of a laboring man, for whom strength is the foremost resource, draws to an end around the age of fifty. On the other hand, the elderly couple or elderly woman without a business or not living with a married child, suffers greatly.

It was by dint of tremendous effort on the part of Angelita Aguirre that her family was able to make the transition to the border city. While her husband was too distant to help her on a daily basis, she ran the household and earned cash while keeping her children in school. I propose that Angelita's experience coming to Agua Prieta was analogous to the dynamics of widowhood. The initial commitment to the border was influenced, in part, by the logic of marketing a home-based business. By moving nearer to shopping in the United States, the dynamic of purchasing consumer goods was reinforced. Angelita utilized machine sewing, an industrial household skill, to earn money while taking advantage of other appliances to realign her domestic labors. Again, like widows with working sons, Angelita received remitted male wages from migratory work north of the border. I used widowhood as a window on the changes that Mexican border women underwent in the early years of the working class; during the breakup of the male mine wage system and transition to the border city, these activities became generalized among women, even though prior to the maquiladoras they were mostly small producers and housewives.

THE HUSBAND–WIFE RELATIONSHIP

The Aguirres were a "border-balance" household. Angelita and Luis comprise one specific arrangement of household power taken in the flux of the new border life, but their experience cannot be securely generalized. In other households, such as that of José and Mercedes Hernández, the husband had more control over the use of remitted money. The literature on Mexican migrant households is likewise contradictory. Richard Griswold del Castillo, in his history of the Chicano family in the southwestern United States, comments that the authoritarian role of male heads of households declined and the managerial role of women heads increased as men went out to migratory work as early as the late nineteenth century (1984:31–32, 34). Ina Dinerman (1982) reported from Michoacán that male migratory work in the United States increased the business activities of women outside the home. She does not make clear who managed the investment of remittances in houses and the education of children (only infrequently in capital investments). On the other hand, Raymond Wiest (1973) differentiated among types of migratory labor from rural western Mexico, and he found that in the case of temporary male migration to the United States, men sent home money and continued to exercise household authority. Referring to industrial migrant labor within Mexico, Frances Rothstein (1983) found that in Tlaxcala male wages were invested by men, not women; and that women withdrew to unpaid housework in migrant families. Therefore, I present a set of dimensions of variation, or questions for ethnographic investigation, if you will, among the arrangements between a husband who is doing migratory work and a wife at home who may have her own earnings.

The first dimension is the relationship between husband and wife. Will the man, making good money in a distant place, send it back to his wife, and in what quantities? This is the point of greatest risk for the woman. Luis told me that he gave his earnings to his wife because when a man is away, he must make a decision to "cooperate" with his wife if he is to return to her. Wiest found that if a husband working in the United States set a definite date of return, he would reliably remit money, whereas indefinite labor migration in some cases was a prelude to abandonment.

Even when the husband is a good provider of support to his wife for daily shopping, this may leave little room for discretion on her part. The second question asks who controls the long-term investments, husband or wife? Jeanne Simonelli (1985:225), who worked in rural Sonora, suggests that women are closer to short-cycle concerns, while male concerns with farms follow a longer cycle. While women in urban, border Sonora did indeed struggle with day-to-day budgeting, they also made decisions about long-term commitments such as houses and children's education.

In turn, what were the long-term uses of remitted money in terms of male and female goals? Do investments of remitted money go toward appliances that women use, or toward tools and materials for a man to set up a workshop? Does the investment go toward spending among friends, promoting a man's local standing, or does it go into a woman's small business? These are questions that help to indicate the actual balance of power in migrant households beyond the formal household headship.

One possible cause of variation is the developmental cycle of the household. Among plantation workers in Guyana, Chandra Jayawardena (1962) found that as men's earnings fall with age, and as women respond by increasing their earnings outside the household, the balance of power shifts so that husbands either bring a greater portion of money home, or conflicts in the marital bond worsen as women assert their claims. Judith Brown (1985) describes three developments among middle-aged women: removal of restrictions; authority over younger kin; and recognition beyond the confines of the household. The Aguirre case combined a historical shift from a male mine paycheck to a border-balance economy with changes in the life cycle that brought Angelita Aguirre into a more prominent role earning money and dealing with public affairs of the household.

Distance of male migration and the nature of local opportunities for female investment may affect household arrangements. Long-distance migrants, such as braceros, remit money home at intervals, thus leaving potential power to wives; male border commuters, like the male migrant industrial workers who return home on weekends, described by Rothstein (1983), carry and control paychecks on their own. The expanding post–1940 border economy provided opportunities for women to guide investments into small businesses they controlled, as with widows in mine towns before them. Studies of communities sending rural migrants, on the other hand, stress investments in houses and other displays that enhance male social and political careers, as well as speculative buying of scarce land, possibly because of limited opportunities for productive investment (Wiest, 1979; Mines, 1981; Dinerman, 1982).

The Aguirre history suggests that in the particular circumstances of the border transitional period—exodus from the male-wage-dominated mines, migratory work by some men in the United States, home-based businesses, and investments in a new urban life—some women had the opportunity to achieve effective power, albeit in untrumpeted domestic locations. Their subtle guiding power is best demonstrated by evidence about long-term family goals such as businesses, houses, and education.

THE RETURN OF PERSONALIZED LABOR RELATIONS

Impersonal labor markets and work relationships were fundamental to the formation of the Sonoran working class in the era of railroads and gigantic mines. After 1929, massive layoffs detached men from corporate hierarchies and corresponding labor unions. Their new workplaces—marginal mines, lumber mills, construction sites in border cities—were small, flexible, and organized through small crews that could move from site to site, be dismissed and reunited, and so forth. (Many instances of migratory labor in the United States also partook of such relationships, although the bracero migrant stream was impersonally organized.) An underlying cultural repertoire for personalized male relationships surfaced when the externally imposed structure of impersonal relationships was removed.

This historical shift coincided broadly with the year (1943) when Antonio Hernández came of working age. As he grew older, he experienced varied possibilities for small-scale working-class relationships, from the restrictive and paternalistic employ of an elite family to a shop of his own, signaling at least the appearance of independence. In Antonio's life we see how the male side (and, in the words and action of his wife, Petra, the female side) of border life emerged in the boom years after 1940, and insofar as many of these relationships and idioms persist, we understand much of border life even today.

Antonio Hernández

When José Hernández left the family farm in Pivipa for Agua Prieta in 1942, the rest of his siblings, Antonio included, were living in Nacozari with their mother. In 1943, however, Juan, the next oldest brother, found employment building an access road to a sawmill in El Sauz, Sonora (a pseudonym), above Agua Prieta in the high pine forest of the Sierra Madre Occidental. Juan brought his three younger brothers and three younger sisters to El Sauz. Four Hernández brothers worked in the sawmill, and all four married in El Sauz. Antonio married Petra Tánori, whose brothers worked at the mill. All three Hernández sisters married in El Sauz, where their husbands labored.

It appears from Antonio's description that the Hernández siblings, along with other workers, were recruited as a group by Telesforo Tapia, Sr. (a pseudonym), to replace a contingent of workers who had been fired in some sort of labor dispute. The Tapia family owned the largest enterprise in Agua Prieta in the pre-maquiladora period, a lumberyard and building supply firm; they and their in-laws have been important political actors in Agua Prieta.

Antonio started employment at 1.50 pesos a day, and when he left in 1957, he was making 4.50 a day—rates that even by the standards of the day were low. The company provided free housing, and credit at the company store; the workers were nominally paid in cash, not scrip, but after deductions for the week's purchases of food at the store, there was little or no hard cash left. Antonio remarked that many workers fled at night from El Sauz without paying the debts they had accumulated. This indicates high levels of debt vis-à-vis ability to repay; it differs from the system of American mine companies that limited credit according to the size of the weekly paycheck. Unlike the mines that attracted more workers than they could employ, the sawmill in the isolated sierra had to entrap workers who otherwise would have abandoned the mill for the border. Antonio recalled that when Juan and his brothers were about to leave the sawmill for Agua Prieta in 1945, when the road project was finished, Telesforo Tapia kept them by promising to give them jobs in the sawmill, houses, and credit at the store.

In 1957, the Tapia company moved its sawmill from El Sauz much further south, to Yécora, Sonora. Antonio and his youngest brother went to Agua Prieta, while the other brothers and the married sisters went to Yécora. This brought Antonio into the border economy, and it behooves us to explore the reasons for his move to Agua Prieta at this key juncture. We begin by looking at the skills Antonio had learned:

> We got tired, at least I got tired, because up in the mountains one doesn't have any opportunity to advance. At least there I learned to do something. When I began, I didn't know anything. I began with a pick and shovel, making a road, but then the company gave me a chance to learn how to drive trucks, learn mechanics, welding, and all that. That I learned in the company.

Of course, growing up in the village of Pivipa, Antonio had not learned to drive, nor had he gained the "metallic" skills that accompany automotive technology.

Timothy Dunnigan, who did fieldwork in highland Sonora (near Yécora, as it happened), observed that even though both mestizo Mexicans and Lower Pima Indians worked for wages in small mines and sawmills, their responses to the frequent layoffs in these marginal operations differed. (Antonio Hernández, having left behind his traces of Opata ancestry and land rights in Pivipa, would be considered a mestizo.) The mestizos would search for another source of wage work, whereas the Pima would retreat into an existing peasant alternative, sharecropping on lands provided by fathers or brothers. Dunnigan (1981) attributes the difference to Pima Indian patterns of generational succession and to the mestizo fund of knowledge, in particular, better Spanish and mechanical skills. That is, each man's life was a small version of the repatriation and Great Depression, and culturally distinctive responses to the challenge of the waged life course are seen.

When Antonio received no indemnity to leave the sawmill, he had to seek a market where he could use his abilities. Though he found transitional work in the nearby mountains of Chihuahua, he intended to search for employment in a distant border city, Tijuana or Mexicali. On his way to Baja California, Antonio passed the house of his brother José in Agua Prieta. José insisted that Antonio stay, and recommended him to the owner of a mechanical shop.

In those early years, Antonio's work was very irregular. Petra supported the family by working as a domestic for a Mexican American woman in Douglas in whom she felt "much confidence." She earned one dollar for a three-to-eight-hour day, five days a week. She crossed the border using a local passport meant for shopping, not employment—that is, she was an undocumented immigrant. Petra commented that in those days (1957) the border inspectors did not stop her even though they knew she was employed, whereas today (1986) they are much more severe.

Petra said that she worked "to help her husband," though she noted that she brought home the principal income for several years. This formulation limits the public worth of married women's work outside the house (particularly employment by others) to its value as a sacrifice for the family (Ferree, 1984). Earning wages did not constitute a valued step for Petra in her life path, the way that home-based businesses did for women who had them.

Petra, though a quiet person, held as her special accomplishment the struggle to get out of rental apartments and into a house of their own. She had to step outside of domestic ideals in order to deal with private and public authorities. As the three of us sat in the Hernández's kitchen, Antonio started the discussion by describing how Petra sought a lot from the municipal president, Dr. Calderon:

> One day an announcement came out in the newspaper that Dr. Calderon was going to give out lots to people who could not afford them. What are you going to buy a lot with if you make 250 pesos a week? My old lady said, "Dr. Calderon is going to give out lots," and I replied, "They're not going to give anything to anybody," and went off to work. So she and a comadre went to city hall to speak to Dr. Calderon, to ask him if it was true that they were giving out lots on this side of the city, and he said yes. . . . When I left work in the afternoon, they had already given her the title to the lot, this lot here.

Petra followed by describing her efforts to get supplies for building the house:

> We put in the floor. Remember that we didn't have money to buy it, and I went to ask for it on time payment. I took the cement on credit, the windows, and the doors.

It is important to realize that hardware store owners, the men with whom Petra had to deal, came from the most powerful families in Agua Prieta. Antonio, with the unpaid help of an older brother, did the physical work of construction.

All in all, Antonio acknowledged the decisive role of Petra:

> I didn't want to come here because we lived in a rented house in the center of town. The missus was insistent on coming to live here. There were just walls,[5] no floors, no doors, nothing, but the missus wanted to come here so as not to pay rent. That was correct, it was very good— why not save on the rent? But one has their hardheadedness . . . .

We must understand that, for Aguapretense, a house is the publicly visible, physical manifestation of a family's ability to live at a socially decent level. Therefore, by dealing with houses, lots, and city services, women like Petra could emerge as important public representatives of their families in a manner never possible in the mine centers, where houses were assigned by the corporation to the male worker according to his standing in the hierarchy.[6]

Until the mid-1960s Antonio continued as a poorly paid helper in several mechanical workshops. He added to the mechanical knowledge he had started to acquire in the sawmill, and he made friendships with a scattering of the ranchers, truckers, and construction bosses. After brief periods working for a number of potential patrons, Antonio finally had the good fortune to encounter a manager he had known at the Tapia sawmill who needed an experienced mechanic to set up the machinery for a *palmillera,* a broom-straw factory. This patron promised to give the tool set to Antonio when the factory was finished.

Antonio opened a workshop of his own with this equipment, and has thrived to this day. He prefers to work independently, though his work is unpredictable, because he consistently earns above the minimum wage, and he has been able to save enough to replace his original equipment as it wears out. He now works in partnership with his adopted son (he and Petra, who have no children of their own, adopted two orphaned children of Petra's brother). Antonio intends to pass the workshop on to the son, who lives in an independent household on the same lot.

Male Relationships in Agua Prieta Since 1940

The friends and facilitators mentioned in Antonio's and other men's life stories have their personal side, but I am specifically concerned with their dimension of power. Power is apparent if we consider some friendships to be vertical, where one man has much greater resources and so is able to make the other an adherent. This is referred to as a patron–client relationship. Other friendships are equal, often guardedly so: webs of horizontal alliance formed at work and play among men of roughly similar power. Each form of friendship has in Mexico, as in much of the world, a specific cultural template that tells how it is to be enacted. My purpose here, however, is less to analyze the well-known phenomena of alliance and patron–client relationships (see Wolf, 1966; Strickon and Greenfield, 1972; Vélez-Ibáñez, 1983; Friedrich, 1986) than to examine the historical context in which these relationships became salient. This question of history—working men uprooted from an older system of power and making their way into a new one—is a first approximation (the male side) to working classness when the institutions of class relationship are not readily visible.

The Structure of Patronage at the Border. The economic and social structure of border cities during the period 1940–1970 inclined poorer men to rely on patron–client ties in order to obtain employment, tools, house lots and construction materials, and security against the perils of illness. Their families had just moved to the border and they needed to stock the new houses, yet there were no company stores to extend credit; there was much work to be had, but it was not to be obtained via accustomed routes of hiring offices and seniority ladders. They were no longer joined together into a union that could put effective laws on the books about job dismissal, disability, and severance pay. Eric Wolf proposes:

> Such ties [patron–client] would prove especially functional in situations where the formal institutional structure of society is weak and unable to deliver a sufficiently steady supply of goods and services, especially to the terminal levels of the social order. (1966:17)

Likewise, for patrons, extending personal obligations to a limited number of laborers had its rationale in the economy of that era. Agua Prieta was growing rapidly, and elite families were benefiting immensely from this growth. The Mezas, the Terans, the Montaños, and the Vildósolas owned lumberyards and hardware firms that supplied materials for building houses. There were restaurant and nightclub owners, always prosperous in a border city. In addition there were older, still important cattle-ranching families—the Morales, the Ortiz, the Valenzuelas, and others—who operated in this export center. Though short-lived (1948–1953), José J. Ortiz's state-sponsored slaughterhouse and meat-packing plant was a setting where many elite managers and common laborers met, members of both groups newly arrived at the border.

In boom times there was a potential shortage of labor for the wealthy employers. The employment they could offer was scattered among a number of enterprises, any one of which (such as construction) might last only a short period. Personal obligation provided a means to retain the commitment of a regular supply of workers.

Another reason for offering ties to clients could have been to assemble a group of followers mobilized for backing in political maneuvering among the powerful. This was not utilized until 1979, for reasons we shall explore shortly.

Patron–client ties in Agua Prieta appear to have been neither lifelong nor exclusive. Just as with Antonio Hernández, men were dropped by patrons when they were no longer of use, or they themselves switched affiliations. This is quite unlike classic forms of patronage, in which clients could deal with only one patron, and bonds of debt and obligation were nearly inescapable (see Burkhalter and Murphy, 1989). At the border, there were many options for workers, including flight to the United States, where Mexican laborers were in demand. Patrons did not want to extend social or material credit to men who could leave so easily. Wolf suggests that alongside a strong institutional framework:

> [The patron's] hold on the client is weakened, and in place of solid patron–client blocks we may expect to encounter diffuse and cross-cutting ties between multiple sponsors and multiple clients, with clients often moving from one orbit of influence to another. (1966:18)

Although Agua Prieta in that era lacked strong institutions, proximity to the United States worked to much the same effect.

The Bonds of Small Work Groups. The profusion of vertical links during the border boom years was intersected by horizontal alliances. At the core were alliances made in the small mines, sawmills, and labor crews characteristic of the 1940–1970 period. These workplaces were operated by small groups of men, frequently in very remote locations and almost always with little direct supervision. Production was obtained by paying the crew as a whole and allowing them to split the proceeds. These loosely organized workplaces relied on a culturally understood ethic of male work relations.

Sonorans use the term compañero (companion) specifically for work partnerships. In one word they combine strict rules for material equality of effort and reward with intimate friendship that guards against the danger of rivalry and disputes. Juan Bautista Valenzuela reminisced to me late one afternoon, sitting in his smithy, describing the old days working in a marginal tungsten mine; and he expressed the ideals, if not the complete reality, of companionship at labor.

The crew agreed in advance on "rules"—that they would split the money evenly; that they would work for each other, so that if one was ill or drunk, the others would work for him and pay him his share anyway; that all the food was bought by all and shared by all—if there were only beans, everybody ate beans. Everybody knew the different tasks, so that they were all drillers, or loaders, or all put in timbers, and so forth, according to need; thus, if one was missing, substitutes were available and the work was not held up. They worked hours according to necessity, not fixed shifts—thus, if the crew needed money, they would work from morning to midnight. Each depended on the others for safety, and they would not enter an unsafe tunnel (surely the incentives of the contract system worked against this).

Sometimes work friends and companions were embittered or separated, but much of the time it was the same gang that *"Díos los hace y ellos se juntan"* (God made them and they get themselves together) as they went from one hillside drift to the next. This differs from the industrial mining mutuality, which it superficially echoes; the group itself continued, even as the workplaces changed.

Egalitarian relationships were encapsulated within patronage bonds of the harshest sort. Just like the sawmill where Antonio Hernández and his kin worked, small mines operated on a chain of debt extended from the wealthy landowner through the mine contractor to the work crew, whose final return for ore was discounted by the food and supplies they used. Over historical time, however, intense horizontal ties could break loose of such limits, for, as we saw, obligations to patrons were not permanent, and men left mines or mills for urban jobs. Yet powerful friendships formed at work could easily be renewed in future contexts, such as the border city. There was a process not only of historical time but also of life cycle time, for these extremely egalitarian small work group relationships were characteristic of men early in the life cycle; youthful bonds of emotion and loyalty can be powerful, practical levers later in life.

Independent Workshops as Social Synapses. Further into the life cycle, and depending on much fortune, hard work, and good connections, a working man can try to establish an independent workshop (*taller*): car repairs, a brick yard, a carpentry shop, sheet roofing, or ornamental ironwork. Moving from wage labor into independent production is an important career goal. Laboring men find that their greatest resource is the strength of their youth, and their wage-earning power declines with age (Balán, Browning, and Jelin, 1973:

199, show this to be true for urban, industrial Mexico]. However, the workshop is not an automatic step forward in the life cycle. It is a challenge, certain prerequisites are required, and only some men achieve them.

First, the man has to learn key industrial skills, such as automotive mechanics, usually through prior employment in the wage sector. Second, the aspiring shop owner has to accumulate tools. I asked questions about the acquisition of equipment in several workshops, similar to the questions concerning household appliances. Three men (a carpenter, a mechanic, and a truck driver) reported that they were equipped by the patron for whom they worked before becoming independent. One blacksmith–mechanic had made his own grinder and drill press, and bought a new arc welder in the United States. One machinist used savings to buy a used American lathe in Agua Prieta. Third, the worker has to have a reputation that will draw clients, a reputation that includes both technical skill and reliability. The man who has been effective at accumulating many personal alliances since youth, both with wealthy patrons and with other working men, will have an advantage here. Looking at these prerequisites, one readily sees that most workshop owners have certain loyalties and obligations to powerful men. Their allegiance spreads in turn to the other members of the shop.

The shop owner is also the principal worker. Additional workers are usually recruited along kinship lines—sons, nephews, or brothers. They are unpaid if they reside in the owner's household, but are paid (at the minimum wage or less) if they belong to a different family budget. Less frequently there are one or two unrelated, paid employees. Authority in the workshop comes from deference to parenthood, age, and work experience, reinforced by the hope of inheriting the shop. There was no formal model of apprenticeship in Agua Prieta, but there was implicit submission to learning.

In addition to the work crew itself, clients, friends, and the anthropologist congregate around the taller. The banter ranges from teasing and jokes, through discussions on technical problems posed by the work, to open commentary on politics and the sad state of the economy. Conversations in this setting have a special weight. Unlike controlled workplaces, physical movement and communication are unrestricted. There is room for free expression, criticism, and even political recruitment on the basis of ties that appear to be simple friendship. The accomplishment of valued life goals by shop owners provides them social recognition—seen in the respect shown to their spoken opinion in conversation—that goes well above their small capital. If younger men are working in the shop, the organization of authority in the workplace gives added weight to communication.

One shop (not part of any family histories) was a center for the right-wing National Action Party (PAN), which was engaged in bitter struggle locally and nationally against Mexico's government party (PRI). Its owner had been recruited into the party after 1979 by a longtime friend, a man of much higher education and social position whom he had known since the early 1950s. The shop owner was one of two key figures organizing party support in his large, predominantly working-class neighborhood, in part through a large sports club centered on this shop. Several young men I spoke with at this shop worked during weekdays in maquiladoras. Their political allegiance to the PAN, openly a party of the conservative rich, was based on loyalty to the shop owner, and did not refer to their explicit place in the industrial working class of today's border cities.

Were we to take the small businesses of women—cooking and selling food, sewing fancy dresses, or selling clothes on consignment—we could make very similar observations about authority over younger women in the household, the freedom of communication, and the place of such businesses as clients of wealthy women. Even more than male workshops, female independent production contrasts with the hemmed-in labors of young women working in maquiladoras, where they are immobile, busy, and closely supervised. Whether we speak of men's or women's shops, these are key social synapses in the organization of Agua Prieta's working class.

The Persistence of Relationships. A cohort of young working men came to Agua Prieta from Sonora's interior during the 1940s, 1950s, and 1960s. They extended personalized labor relationships both upward and sideways—nearly always a necessity in that era of transition. Since 1965, Agua Prieta has had a large and often impersonal factory labor market centered on the maquiladoras. Many of the older relationships have fallen by the wayside, but to a surprising extent ties formed in the earlier decades continue to structure the economic and political life of Agua Prieta's working people.

Some members of the 1940–1970 cohort, now (1986) in their forties, fifties, and sixties, have ascended into key positions. This applies both to leaders in elite families and to accomplished senior members of the working class, who tie together a wide range of former compañeros, friends, and family members. Although it is impossible to recite personal details without exposing my informants to troubles stemming from Agua Prieta's embittered politics, every interviewed male working-class activist, whether belonging to government or right-wing opposition parties, was recruited by a party leader from an elite "political family" with whom he had had a prior vertical friendship.

Although Agua Prieta's working class today has an unusually uniform economic character given to it by the maquiladoras, one cannot deduce its social and political organization according to some expected notion without taking into account how relationships have formed and crystallized over time. Nor is this simply a phenomenon of historical lag, for key elements such as the organization of communication and political interests of the independent workshops are a basic and recurring feature of border working-class life.

THE BORDER SETTLEMENT PROCESS:
SUMMARY AND CONCLUSIONS

The border settlement process is important from two points of view. The distinctiveness of border city life—described in brief as considerable consumption very much determined by the availability of dollars, and an unusual combination of impersonal migrant employment in the United States with highly personalized channels for resources in Mexico—crystallized during the period from 1940 to 1970, though it was not without antecedents.

The process holds comparative interest as well. When the families of miners are removed from their encompassing institutions—the industrial workplace, the town dense with working people, and the labor union—they present us with the intriguing problem of a working class without any of the easy touchstones so often used to analyze proletarian life. The naming of absent attributes being an inadequate response, we have to ask what the substantive characteristics of a different kind of working class are. The first step is to look at the politics of urban land in order to understand that even in the absence of political relations which refer to class, working people cannot avoid settling into their new lives within a structure of power relations.

Agua Prieta's Urban Structure: Land and Politics

The key to Agua Prieta's urban form was already in place when families arrived at the border. In 1915 Plutarco Elías Calles (the revolutionary chieftain of this border town) mandated a "local agrarian commission" based in Agua Prieta. It distributed seven-to-eight-hectare lots of "abandoned" or "enemy" land. The *ejido* of Agua Prieta was officially in existence by May 1925. Why this early agrarian distribution in a desert city with only marginal farmlands and no peasant traditions? The agrarian commission, and later the ejido of Agua Prieta, in fact served an urban function: to distribute house lots. In the early years house lots and small farm plots in the first ejidal zone west of the railroad tracks (Barrio Ferrocarril) were given to veterans and other local adherents of Calles (according to interviews with descendants of the early residents of that area; also Cumberland, 1972:231; Sanderson, 1981:236; Radding, 1985:272–273).

Over the years, the location of the ejido has shifted, but it always has been on the growing edge of the city, and it has always served the purpose of opening up lands for residential lots. Since the 1940s, the main operating method has not been to enroll families in the ejido, but extralegally to subdivide and rent lots to outsiders. Later the neighborhoods so formed are placed within the municipal boundaries so that families can legally hold private title to land ("regularization"), as they could not in the ejido. From Calles on, obtaining house lots and regularization have been strictly related to the governing political groups of this city.

The ejido was used to open up land for the flood of families arriving in the 1940s and 1950s. In the large Barrio Ferrocarril neighborhood, lots were extralegally sold for forty pesos—ten for the municipal *síndico* (receiver or recorder) who controlled the sales, and thirty for the ejido—with a subsequent rental payment to the ejido of two pesos a month. This was cheap for urban land, for in the late 1940s forty pesos would have been about ten days' work, while the monthly two pesos was less than a day's work. Large areas of house lots to the east and southeast of the city were sold directly, with proper title, by the municipal government. Another wave of ejido subdivision started in the mid-1970s, creating the Colonia Ejidal first on the periphery southwest and then due south of the city; as I was leaving in 1986, the legal regularization of this area was emerging as a possibility.

Obtaining and regularizing house lots brought families into the political arena, but in a curious manner that created a superficial noninvolvement in politics. In order to understand this, it is necessary to sketch the history of governing political groups in Agua Prieta. From the revolution through the 1940s, Agua Prieta was dominated by men who came from the immediate military and political associates of Plutarco Elías Calles, who had made this city his home base during the revolution. In the 1940s, as Agua Prieta began its rapid growth, a younger generation of families, based more on commerce and construction/hardware, slowly but surely entered the political arena, their way smoothed by marriages into older families. During the late 1930s and the 1940s, elections for municipal president in Agua Prieta had become disputatious, because of alliances with state and national politicians too complicated to explain here. An election in 1949 brought heated public participation, and when the result became apparent—the victory of a major figure from an important cattle family who had key state allies over a more popular, smaller rancher—its aftermath required a halt to overt mobilization of political followers. From 1949 to 1979 Agua Prieta settled down into a "politics of apathy" (Hansen, 1977:142ff.).

This was carried out through the system of distributing and regulating urban land. Oral histories report that the victorious 1949 candidate promised residents of Barrio Ferrocarril that he would transfer lot titles from the ejido to the homeowners. The period of apathy coincides with the period of family immigration to Agua Prieta; predictable, cheap, and fairly wide-open provision of the most desirable good, land for houses, made quietness possible. My argument is that the politics of Agua Prieta was "nonpolitics"; the narrowing of focus from the broad class concerns of the mine community to the seemingly familial concerns of lineal accumulation on the border was structured by this invisible political bargain.

The agreements within Agua Prieta's "political families," the second generation of the group of the 1940s, broke down in 1979 over a disputed candidacy for municipal president; this local conflict joined into a national elite split between the governing PRI and the right-wing opposition PAN (Moncada, 1985; Guadarrama, 1987). For reasons of larger national considerations, active mobilization of political followers in Agua Prieta was resumed, following the lines of personalized vertical alliances as described above. Promises to regularize titles on large areas of ejidal land have been one weapon in the government's arsenal; a corresponding issue, improvement of municipal infrastructure, was expertly manipulated by the opposition.[7]

The system of distributing house lots had one other important consequence for the social structure of the border working population. Lots were distributed piecemeal, as families requested them, making the city a social patchwork (though there are gross differences of social status between neighborhoods). Since lots, not houses, were distributed, each family built a house according to its economic capability. This contrasts with the mine company towns, in which house assignment by occupation and nationality provided for clear social geography. At the border, residential and other community alignments were relatively independent of workplace alignments.

The Family Settlement Process

Resettling at the border required families to solve a series of problems—how to obtain income, where and how to buy goods, and so forth—in a place very different from the ones they had left. The fundamental economic impetus in Agua Prieta before the advent of the maquiladoras was migratory labor across the border. However, for immigration statuses such as bracero, commuting worker, or undocumented entrant, the location of work was legally separated from location of residence, social relationships, and potential political involvement. This disjuncture meant that Mexican workers and their families had no way to act as a group regarding their conditions of labor or wages except through the Mexican consulates; border residents responded case by individual case, trying to change their visa status or that of family members within the U.S. immigration bureaucracy. This has been an important cause of narrowing to family concerns.

The American side was the source—directly and indirectly—of the majority of Agua Prieta consumer goods and utilities. The evidence and details about border consumption will be presented in the next chapter; here it will suffice to note that border residents could obtain credit in Douglas to buy appliances needed for women's work, and furnishings required to equip houses of families new to the border. Back in Mexico, house construction materials, expensive and obtained on extended payment, were provided by a few powerful commercial families. Lines of credit and sources of goods were important relationships that some person in the Mexican household had to manage carefully.

Families living at the border invested in longer educations for their children. No longer could a young man like Luis Aguirre drop out after three years with the realistic expectation that he would work in the mine, nor could a girl leave school, as Angelita Aguirre did, to help her widowed mother. In the families I interviewed—and greater quantitative evidence certainly would be needed—children stayed in school for noticeably longer periods: girls at least through primary school, and boys into secondary school. Even persons who ended up in blue-collar work possessed these minimums of education, and there were several families, like the Aguirres, whose sons and daughters had gone much further.

Therefore, whether looking at housing, or lines of consumer credit, or educational investments, the border household required a person or persons with a sense of the long-term trajectory of the family settlement process. Several roles inside the household were recombined. At the crux was the negotiation of power between husband and wife. Women, though they took on the added burdens of running households while husbands were away as migratory laborers and children were staying longer in school, also assumed, in some families, the power of managing long-run goals and presenting the public face of the household when dealing with municipal authorities.

To this was added the problem of unpredictable or periodic male income, since men were either remitting money from the distant United States or laboring in the Mexican casual employment market. Some women, such as Angelita Aguirre, filled the need for daily income by operating a small business, while others, like Petra Hernández, dealt with her husband's irregular employment by working as a domestic. Women therefore had to establish their own network of clients and contacts.

Men faced a different set of problems, stemming largely from the lack of an institutional structure of work such as that found in the industrial mines. They had to link an ever-shifting series of positions. Since this could not be done through formal mechanisms, it had to be done by retaining personalized relationships with more powerful men who might be employers. In the border setting, this meant sustaining a varied set of potential patrons.

Each household, then, had dozens of complex relationships extending outward: employers, creditors on two sides of the border, the municipality or ejido, the U.S. immigration system. These institutions and individuals were distinct entities, not, as in the mines, multiple manifestations of one encompassing corporation. Furthermore, there were at least two different agents of the household, the wife and the husband, each operating on a separate agenda and interests. The working class in the border city had a heterogeneous community form (besides the Agua Prieta material, see, on the border cities of Ensenada and Ciudad Juarez, Ugalde, 1970; 1974).

Heterogeneous Versus Unitary Working-Class Communities

A heterogeneous working-class community lacks the direct, one-to-one overlap between key domains of life—workplaces, labor and employment relations, residential patterns, consumption, and political arenas—that characterizes the unitary structure of company (or single-company-dominated) towns. Agua Prieta was not dominated by a single enterprise with a linked system of workplaces, as were the mines; not only were there many employers, but work sites spanned two nations. Miners were overwhelmingly adult males; at the border each household had men and women, older and younger persons, all earning money. They worked in diverse modes: formal employment, informal sales, independent production, and so on. In politics, the same pattern holds: In the mines one employer confronted, by the 1930s, one labor union; that union connected working people—dissidents and adherents both—to the Mexican state. Border working people related to several domains of power, the most important of which, the United States, they had little chance to address. Divisions among miners cannot be compared with the true structural heterogeneity of the border working class.

Fundamentally, the social structure, the lines of inequality that dispose people to understand themselves and act within and on power, differed in the two settings. Men were ranked by their position in the industrial hierarchy of the mines; as heads of households were ranked, so were their wives and children. Before nationalization of the mines in the late 1950s, the basic division between Mexican and North American was there for all to see. The heterogeneous working population of the border was part of several orders: a complicated local status and power system, including criteria of consumer goods, house appearance, personal relationships, and political pull; as well as the class inequality between Mexican labor and U.S. employers. An important feature of the heterogeneous situation, furthermore, was that many housewives were social actors distinct from their husband's occupation, some of them managing concerns of the household, such as education or investment, that deeply affected their place in the future social order.

I have drawn this contrast within the terms of a specific historical transformation, and therefore these cannot be taken as a list of features applicable to all ethnographic cases. Nevertheless, border Mexico fits the wider literature about working peoples. Within Latin America, for example, one can contrast the industrial community described by June Nash (1979) for Bolivian tin miners with the large literature in urban Latin American studies that emphasizes diverse sectors of employment (Roberts, 1978). Ethnographies of southern African miners (Wilson, 1941–1942; Epstein, 1958; Powdermaker, 1962) contrast mine compounds with more heterogeneous town sites. William Kornblum (1974) contrasts factory and neighborhood politics (ethnic groups are unified in the former, divided in the latter) in a steel-mill district of Chicago. The linkages between working-class housing and enterprise type are drawn in a particularly clear, insightful manner by Neuma Aguiar (1983) for a plantation, a government irrigation project, and a factory neighborhood in Brazil.

Peter Lloyd (1982) uses the complicated, heterogeneous character of urban working populations to argue that the concept of working class, which he thinks of as a clear-cut industrial work force plus community, is not adequate for the anthropology of the Third World. The Agua Prieta case, however, is undeniably part of a historical continuum of working classes in northeastern Sonora. The analysis of the "waged life" shows that deeply rooted patterns of work and consumption continued at the border. The heterogeneous form cannot be judged according to its fit or failure to fit assumptions originating with unitary working communities. The border case shows that it is indeed possible to analyze the lines of heterogeneous communities as working classes, paying due respect to the ethnographic evidence.

6. Agua Prieta in the Maquiladora Period, 1967–1986

INTRODUCTION

In 1967, Agua Prieta received its first factory under the Border Indus-trialization Program. Two decades later (June 1986) twenty-six plants were in place, employing over 6,400 people (Stoddard, 1987: 19). What do we learn from setting these workers in their time and their place? Previous studies of origins of maquiladora workers have established that the majority moved to the border with their natal families, not in the immediate past but as much younger children accompanying their parents (Fernández-Kelly, 1983:58–60; Peña, 1987:133). Their origins lie precisely within the border settlement process during the decades after 1940.

In their history of women's work in industrializing France and England, Louise Tilly and Joan Scott (1978) developed two related models of wage-earning households, the "family wage economy" and the "family consumer economy." The majority of maquiladora employees, especially women, are "working children" who live with one or both of their parents, and contribute part of their wages to the household budget. The concept of the family wage economy pro-poses that this role is determined by the working-class family's need to purchase most of the items of daily existence:

> For increasing numbers of women, as well, the essence of work was earning a wage. Since they were members of family wage economies, their work was defined not by household labor needs, but by the household's need for money to pay for food and to meet other expenses, such as rent. (1978:104)

The family consumer economy broadens these needs to include the wide range of new consumer goods:

> The goal of working families in the mid-nineteenth century had been to earn enough to subsist. As many family members worked as were necessary to earn a "target income" which would maintain a minimum level of subsistence. By the early twentieth century the higher wages of men particularly and the availability of cheap consumer goods raised the target income of working-class families. Necessities now included not only food and clothing, but also other items that once had been considered luxuries. What we have termed the family consumer economy, then, was a wage-earning unit which increasingly emphasized family consumption needs. (1978:176)

Tilly and Scott draw the distinction between the two forms of working-class economies for a specific historical purpose: to account for the relative decline in Western Europe of women's labor force participation as men's earning power rose. For the circumstances of the Mexican border, however, which combines low real wages with prolonged exposure to the many consumer goods on the U.S. side, it seems appropriate to unify the models of the family wage economy and the family consumer economy. We should therefore look to the history of consumption and purchasing power in the border settlement process for the key to the amassing of a "working child" labor force.

The young female operatives—it is predominantly young women who work in the maquiladoras—put up with tedious tasks and poor remuneration. They fulfill the need of their families to bring in a steady paycheck. Such self-sacrifice is referred to as the "subordination" of women (Nash, 1980; Young, Wolkowitz, and McCullagh, 1984; Fernández-Kelly, 1983, applies this concept to the maquiladora workers). However, women are subordinated to households and larger economies in many different circumstances, and for many kinds of paid and unpaid labor. It is unsatisfying to explain the efforts of young women at the border by reference to a general condition. For this reason it is necessary to set maquiladora women in a regional context, in a longer stretch of history, and in relation to their fathers, mothers, and especially brothers, some of whom work beside them in the factories. This is an attempt at a two-gender analysis of the maquiladora working class, for although women are numerically preponderant, they are a majority in an unequal relationship to a smaller number of factory men.

CÓRDOBA FAMILY HISTORY

When Carlos and Francisca Córdoba married in 1940, they could well expect to spend the rest of their lives in the shadow of the mine's hoist tower. Carlos labored in Santo Domingo from 1936 to 1958, except for employment in Pilares de Nacozari while Santo Domingo was not open, and in another mine south of Agua Prieta until 1972. Yet Carlos and Francisca's children did not become miners. Instead, they were among the first workers to enter Agua Prieta maquiladora doors in 1967, and various among them labored in the factories through the mid-1980s. The length of the Córdobas' collective working experience is important: Roles for the children developed during several decades while the family shifted and set-tled; and the younger Córdoba generation—Jorge, Francisco, Guada-lupe, and Luisa—have substantial portions of their life stories to tell us, permitting contrasts among them to emerge.

Although Carlos did not finally break with the mines until 1972, the rest of his family had committed themselves to move away years earlier; the reasons for this are of considerable interest to the forma-tion of the border family economy. As it matured, the Córdoba household shifted its concentration from the adult male wage earner to investment in education and placement of children in an advan-tageous job market. This is proven by a complicated household mi-gration history with multiple residences at a given time (for basic definitions I follow Bender, 1967, and Goody, 1972; Carter, 1984 en-joins us to follow actual sequences of household histories).

The Córdoba household split in 1956. The reason was the need to continue the education of the eldest son and daughter (born in 1944 and 1948, respectively). The small mine town of Santo Domingo had only an elementary school, and the nearest secondary school was in the city of Nacozari de García. Francisca went to Nacozari to care for the two older children while her mother, Amalia, cared for the youn-ger children and her son-in-law in Santo Domingo. That is, the Cór-doba households were composed of two residential units with one source of income (Carlos in Santo Domingo) but two sources of un-paid labor (Francisca and her mother in Nacozari and Santo Do-mingo, respectively) (Figure 6.1).

The residential choice of Nacozari de García was significant. The mine having closed, no longer was it a male wage center; Carlos was justified in remaining with his job in Santo Domingo. But instead of

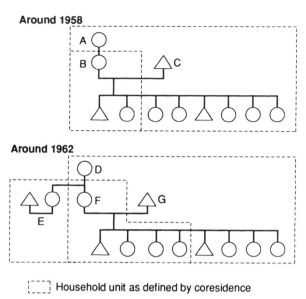

Around 1958

Around 1962

⌐⌐⌐⌐ Household unit as defined by coresidence

A. Amalia Galaz. Household work in Santo Domingo
B. Francisca López. Household work in Nacozari
C. Carlos Córdoba. Wage work in Santo Domingo
D. Amalia Galaz. Household work in Esqueda
E. Help with housing in Agua Prieta for Francisca López
F. Francisca López. Household work in Agua Prieta
G. Carlos Córdoba. Wage work in Esqueda

Figure 6.1. Córdoba household arrangements during migration

preparing his eldest son, Jorge, to follow in his footsteps, the family invested in a formal education for both son and daughter that could best be utilized in labor markets other than mining.

Similarly complex household arrangements were made during two subsequent moves. After a period of unemployment following Santo Domingo's demise in 1958, Carlos found work as a diesel mechanic at a fluorite mine near the town of Esqueda. From 1959 to 1962, the Córdoba households were arranged in the following manner: Francisca lived with Carlos in Esqueda during the week, to care for him and the six younger children, while her mother cared for the two older children and the house in Nacozari; the whole group would reunite in Nacozari on weekends.

In 1962, as the next set of offspring was ready for secondary school, a portion of the family moved again, this time to Agua Prieta, with the help of Francisca's older half sister. Francisca resided in

Agua Prieta with the four oldest children (three in secondary school
and the oldest son working), while her mother stayed with Carlos in
Esqueda to care for the four younger children still in elementary
school. By 1965 the children were all in Agua Prieta, while Carlos
remained working in Esqueda and his mother-in-law kept the house.
On weekends they would come together in Agua Prieta.

The final turning point in the Córdoba story came in 1972. The
fluorite mine in Esqueda closed, and Carlos wanted to take a job
working with an engineer in the new La Caridad project, isolated in
the mountains above Nacozari. But Francisca and her children refused to leave Agua Prieta. By that date, the two youngest daughters
were in secondary school, which they could not have attended in the
mine development zone. Four of the older children were working in
maquiladoras. The family debate and decision to stay in Agua Prieta
in 1972 marked the completion of the shift from the adult male
mine economy to the multiple-worker border economy. In keeping
with the developmental cycle, earnings for the household had
shifted from father to children. This turning point also shows how
husband and wife had different interests in choosing migratory locations according to their alignment in both labor and consumer markets (with women bearing children's interests in mind).

The first major investment the Córdoba family made in Agua
Prieta was a house. When Francisca came to the border in 1962, she
and her children moved in with her half sister, then resided in rental
apartments. In 1965, Carlos and Francisca bought a house lot from
the municipal government (city, not ejido, land). It cost two hundred
pesos for the lot and fifty pesos for a building permit, at a time when
Carlos was earning fifty pesos a day. They responded to my inquiries
that they had not needed any "pull" (*palanca*) or political involvement to get the lot. The building materials were bought from a hardware firm owned by an Agua Prieta politician with credit extended
to Jorge, their oldest son. The plumbing was bought, straight cash, in
the United States. They hired a mason to do the basic foundation,
walls, and roof; Carlos, in Agua Prieta on weekends, and his two
sons did the ceiling, floors, windows and doors, wall plastering, and
such, and Carlos baked the bricks himself in Esqueda. His sons did
the electrical wiring.

The oldest son, Jorge (born 1944), started to work in a wood products factory in 1962, soon after arriving in Agua Prieta. The Córdoba
family began a working child economy even prior to the advent of

the maquiladoras. Evidence about the financing of the house supplies seems to indicate that Jorge's income had become as important to the household as the father's. In 1967 two daughters, aged nineteen and eighteen, and one son, aged sixteen, went to work in a maquiladora. Both girls had finished nine years of school; the son was attending school at night. By 1969 five children, all living at home, were working in the factories: three daughters as operatives, one son as a foreman, and one son on a maintenance crew.

Carlos continued to work, however. When his mine job came to an end, he looked for occasional work in Agua Prieta repair shops. Finally, he had the opportunity to buy a used lathe from a shopowner going out of business. With this crucial tool, his many years of experience, and his reputation for skilled work, Carlos was able to launch a machine shop, the culmination of his life's labors. At the age of seventy-seven (1986) Carlos continued to operate his business two, three, or more days a week.

The Córdoba family pooled several incomes to equip their new household in Agua Prieta, especially in the years immediately after completing the house in 1969. In fact, Jorge bought a television "for his father" in celebration of the completion of work on the house. The family also gathered money to buy a small electric refrigerator, the first the family had owned. They replaced it in 1973 with a large refrigerator-freezer bought secondhand in Douglas. The employed children pitched in to meet its forty-five dollar price. It was purchased on the occasion of Jorge's marriage, with the purpose of storing the meat from a cow that the godparents of the marriage were contributing as part of their sponsorship of the ritual. In the same year (1973) Jorge made another major contribution to the family by buying his mother a new sewing machine, to replace the one inherited from her mother in 1940, for 1,500 pesos (120 dollars at the exchange rate of the time).

In 1972, the family as a whole bought a new, large wood-burning stove to replace the stove that was part of the household's original 1940 equipment. Although purchased in an Agua Prieta store, the fact that its purchase price was named in dollars (four hundred dollars) probably indicates that it came from the American side. In 1982 the Córdoba household, now supported by the working father and two working daughters only, bought a butane-fueled stove, a set of cabinets, a counter, and a dishwasher for 50,000 pesos (roughly 250 dollars) from a friend who was moving. A similar personal arrangement permitted them to purchase bedroom and living room furniture in the mid-1970s.

Another set of bedroom furniture and a china cabinet were purchased for the family by "the daughters" (there were six). They made payments of at least five thousand pesos (four hundred dollars) to an Agua Prieta furniture store. The china cabinet holds glass and ceramic mementos given to Francisca Córdoba by three daughters, a daughter-in-law, a comadre, and two nieces who had been guests of the family when they came from out of town to seek factory work. Just as the gifts ascend from daughters/daughter-in-law to mother, so the mother provides child care for her grandchildren when her daughters are at work or shopping in Douglas.[1] The term in Spanish for such gifts, *recuerdos*, was used specifically for symbols of personal relationship that, in this case, represented an important exchange in an economy where younger women had access to cash and older women provided unpaid labor.

The details of the Córdoba material culture history demonstrate the confluence of a historical process, the consumer environment of the border, with the family developmental cycle. The result was an outburst of children born in the 1940s and 1950s maturing and working for the goals of family accumulation. Through the 1970s, all the children save one daughter married out of the core household. Because the marriages were spread out between 1972 and 1984, the household always had at least one working child at home. This combined with the slowing down of needs for material provisioning to result in a household that relied on resident working children and the father to fulfill the ongoing need for income.

In 1986 the central Córdoba household was composed of the elderly parents, a divorced son who had returned home (his children live with his former wife), and an unmarried daughter with her daughter. The father, Carlos, pays the monthly bills (gas, electricity, water, taxes) by saving from his fluctuating workshop income; in 1986, he estimated that he earned five thousand pesos (roughly ten dollars) by charging clients for a day of labor on top of the cost of materials. The resident son, Francisco, earned two and a half times the minimum wage as a mechanic in a maquiladora (26,000 pesos, or 52 dollars weekly). He contributed 5,000 pesos and a 1,200-dollar grocery store voucher to the Córdoba household; he was also supporting his children. The resident daughter, Teresa, earned the minimum wage (11,550 pesos, or 23 dollars weekly) as a maquiladora operative. She contributed a fifth to a quarter of her earnings (2,000–2,500) directly to the household fund; she spent most of the remainder on her three-year-old daughter. The mother, Francisca, did not earn money, but she managed the contributions to household funds.

The remaining six children each live in neolocal, nuclear households (a married daughter and her husband live in a small house on the family lot, but they maintain a separate budget). Each of these families is sustained by a single wage gained by the husband (two of them from maquiladoras, and four not). None of the five married daughters worked as of 1986. This is a product of regular (but not inviolable) patterns of employment change at marriage. The Córdoba daughters stated that they left the maquiladora when they were wed, a phrasing that is a cultural convention—the real date of exit was, as we shall see, more complex—but this did express the nature of the new household. In contrast, sons stayed in the labor market, and marriage brought no direct change in their employment. In effect, male-wage-earner nuclear households hived off from the complex wage-earning parental household.

These filial households were reported to me as completely separate in terms of budgets, but in fact there was considerable sharing of child care and groceries, especially on weekends. One daughter married a Mexican American from Douglas; another married a man in Agua Prieta and later immigrated to Douglas. With the help of cars and local visiting passports, the Córdoba grand-family effectively spans the international boundary (Figure 6.2).

Among the various members of the Córdoba family, I will focus on the careers of four children who have worked or are working in maquiladoras: Jorge, the oldest Córdoba son (born 1944); his younger brother Francisco (born 1953); and their sisters Luisa (born 1948) and Teresa (born 1949). Today Jorge is a section foreman and Francisco is a mechanic, both earning over twice the minimum wage; Teresa, after seventeen years, remains a line operative paid no more than the minimum wage; and Luisa has dropped out of the maquiladora work force altogether.

All four were reported as essentially equivalent in formal education, having completed secondary school.[2] However, there were important differences in informal education. Jorge and Francisco grew up working alongside their father, a skilled machinist and mechanic. They learned from books, not just observation and participation, for Carlos bought an instructional course in diesel mechanics for them.

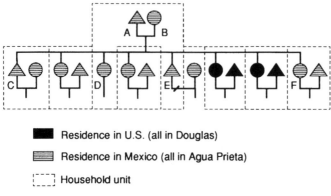

Residence in U.S. (all in Douglas)

Residence in Mexico (all in Agua Prieta)

Household unit

A. Carlos Córdoba
B. Francisca López
C. Jorge Córdoba
D. Teresa Córdoba
E. Francisco Córdoba
F. Luisa Córdoba

Figure 6.2. Córdoba grand-family: constituent units and cross-border locations

As young men they also spent days tinkering with cars, gaining yet more knowledge in the process. This informal education dovetailed with factory management ideas about appropriate training and job placement for men versus women. Francisco's first job was as a maintenance technician trainee in an electronics factory. His sisters entered at the same time (one in the same factory) as line operatives.

Women learn equally valuable skills in the family. Both Teresa and Luisa know how to sew and cook. However, male-associated mechanical skills are directly applicable to the factory tasks to which they are assigned, whereas women's work and knowledge are divided into two spheres, factory and home. The skills involved in sewing on a machine at home are not similar to the operation of a large industrial sewing machine, several women insisted—to say nothing of the novelty of electronic assembly.

Men and women differ not so much in possessing bodies of knowledge as in how the factory social system makes male mechanical backgrounds "relevant" and women's sewing backgrounds "irrelevant." This is, in part, a product of unequal socialization of males and females. Although both boys and girls go out to work in their teens, long periods of stop-and-go employment are tolerated, even expected, for young men, while young women persist in holding a

job and thus steadily contributing to the household fund. At this
stage of life, creation of lasting friendships is more important to
boys than is sustained work. Young men also investigate many job
locations and possibilities in order to place themselves in a good
starting point to advance in skills and connections. The early years
of Francisco Córdoba's work history, which included training in one
factory, employment in another, and even an exploratory voyage to
the United States, demonstrate this pattern. Ironically, the erratic
labors of young men prepare them for a life of employment, while
the dedicated efforts of young women provide them only dead-end
jobs, and demands from their families.

The perspective afforded by the study of several generations of
family history is valuable for explaining unequal roles of maquiladora men and women. The male life course during the border
settlement decades was a sustained attempt to bring home income
despite complex employment, including stretches between jobs.
Men found it necessary to explore personalized relationships and
flexible work skills. Women dealt with unpredictable or migratory
male employment by sacrificing part of their labor time to earning
money while providing unpaid effort for the household economy according to the current balance of income and household necessity.

Although the maquiladoras appear to have broken drastically
with the past, replacing women's roles as housewives with women's
roles as wage earners, in fact the young women who work in the
factories are doing so in coordination with the older women who
work as housewives. In accord with Fernández-Kelly (1983), women
work in maquiladoras as part of a household economy. They work to
provide the immediate cash flow. At the same time, they are also
responsive to many types of sudden demands for extra unpaid labor
in the household when children get sick, elderly parents are taken to
the doctor, and so forth.

The nature of the assembly operative jobs filled by women makes
this possible. There is a large pool of very similar positions in a
number of different factories. Almost all pay the same minimum
weekly wage. While experience and skill are valuable for assembly
work, there is little reward for such ability; there is no ascending
career track because one operative position is no better than another.

The male role is also shaped by the household economy. The majority of male maquiladora employees in the 1986 resurvey sample

were the sole support of their households (see below). Men differ from women, however, in that they try to provide for the household economy by organizing a work career that will sustain their earning power through rough spots. They attempt this by accumulating alliances and skills in the same manner as their fathers, though they now operate in the context of personalized employment networks inside the maquiladoras. Men have much greater access than women to nonoperative jobs, positions such as mechanic and supervisor paying more than the minimum wage, for which there is a recognized and well-rewarded career ladder for skill and experience.

The work histories of the four Córdoba siblings demonstrate how male and female careers contrast; I concentrate on their reaction to the key juncture posed by unemployment. Francisco had spent a long period working for one electronics factory in Agua Prieta that, in its time, had been the largest employer in the city. He had ascended from trainee to foreman there. In spite of this, in 1982 Francisco departed without severance pay when this operation declared bankruptcy. After passing through several minor jobs, in 1984 Francisco obtained a very desirable position in a relatively new electronics plant. He was connected into this job through his closest friend, a foreman at that plant, with the approval of the plant manager, a former maquiladora union official. Even though this was an extremely high-pressure operation that forced Francisco to work exhausting amounts of overtime, he was fiercely loyal to this factory. In light of Francisco's previous experience, repaying faith to his connections can readily be understood.

Jorge had begun work as a laborer in a factory that antedated the maquiladoras. Over the years, this place has proven to be an important source of subsequent male alliances. Jorge has worked as a mechanic and as a foreman at a number of maquiladoras since 1967. At least twice, in 1974 and 1984, he lost his job as part of major layoffs. Unlike his sister Luisa, Jorge returned to the labor force. His ability to do this depended on the web of repute among men. When I first met Jorge, the electronics firm where he worked had gone bankrupt. The next year he joined a small operation where imported satellite dishes were assembled—a job, but clearly a marginal one. In the spring of 1986, Jorge suddenly obtained a position in a major American multinational operation in a department where there had been problems with high rates of defective items. He was hired on the basis of his reputation as a tough supervisor and experienced mechanical troubleshooter.

Francisco and Jorge had been able to switch firms and survive numerous layoffs while advancing in their careers. Their sister Teresa, after seventeen years in many, many factories, had not been able to advance beyond the level of operative paid the minimum wage (one position, as a quality control inspector, paid slightly above the minimum). Teresa alternated between wage work and unpaid work according to the needs of the Córdoba household at a given time; she persisted in working despite lack of advancement in part to provide for her daughter.

During my visits from 1984 to 1986, Teresa passed through four jobs. She left the initial position because her mother was bedridden with rheumatism. She had to take up the slack of household tasks as well as be home to care for her child, which her mother would normally have done for her. When Teresa returned to work, she quickly went through three factory jobs before settling on tagging electronics parts because it was low pressure and close to home, thus leaving her with energy for her daughter. Shortly afterward, I talked with her, and she was angry enough at being called back early from her vacation to reveal how worn the endless job track made her feel: The plants just come and go, slow down and speed up; there were too many jobs to tell me about.

Luisa did not return to the labor force after being laid off. She continued working after marrying, but she dropped out of the job market in 1977, when she was released from a position she had had for almost a decade. The combination of the external action of the factory, and a role in a household economy in which her husband was working (in contrast with Teresa's situation), ended Luisa's work career.

The divergence between men and women was encapsulated in a conversation involving Teresa, Francisco, and Jorge. The brothers argued that turnover of employees reflected the basically unreliable and screwed-up character of people, expressing the supervisory point of view associated not only with that position but also with the male career. Teresa demurred; she said that the factories hardly made it worth staying, and illustrated her point with one factory that announced "great" new bonuses for 100 percent attendance: five thousand pesos, or ten dollars, paid weekly—but only after three perfect months. Who, she asked, undoubtedly with her daughter in mind, could do that?

As simple an expression of deep-rooted imbalance between men and women within Mexican life as this conversation may seem, the mention of bonus money should give us pause. Ten dollars for good attendance is an exercise of power when people earn little more than twice that much in a week. Compensating for a pay scale fixed entirely too low with a bewildering array of bonuses not only makes each factory seem unique, it divides the potential rewards for being a working man from the possible returns to a laboring woman. Up to this point I have addressed culture, specifically social organization: what the Córdobas, and people like them, have made of their lives. To this I will add power—family, factory, and international—that makes actual the diverse potentials within culture.

BORDER CONSUMPTION

Since the turn of the century northeastern Sonorans have obtained consumer goods from the United States. Agua Prieta was the epitome of this pattern. In common with all of Mexico's northern border (especially the northwestern section), it was virtually cut off from the rest of the nation. Little in the way of supply reached this isolated outpost, and therefore until 1979 Agua Prieta was permitted the special status of "free perimeter," which allowed U.S. goods to be brought to the city without tariffs. The settlement was surrounded with fences on its interior side, as well as the border side, and traffic south had to pass a domestic customs gate.

A survey of expenditure patterns of maquiladora employees in 1972 provides evidence about the extent of Agua Prieta's consumer dependence on Douglas (Ladman and Poulson, 1972). Factory operatives reported that they directly spent an average of 39 percent of their paycheck in Arizona (managers reported spending 59 percent). Ladman and Poulson further estimated indirect expenditures, with the result that more than half of total expenditures (52 percent) finally ended in the United States.[3]

The border pattern of shopping in the United States combined with a long period of rising buying power and a stable rate of exchange between the peso and the dollar to create a powerful set of consumer expectations among the households that arrived in Agua Prieta in the 1940s, 1950s, and 1960s. Real wage levels in Mexico fell precipitously through the 1940s, and hit bottom in 1947. At nearly the same time—1948 through 1953—a series of devaluations devastated the border trade (Sandomingo, 1951; Jeffrey, 1951). This trough in purchasing power coincided with the ultimate collapse of the Sonoran mines and the flight to the border. From this moment at the bottom, families gradually ascended.

The national real wage index rose fourfold over the next thirty-one years (1947–1978) and, especially important for border consumers, the peso retained its strength against the dollar from 1954 to 1976. This long favorable stretch corresponded to the period when families were settling in: building houses, filling kitchens with stoves and refrigerators, buying beds, tables, and chairs.

At the border a trade developed in used goods brought from the United States to Mexico. Kitchen appliances stood out among the items in this trade, as well as salvaged materials from demolished houses (doors, windows, plumbing, and electrical wiring), which were particularly in demand during the home-building years.[4] Another channel for inflow of consumer goods was generous lines of credit extended by Douglas stores and banks to Agua Prieta households, with Mexican American kin cosigning. Both types of trade depended on stable exchange rates to permit Mexican consumers, whose incomes were set in pesos, to make purchases of goods whose price originated in dollars (whatever the currency of the final sale).

A standard of living arises from the combination of external economic circumstances—the real wages of the working class—and the family and community history experienced by each succeeding generation. During the period described above, the working people of border cities such as Agua Prieta came to expect certain "decencies" (Schneider, 1980:328). Neither strict necessities nor luxuries, such items can reasonably be expected at some point during a lifetime, and convey to the household a standing above abject poverty.

That border working families do indeed possess such objects is demonstrated by the 1978 survey of Agua Prieta maquiladora workers (Seligson and Williams, 1981:50–53). In their households 73.2 percent reported ownership of a refrigerator; 52.0 percent, of a television set; 49.3 percent, of a washer; 42.3 percent, of a sewing machine; and 34.1 percent, of an automobile. Indications of decencies in house construction abound: 93.5 percent of houses had indoor plumbing, and 97.6 percent were wired for electricity. These are two of the most expensive items in building a house.

The standard of material existence brought the need to earn cash, especially for maturing children to work and contribute to the improvement of the common household. In the older mine economy, access to consumer subsistence and appliances came nearly entirely through adult males, as organized in the company store payroll system. By the time families reached the border, male employment, though often effective at bringing in bursts of cash, had become complicated and frequently unreliable. It was not just a matter of male unemployment or underemployment. This existed in some cases, but in others it was not a factor. A family consumer economy lacking a historical basis in rising adult male wages (such as that described by Tilly and Scott for developed countries in this century) simply pushes "working children" harder.

MEXICO'S ECONOMIC CRISIS AND THE BORDER

Mexico's economic crisis after 1982 has affected the border zone in specific and severe ways. The nearly constant devaluations of the peso—by 1987 reducing the Mexican currency to a hundredth of its equivalent in 1982 dollars—closed channels through which border city residents had obtained American goods. The devaluations were worse at the border than elsewhere in Mexico, for this region suffered speculation and exaggerated declines in the peso's value.

Mexico now owes over one hundred billion dollars in foreign debt. Although the principal on the debt is effectively not being repaid, Mexico pays over twelve billion dollars annually in interest. The net balance of exports over imports has to increase in order to raise the foreign exchange to fund this costly stream of dollars departing Mexico (Cornelius, 1986). Factories at the border are an important part of debt-driven export development. They compete with East Asia and the Caribbean for extremely low-cost manufacturing markets. To retain American employers, the Mexican government has had to reduce the real wage. Increases in the officially mandated minimum wage, the standard pay of the vast majority of employees in the maquiladoras, are deliberately and consistently set at ceilings below projected rates of inflation (Bortz, 1986:41–42).

The loss in household purchasing power at the border has been measured. In late 1981–early 1982 James Greenberg (1981–82) surveyed ninety-three households in two working-class neighborhoods of Agua Prieta, Barrio Ferrocarril and Colonia Ejidal. In March and

April 1986, I was able to recontact sixty-three households. Of those households, fifty-eight provided information on total household income from all sources.[5] The average income of the fifty-eight recontacted households had been 3,213 pesos a week in 1982; in 1986, it was 30,253 pesos a week. However, the 1986 figure was seriously distorted by one household that reported 180,000 pesos in weekly sales revenues from a prosperous bakery rather than the actual income to the house, which is unknown. Dropping this case from both 1982 and 1986, the average for 1982 was 3,217 pesos, and for 1986 it was 27,626 pesos.

It remains to figure out what these numbers mean in constant purchasing power. There are two manners of doing this, each with its own faults. One can convert the pesos into dollars at the free-market exchange rate of the time; the exchange rate deflator was 19.0.[6] This deflator assumes that all border spending ends up in dollars; 52 percent of Agua Prieta spending did in 1971, but after repeated devaluations we cannot be sure to what extent people have shifted from more expensive U.S. sources to less expensive Mexican products.

Alternatively, one can deflate using the official price indices published by the Banco de México (*Indicadores económicas*, May 1986:Cuadro III-9). The problem with these is that there is reason to suspect that for political reasons these figures underestimate the real increases in the cost of living (Bortz, 1986). The figures for the border city of Ciudad Juárez were used as the closest approximation to Agua Prieta. The arithmetic ratio between the indices for April 1986 and January 1982 is 14.3.

Using the price index deflator method, real April 1986 household income was 1,932 pesos weekly—60.1 percent of what it had been in January 1982. Using the more extreme exchange rate method, 1986 household income was 1,454 pesos in 1982 terms, a fall to 45.2 percent of 1982. An accurate figure probably lies somewhere in between; whichever figure we choose, the harm to household budgets is palpable.

Similar methods can be applied to the factory paychecks. In January 1982, the minimum wage was 1,960 pesos weekly; at 26.26 pesos to the dollar, this was worth $74.64. The minimum wage in the first half of 1986 was 11,550 pesos weekly, $23.10 at 500 to 1, the going exchange rate at the time. This is only 31 percent of the 1982 dollar value of the wage. Alternatively, using the price index method, the

1986 factory check was worth 42 percent of what it had been in 1982.

Bringing home a steady stream of cash is one of the roles of the maquiladora employee within the family as a whole, and the nonpay benefits, such as enrollment in the national medical system, though important in other ways, do not help in this critical respect. Devaluations and repressed real wages have made fulfilling this role much more difficult. At the same time, many more of the now-cheapened factory jobs are available to any given family.

"WORKING CHILDREN" IN THE MAQUILADORA LABOR FORCE

Factory sound trucks drove around the neighborhoods of Agua Prieta, urging people to come with promises of special bonuses. Factories needed workers; the logic of debt-driven exports had succeeded. Prior patterns of border family culture changed or, better said, amplified in this power context of U.S.–Mexican economics.

In Agua Prieta, as in other border cities, more factory workers have responded to a lower price, a curious turn of events. This provides a useful test for the presence of the family wage/consumer economy. Tilly and Scott propose that in the family wage economy, "The composition of the household no longer was dictated by a need for household laborers, as in the family economy, but by a need for cash" (1978:105). I hypothesize that if the family wage economy exists and operates in this manner, then we should see a response in the internal balance of households as they desperately attempt to retain a decent life. I will measure whether the proportion of persons sent out to earn wages increases relative to the total labor available within the household. I expect to see the intensification of wage earning occur in specific types of labor, in particular, among female working children.

I will examine the change in wage labor participation from 1982 to 1986 among the sixty-three resurveyed households. In analyzing the results, I have used ethnographically appropriate categories that are stronger than gross demographic aggregates, dividing the work force simply by age and sex. In order to recognize the fact that the ability of each household to supply workers to the labor market is determined by the domestic cycle (some could send only the two parents, while others have numbers of adolescent and older children), I have measured labor participation against the numbers of "available" workers. "Available workers" are all persons over the age of sixteen, either male or female, regardless of whether they are in fact working or looking for work; I also included several young people under the legal working age of sixteen who were already employed, all of them in maquiladoras.

This definition does not presume that married women with children at home are not available since, in the maquiladora context, it is conceivable that they might be. In other words, this assumes that if the household had to, it could send anyone out to work, and then asks who in fact does go forth. The power of the "available worker" approach is that it measures changes in the use of labor household by household, and therefore directly addresses the family wage/consumer economy.

I have also divided types of available and actual workers according to what we have already learned through ethnography and family history. The categories reflect fundamental roles in the organization of households. "Working children" are defined as single, separated, divorced, or widowed children and grandchildren living in a household with their parent(s) or grandparent(s), whether or not they have offspring of their own. Such "children" can range in age from sixteen to the forties, because the criteria are that they are not currently married and that their earnings are pooled into a parental economy. I have included in this group workers with children of their own, especially women who are separated and live at home, because it is my experience that they work for wages while mothers or grandmothers care for their children. I will subsequently discuss the important differences between separated and single working children.

The remainder of available workers are "nonworking children." This group can be subdivided into available "working parents," who are parents or grandparents but do not fall into the group of working children discussed above. That is, they are parents working to support children who have not reached working age. There remains a residual "other" category composed of kin, such as cousins or aunts, living in the household.

The purpose of these data is to identify types of family wage/consumer economies, and in particular to isolate the changes in the working child economy of the maquiladoras. I have therefore devised three tables that focus our attention on these distinctions: all households containing available working children, whether or not actually employed, and whatever else the household membership

Table 6.1. Maquiladora Labor Force Participation: Households with Available "Working Children"

	1982		1986	
Available Workers	No.[a]	Percent	No.[a]	Percent
Available female "working children"	26	100%	29	100%
Employed	19	73	20	69
Maquiladoras	14	54	19	66
Underemployed	0	0	0	0
Not employed	7	27	9	31
Available male "working children"	33	100	35	100
Employed	11	33	15	43
Maquiladoras	7	21	7	20
Underemployed	8	24	5	14
Not employed	14	42	20	57
Available female "working parents"	18	100	21	100
Employed	4	22	4	19
Maquiladoras	2	11	2	10
Underemployed	3	17	1	5
Not employed	11	61	16	76
Available male "working parents"	17	100	20	100
Employed	13	76	18	90
Maquiladoras	1	6	2	10
Underemployed	1	6	2	10
Not employed	3	18	0	0
Other available female workers	2	100	4	100
Employed	2	100	0	0
Maquiladoras	1	50	0	0
Underemployed	0	0	0	0
Not employed	0	0	4	100
Other available male workers	4	100	4	100
Employed	3	75	2	50
Maquiladoras	1	25	0	0
Underemployed	0	0	1	25
Not employed	1	25	1	25

[a]Number of cases: 1982, 27 households; 1986, 28 households.

was (Table 6.1); households solely with one or both available working parents (Table 6.2); and miscellaneous, which mainly consisted of solitaries and joint families formed by married and unmarried siblings without parents in the house (Table 6.3). Households are categorized according to their situation at each of the two dates.[7]

Because gender inequality is basic to all types of work, especially in the maquiladoras, I have divided all types of workers (such as working children) into separate male and female categories. I expect to see greater labor force intensification by women than by men. For each category of available worker, I have calculated two rates. One is the total employment rate, whatever the job. The other is the rate specifically for maquiladoras. The phenomenon of labor force intensification is measured as an increase in the actual numbers employed (especially in the assembly plants) relative to the number of available workers for each household role type.

In 1982, 41 percent of all households had maquiladora workers, while in 1986, 52 percent did; there was a net increase of six maquiladora workers (from forty-one to forty-seven). If we look at Table 6.1, we find that it has been female working children who have intensified their labor in the maquiladoras. The rate of use of available workers in this category has risen from 54 percent to 66 percent. Of

Table 6.2. Maquiladora Labor Force Participation: Households with Only Parent(s) Available for Working

	1982		1986	
Available Workers	No.[a]	Percent	No.[a]	Percent
Available male "working parents"	28	100	27	100
Employed	23	82	23	85
Maquiladoras	6	21	6	22
Underemployed	5	18	4	15
Not employed	0	0	0	0
Available female "working parents"	30	100	27	100
Employed	6	30	5	19
Maquiladoras	5	17	3	11
Underemployed	3	10	3	11
Not employed	21	70	19	70

[a]Number of cases: 1982, 30 households; 1986, 27 households.

Table 6.3. Maquiladora Labor Force Participation:
Other Households

Available Workers	1982		1986	
	No.[a]	Percent	No.[a]	Percent
Available male workers	12	100	11	100
Employed	9	75	8	73
Maquiladoras	3	25	7	64
Underemployed	2	17	0	0
Not employed	1	8	3	27
Available female workers	9	100	7	100
Employed	2	22	2	29
Maquiladoras	1	11	1	14
Underemployed	1	11	0	0
Not employed	6	67	5	71

[a]Number of cases: 1982, 6 households; 1986, 7 households.

the overall increase from 1982 to 1986 of six maquiladora workers, five can be accounted for by this group alone. On the other hand, male working children have contributed nothing to this intensification; the number of maquiladoras has remained constant and utilization of available male children has, in fact, dropped.

Another group that appears to have an important role in maquiladora employment is male "nonworking children." In fact, there were ten married males working in the factories in 1982, and twelve in 1986 (this figure was arrived at by combining cases which occurred in all three household tables). This was the largest group after the female working children. On the other hand, married women decreased their maquiladora labor force participation from eight cases to five; there was one single female head of household who worked in the factories in both years. Married women report very low rates of employment, but in surveys such as this it was normal for housewives to report "no work" when in fact they had small sales or home-based businesses.

It has been suggested that male unemployment and underemployment (that is, work at very low remuneration or reduced numbers of hours) are a cause of female maquiladora work (Fernández-Kelly, 1983:56). It is possible to test this proposition with the data. I defined underemployment as work providing less than the minimum wage in a week. Day labor, firewood cutting, and employment by others in small workshops were types of underemployment. The data do not show that unemployment and underemployment of male heads of households caused female working children to enter the maquiladoras. Even as young women intensified their wage labors from 1982 to 1986, their fathers also found work. The differences among types of households in male "working parent" employment are not significant. To examine the question further, I separated out all households with active female maquiladora workers. Their rate of male parental full employment was 79 percent, a depressingly low figure but not significantly different from the rate of 85 percent in all households (the difference in percentages is accounted for by one case). Since unemployment and underemployment of fathers do not account for the labors of their daughters, we must look to border consumption, and in particular the need to preserve eroding family incomes.

The data do show shockingly high rates of male working child unemployment and underemployment. This is an important finding in need of explanation. Some young men may have been working in the United States. Since this was an impersonal survey, people did not refer to undocumented aliens as freely as they did among the families with whom I had lasting relationships. By indirect means, counting young men who were listed in the 1982 household census but not in the 1986, and not accounted for by marriage or otherwise leaving the household, I estimate that in 1986 at least seven male working children may have been in the United States.

The 1982–1986 evidence strongly affirms Fernández-Kelly (1983), who has provided the most important analysis of why women are concentrated in maquiladora work. Basically, she argues that young or separated women work in factories because they are the group within households most powerfully dominated by obligations to contribute to the family wage economy. At the same time, certain branches of manufacturing capital are in particular need of women who are dedicated and will accept low wages. The 1982–1986 period is especially useful in testing this analysis, since it was a time of very rapid decline in real income; that is, it was a time when the family wage economy required compensatory wage earning. My data show that female working children were indeed the group who responded the most.

The data also support, in a more indirect manner, the propositions about male versus female work careers in the maquiladoras. I identified two crucial worker types in the data: female working children, and married males, usually heads of household who were the only source of wages. The women enter or return to work as key contributors to the family wage/consumer economy of the border cities, while men work in factories as part of a lasting career. This again points to the importance of studying the roles and interests of males in the maquiladoras in relation to and contrast with females.

The underutilization of available male working children is very striking in these data, especially considering the severity of the economic crunch and the rapid expansion of maquiladora employment. As the factories drew a larger Agua Prieta work force, why did the gender selectivity not lessen (leaving aside male careerists)? The answer cannot be established from the data at this point, but from my friendships with young men, I would say that there was a misfit between the erratic "searching and learning" life path (including voyages to the United States) and the tedious, highly restrictive discipline of the maquiladoras, which was the basis for hiring and retaining line operatives.

THE PAYCHECK AND THE ORGANIZATION OF POWER
WITHIN THE HOUSEHOLD

The family wage/consumer economy is made up of several specialized activities and roles. Certain members, for example, may be on the lookout for good buys or exchanges in used appliances, while others may operate small workshops that pay better than the daily minimum wage but are less reliable than steady employment. The role of the maquiladora worker, as we have learned, is to bring in a predictable flow of cash needed for expenses such as shopping or utility bills. In fact, among the households in which maquiladora workers resided (52 percent of all 1986 households), three-quarters of their total income (74 percent) came from factory paychecks.

The distribution of earnings within the household became increasingly tense during the 1980s as the value of the maquiladora wage fell. By the spring of 1986, forty-eight hours of effort were worth no more than twenty-three dollars when shopping in Douglas. This crisis provides an unusual opportunity to expose the lines of power within the household that lay hidden in boom years. Conflicts over the amount of income that maquiladora working children were expected to bring home were audible.

The crux of power and conflict was the proportion of the paycheck put into the hands of the family manager, and the proportion retained for individual use. Roberta Baer encountered consistent patterns of income pooling in Sonora, whether rural, urban migrant, or urban born. She reports that "with regard to allocation of income, at all household income levels the husband's income is generally used for the main household expenses" and "in most cases [wives'] income is used for general household expenses or food" (1984:187, 189). However, Baer writes:

> In those households where children or other relatives are working, the pattern in Sonora is that these other workers generally contribute only a portion of their earnings to the husband or the wife of the household, retaining the rest of their income to dispose of as they choose. (1984:191)

It was the balance of such contributions that Agua Prieta families contested.

Among the twenty-eight households in Agua Prieta that contained working children, sixteen reported a reduction in effective income because children withheld a portion of their pay for personal uses.[8] In these households, this amounted to a reduction to 69 percent of total income. People usually stated that the split of their children's paycheck was half to the household, half for themselves. This was a formulaic response, and although it may have served as a rule of thumb for dividing money, I know from households with whom I had much more frequent visiting relations that the pie was sliced in more particular ways that reflected the balance of interpersonal relationships within the household.

The various money-earning and saving strategies within the household were not equal, nor were the persons concerned. As we learned above, the Mexican government has consistently set the levels of minimum wage increases lower than the rate of inflation. Because this process of wages falling behind prices is readily visible, wage earning has become devalued among Agua Prieta families. One statement was repeated so often that it served Aguapretense as a stereotyped model for understanding the economic crisis. It was said that it would do no good for factory workers to strive to raise their wages, because inflation would just rise to match them; instead, it was prices that had to be lowered. I heard this from persons making the minimum wage.

On the other hand, investing in large consumer durables with an eye to reselling was an effective way to beat inflation. This was the domain of senior men or women, depending on the item. Another valued strategy, possibly the post powerful, was maintaining a privileged job or commercial relationship with an important elite. This was usually the domain of men, though some women in commerce also utilized this strategy. The logic of prices required senior men and women in households to extract as much cash as possible from working children so that they could shift household income into inflation-beating strategies. This worsened pressure and conflict between generations in families.

Male and female working children differed not so much in the proportion of their pay that they brought into the household as in their degree of responsibility toward the job. Young women would tolerate the tedium and even terrible conditions of an assembly plant in order to continue to bring home needed money. Or, like Teresa Córdoba, they would abandon a decent factory position in response to a sudden pressing need in the household (her mother's illness), and then have to return to the exhausting job search. Young men were more responsible to their individual life path, and would leave a steady but dead-end operative job to explore a work possibility that seemed more promising or exciting. Even though young women retain part of their income, they are the group most narrowly constrained in the household economy.

Not all working women were equal in the degree to which they were subjected to household economic needs. Among the twenty-five female maquiladora workers in the 1986 resurvey, five were single, separated, or divorced, had children, and lived with parent(s) or grandparent(s). Fourteen were single, childless daughters living at home (the remaining six cases were married women). The working daughters with children left them with their mothers or grandmothers. In turn, they were the most bound to the demands of senior women, who were managers of the household funds. This was somewhat disguised because the group of separated mothers reported paying less than half their income to the home. However, they reported spending virtually all the remainder on clothes and other needs of their children, which in effect replaced a major expenditure by the household as a whole. Much less leverage could be applied by mothers to childless daughters. One anonymous interviewee complained about the contributions by her daughter. The house got 3,000 pesos of her daughter's 11,550-peso minimum wage, and the rest went to her "for clothes." The mother added, "How nice it would be if she brought it to the house."

Part of single working children's personal expenditures is for cooked food at lunchtime, and part for transportation—though most walk to work in this small city—and some goes for dances on weekends, and clothes. Jeans and clothes are sold on the installment plan in Agua Prieta stores. These expenditures, less important though they may appear, were necessary to the young people of the city (see Fernández-Kelly, 1983:138–139). As Tilly and Scott noted for Europe, the location of youthful socializing has changed from inexpensive rural public settings to urban commercialized ones (1978:186–187). Mexican small town dances have sponsors and charge money, but this does not compare with the cost of large discos and sponsored dances of the border city. In turn, Tilly and Scott connect the spending on leisure activities to a new structure of marriage. Marriage is now the "union of two wage-earning capacities" and money no longer invested in dowries instead is used to maintain an attractive appearance among the social groups of youth within which marriages are made (1978:191).

The choice among marriage partners could mean the difference between starvation and stability for Agua Prieta women. My analysis of 1986 household budgets (Heyman, 1988:365–374) shows that households headed by a single male wage earner making one minimum wage or less, such as a construction laborer, could not afford sufficient food for a given family size even if they spent not one cent on anything else. On the other hand, the most prosperous households were headed by single male money earners—but they had well-placed jobs or businesses that paid several times the minimum wage.

However, when young women with their eye to the future invested part of their pay in the social life of their generation, they took away from the satisfaction of parental demands. This explains internal family tensions over single daughters' wages. I speculate that young women are now undergoing the conflicts of individualization of waged life similar to those of young men generations earlier. Though Tilly and Scott are proponents of the concept that women are subordinated to the family wage economy, they write:

Even when daughters remained at home, as happened more often in urban families, or when whole families migrated to textile towns, the fact that they earned wages had important effects on family relationships. Family members were no longer bound inseparably to a family enterprise. Instead, the goal became earning enough money to support the minimal needs of the group. The family wage was the sum total of individual members' contributions. Inevitably, in this situation, contributions became individualized. One might work with other family members, but this was not necessary. . . . Ultimately, the wage (however low or unfair) represented remuneration for an individual's labor. (1978:119–120)

We can hardly feel certain, however, that young women of the 1980s will follow the course of young men of the 1930s who did break with families; we can just as easily envision that this will be a recurrent tension.

POWER IN THE FACTORIES

The operation of assembly plants requires that management exercise power for two reasons: Workers should assemble the maximum number of parts during the time they are paid; and foremen and other ranking personnel should act for the interests of the management, rather than sympathizing with their subordinates. To fulfill these requirements of power, the maquiladoras rely heavily on the gap between women and men.

The 1986 survey shows great disparities between male and female maquiladora employees in occupation and pay level. Ninety-two percent of female maquiladora employees were operatives. Only one out of twenty-five women (a bilingual import-export administrator) earned more than the minimum wage. Fifty-six percent of men (twenty-three total cases) were operatives, but males dominated positions that were either ancillary or supervisory: manager, foreman, technician, truck driver, mechanic. All but one of these positions (ten in total) were filled by men. Several of the males in operative roles were adolescents and in line for training as technicians. Six men made at least one and a half times the minimum wage, while seventeen were paid the minimum.

The division between minimum-wage position and above-minimum-wage position is a watershed. At a time when the minimum wage was 11,550 pesos weekly, the average pay among those males earning above the minimum in the maquiladoras was 30,200 pesos.

Men are, or aspire to be, wage-earning heads of household during their life course, and the goal of a paycheck well above the minimum serves as an effective incentive for them to adhere to management desires. The manner in which this is arranged will be explored shortly.

Women, as we have seen, respond more directly than men to the pressing need at home for money right away. The minimum wage is set by the Mexican government, and does not directly refer to the factory power structure; it has to do with the need to attract export industries to offset the debt. Laid on top of the minimum, however, is a complex set of bonuses, piece rates, loans, shopping chits, and awarding of overtime. It achieves its power to motivate rapid and precise work[9] from the fact that the minimum wage has been set so low, and family needs are so great. In the 1986 survey, among those persons who detailed their bonuses and such, these amounted to an average per worker of 3,203 pesos a week, roughly 28 percent of the minimum wage.[10] While this may seem like a measly six dollars to a U.S. citizen, it was a desirable sum amid economic suffering in Mexico.

My interviews also revealed four loans from maquiladoras amounting to an average of 16,250 pesos. These loans could not bind individuals to jobs and did not carry interest, so they are best understood as a favor done by the factory to workers in need, which in turn put them under obligation to the management. A few maquiladoras, in admirable response to the erosion of consumer power, provided employees with vouchers redeemable for groceries.

The pay structure was the most important manner by which gender roles were manipulated in the factories. Pay levels were clearly divided along gender lines, and bonuses were used to manipulate and reinforce the role of women as self-sacrificing earners of cash income. Their importance to Agua Prieta maquiladora operatives was shown by their conversations comparing small advantages in bonus pay between factories. Direct material incentives in the context of very low real wages seem to me to have been the foremost exercise of power over women workers' lives.

The key to the management of maquiladoras was a division of labor between American general managers and Mexican, often native Aguapretense, personnel managers (this applies to American-owned multinational subsidiaries; the two roles were combined in smaller, locally owned subcontractors). While the general manager made fundamental decisions such as the production level of the plant, the personnel manager decided who was hired and who was laid off. This system shielded American managers from potential conflicts and criticism, and made them appear more neutral than they really were (see the interviews with maquiladora workers in Iglesias, 1985:e.g., 27–28).

The arrangement tapped the vast local knowledge of Mexican personnel managers about individuals, their pasts, and their personal qualities. While the chains of gossip provided power over women workers, they were especially valuable for controlling working men who, since their youth, have operated within a sphere of personalized alliances. This was called the *rebuscada* (literally, the "extra search"), and it referred to inquiries into personal gossip about a job applicant after all the formal job experience and skills were weighed. The term was applied specifically to male factory jobs.

As we have seen, men attempt to assemble a life's career of ascending skills, jobs, and connections, though many fail. Men use connections to string together employment despite layoffs and job switching. The rare position paying more than the minimum wage is especially desirable. If the local maquiladora manager hands one of these jobs to a working man, he can expect in return a powerful sense of obligation phrased in terms of vertical friendship. Such ties bind the men who work in critical occupations, such as section supervisor, to the interests of the factory management; they even pervade the goals of male workers such as technicians and trainees who aspire to advance. Francisco and Jorge, for example, manifested a consistent adherence to the goal of maximizing production in interviews I conducted about maquiladora work.

There was one central union for most of the maquiladoras in Agua Prieta, especially the large, U.S.-owned ones. Officially recognized unions in Mexico are part of the political networks of that nation's ruling party (on the maquiladora unions, see Carillo and Hernández, 1985:Chapter 4). Because low wages are an important part of the Mexican government's export strategy, official unions will not challenge this fundamental feature of the maquiladora system. The union in Agua Prieta, however, has played an important role in other ways. The union local first gained prominence during the mass layoffs of 1974–1975, when it negotiated several settlements of severance pay in lieu of the legal norms.

During the mid-1980s, the union was striving to change the legal tenure of newly hired workers from in-plant contracts to collective bargaining contracts. There are three types of tenure (de la Rosa

Hickerson, cited in Peña, 1987): in-plant contracts, which convey indefinite tenure; collective bargaining contracts, in which the worker's tenure is renewed periodically; and contracts of twenty-eight days for trial or temporary workers. By switching from in-plant to collective bargaining contracts, workers no longer indefinitely accrue time in the plant and can be released by not renewing the contract. Because severance pay increases rapidly with time, this can save the maquiladora considerable expense.[11] Workers go through the union, rather than directly to the factory, to sign the collective contract. Women workers driven into the labor market by their family's need for cash have to accept the union.

I assembled two case studies of conflict in the maquiladoras. One case involved individual grievances over money owed when a factory was closed; the other involved a strike at a nonunionized, and often abusive, factory. I cannot provide the details of these two cases because I promised confidentiality to my informants, and descriptions of personal roles would inevitably reveal the identities of the actors in a city as tightly knit as Agua Prieta.

Certain points can, however, be summarized. A working married woman pursued pay grievances; she had to work, but she did not passively accept the abuses piled on her. She had recruited a small network of fellow complainants among her former coworkers, both male and female; this network was interlocked with relationships of kinship (a sibling and cousins). Despite her informal support, however, this woman's pursuit of the case was frustrated by the lack of interest of the union (it had been a nonunionized plant) and by the governmental labor arbitration system, which makes a trip to the state capital to appeal grievances expensive and most likely unrewarding.

In the strike, a man and a woman had opposing roles in the complex aftermath involving internal factory and union politics. A widow was a key opponent of the factory manager and was experiencing considerable pressure aimed at forcing her out of her job. A young man, who was working for the plant manager behind the scenes, had been promoted from operative to technician trainee. I was able to identify his family as one with connections to the maquiladora union, both political parties, and key Agua Prieta elites.

My material therefore affirms the important arguments of Devon Peña about power and conflict in the maquiladoras (1987). He looks at the gender hierarchy on the shop floor and emphasizes the diverging interests of male line supervisors and female group chiefs. The official union system cuts off open protest, so information networks are created on the basis of off-work relationships, such as neighborhood and kinship, as well as of small work groups. Peña also stresses that the vulnerability which places women in cheapened jobs cannot be translated into an assumption of weakness or passivity over workplace issues.[12]

IMMIGRATION

As families nestled into cities along the Mexican border, and as their children matured, some branched by marriage and by jobs onto the U.S. side of the line, forming a modern version of the cross-border family. I propose that current immigration from border sources and maquiladora employment have the same historical antecedents in the family settlement process, though evidence shows that maquiladora employment does not in the short run cause immigration (Seligson and Williams, 1981). Nor can the social organization from the point of view of migrants themselves be separated from lines of force, just as I argued for the factory system. The escalating urge in the United States to strictness at the border and the attempt by Mexican families to secure a decent life "outside the law" (The Mexican American Tapes, 1984) ends in the ironic result that neither is the law enforced nor is the life decent.

The eight children of Juanita and Pedro Durazo live in both countries (Figure 6.3). The elderly parents and three sons live in Agua Prieta; two of the sons are maquiladora employees. Four siblings are legal immigrants to the United States—two by marriage to U.S. citizens, one by his job skills, and one after many years as an undocumented worker and parent. At a Durazo reunion on July 4, 1985 (a date chosen because the children living on the U.S. side could get away to their parents' house in Agua Prieta), Ester Durazo, whom I met for the first time, spilled out to me in a rush of words her harrowing story of abandonment and immigration by desperation. Her brother Tomás, whom I often visited at his house in Agua Prieta, recalled how settled he became in the United States—"even a driver's license"—with the distance of an era that he had left behind.[13]

The Durazo family came to Agua Prieta from Moctezuma in 1946. In Agua Prieta, Pedro found much work, though of an irregular

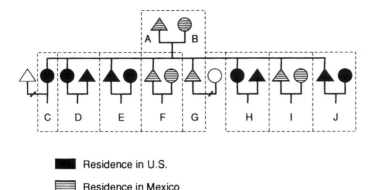

Figure 6.3. Durazo grand-family: constituent units and cross-border locations

character. This included gardening in Arizona (he entered the United States without documents). Thus Pedro, who started his work life in the United States in the 1920s and for several decades moved out of the casual labor market, again responded to the insatiable demand in the United States for labor, though now without the chance to immigrate legally that he had had the first time.

However, by the time the Durazos reached Agua Prieta, Pedro's earnings had lessened in importance. The family subsisted on the work of their eight children, beginning with the two eldest daughters, Ester and Adela. They worked as secretaries after they left secondary school (1946 and 1947, respectively). The Durazo household anticipated the working child pattern of the maquiladoras, starting nearly two decades earlier. In 1950 Ester married in Agua Prieta; Adela continued to work and live with her parents until she married and immigrated in 1957 with her husband, an American citizen.

Ester's husband abandoned her in Tijuana with two tiny sons. In those days (1954) before the maquiladoras, finding employment in

Mexico was hard for a divorced mother, so Ester decided to slip across the U.S. border. She made her way to Los Angeles, and there found work in a garment factory, stretching her pay to cover child care and household expenses.

In 1960, Ester remarried, this time in Los Angeles, though she was there without documents. Again she was divorced. For a year Ester returned to Mexico, where she lived in her parents' home, working days while her mother took care of her two sons and her two daughters from the second marriage. Ester decided to return to California to raise her children; there, she explained, they would have better chances for schooling and work. She remained on the American side for six years, in constant fear of her young family being deported. Finally, seventeen years after her first venture into California, Ester became a permanent legal resident in the United States under the provision in force before 1976 that allowed U.S.-born children under the age of twenty-one to sponsor their parents (Massey et al., 1987:281).

Tomás, born in 1943, also went to the United States as an undocumented alien. In 1965 he crossed the border openly with a "local passport" meant for shopping and visiting. He then violated its conditions by leaving the 12.5-mile perimeter to look for work. Tomás accompanied his brother-in-law, a resident alien, to New Mexico. There he found work in a guano mine:

> They paid me $1.25 an hour. I worked as a winch operator. Only I didn't last more than four months. Immigration got me. . . . They owed me for a week. They paid me everything, didn't take anything away. The immigration officers treated me very well there, they took me to Lordsburg to eat in a restaurant without paying. Afterwards they let me loose [at the border] in El Paso, Texas. It was January and snowing, when I crossed to Ciudad Juárez. From there I came to Casas Grandes, Chihuahua, got a plane to Cananea, and from Cananea to Agua Prieta it took me three days—for three days it snowed.

After working in Agua Prieta at various unskilled jobs, Tomás returned to the United States. This time he headed for California:

> Then in '67 I returned to the U.S., this time to California, with my sister in Stockton. There I worked in the fields. . . . Also in Stockton I worked in sidewalk construction, my sister and I tore out sidewalks, then the cement mixer came, and we also laid them. We worked right in front of the Immigration offices—there is a lot of Immigration Service in Stockton. Well, I bought a truck there, a big one, and we came back to Agua Prieta for a visit. In 1967 I began to work in Agua Prieta carrying

shipments, cattle, cement, whatever. In 1971 I sold this truck because work got very scarce. I didn't do anything for two or three months and then in '72 I went to the U.S. another time. I worked three years in a lumberyard in Tucson.

The lumberyard was owned by an Anglo-American, it had a Mexican-American foreman, and almost all undocumented Mexican workers. Tomás was thrown out once by the authorities. This time he returned within fifteen days, knowing that he had a job waiting. Of all the periods of U.S. immigration, Tomás lasted the longest in Tucson; it was there that he took out his driver's license.

Ultimately Tomás quit his life in the United States. I asked him why, and he replied:

> Because I was a bachelor, I wasn't saving money. I spent it all on dances, women, and beer. One day I began to think that all alone I didn't have any reason to be there, it would be better if I returned to Mexico. I left work because I was tired of it, and came here [Agua Prieta] to look for something better. Here things have gone well. Afterwards, even better—I married in 1977.

Tomás phrased in terms of his marital status the gap he felt between Mexico and the United States: his surprising feeling that he could save more as a married man, the contrast between working for others and his success working for himself, and so forth. By contrast with Ester and her children in California, Tomás shows the pattern in which a migrant's social being remains in Mexico even while he is laboring in the U.S. for instrumental ends.

When Tomás returned to Agua Prieta in 1975, he bought a used backhoe with a thousand-dollar loan from a brother who was a permanent resident on the U.S. side. Tomás has worked in Mexico since 1975 as an independent contractor, hiring his labor and equipment to ranchers and construction contractors. He has had a patron, a member of an elite family, who has bought new equipment for him, as well as arrangements with two elite businesses, exchanging his work for materials for a new house.

Tomás's story fits the stereotype of Mexican immigration, the single, young male voyaging without documents in search of a job. It behooves us to minimize our stereotypes by noticing other Mexican immigrants: legal permanent residents (Portes and Bach, 1985); female undocumented immigrants (Solórzano-Torres, 1987); and family groups (Chavez, 1988). Leo Chavez suggests that the term "binational family" be applied to households such as Ester's that include members of various citizenship and legal statuses, such as an undocumented parent with U.S.-citizen children.

Ester Durazo immigrated out of immediate necessity, and she was driven into returning by the continuing need of her family. Women's life courses have been based on learning domestic skills and refining kin and social bonds, accumulations that take place within Mexico. However, divorce and abandonment are a regular enough feature of women's lives that women do migrate to the United States in circumstances other than as half of a married pair. It is such women and small children who are hurt most by the U.S. enforcement system. As in the case of Ester, it is difficult to establish the regular location and earnings needed for stable residence; families with children grow up in a climate of terrible insecurity (The Mexican American Tapes, 1984). This group can least afford the dangers of returning to enter the United States again, after they are intercepted by U.S. authorities or visit parents and grandparents.

Tomás recapitulated the experience of his father, Pedro, to an amazing extent: He went out of a sense of adventure, he learned to drive a truck, and when he married, he showed that he retained his social personhood in Mexico. Clearly, this is a repeated pattern in the male life cycle. Such a pattern is in want of explanation, however. Why do generations in the same family cross the border in search of work?

Pedro's money from the United States did not mean that his son could build on his success, for Pedro had gone bankrupt and lost the truck long before Tomás went across the border. Working people in twentieth-century Mexico who manage to accumulate a few resources, such as a truck or a workshop, have difficulty in passing that accumulation on to their children. Mexico's social system is among the most polarized in the world (Hansen, 1971:72ff.; Hellman, 1983:103).[14] Young men must go to the U.S. labor market simply to stay in place. The Mexican male life course is caused by the need of each generation to recapitulate the tools, funds, and alignment toward a work life; this is embodied in ideas of adventuring and learning while laboring in the United States. This argument, that Mexicans immigrate because of a history of rapid economic development in which the rewards have been unfairly distributed, should be distinguished from the commonplace American assumption that Mexicans flee a uniform, perhaps inherently Mexican, state of poverty.

Though Tomás repeated his father's experience, the power context had changed. It did not matter very much in Pedro's day that he went to the United States as an undocumented entrant—there was virtually no Border Patrol, the risks were few, and he could nearly as easily have gotten a proper visa. Tomás was ejected several times, while obtaining legal resident status was hemmed in by quotas and complications. The patterns of immigration from Mexico have changed far less than U.S. policy.

THE STRUCTURE OF IMMIGRATION

Immigration today is channeled not only by supply and demand; government affects it, both positively and punitively. In a series of acts of legislation begun in 1965 and completed in 1976, U.S. immigration laws took the basic form they have today: First, Western Hemisphere nations such as Mexico were brought under the restrictions on total hemispheric visas, to which they had not previously been subject; then Mexico, like all the other nations, was made subject to the twenty-thousand visa quota limitation; and a new system of immigration preferences, nine in all, was imposed on what had once been little defined (Cafferty et al., 1983:Chapter 3). Employment certification was reduced in importance (though it was retained); the new general principle was family reunification.

Three preferences—spouses of citizens, unmarried children (under twenty-one) of citizens, and parents of citizens over twenty-one—do not have to wait out the national quota, and thus enter within a matter of months. Four kinship preference categories must queue up within the national quota: unmarried sons and daughters, over twenty-one, of U.S. citizens; husbands, wives, and children of legal permanent residents; married children of U.S. citizens; and siblings of U.S. citizens over twenty-one. Each preference has a specified percentage of the quota assigned to it.

There are two more preferences, both based on employment. One is for professionals, artists, and scientists; and the other is for workers who can show a job offer and certification by the Department of Labor that U.S. workers are not available.

At the heart of the legal structure of U.S. immigration lies an ideal model of a nuclear family household. In practice, the nonquota, high-priority kin—married couples, children, or parents of citizens— form two generations of nuclear families. It leaves open the possibility for a citizen's family to be lineally extended upward.

Surrounding the nonquota nuclear family core are quota kin. They are bilateral consanguines one step removed from ego (siblings, married children, etc.). Two preferences are less valued (e.g., adult children at home) versions of the nuclear family household. The married children preference would allow for a second nuclear family joined downward, and the sibling preference, for lateral extension of kinship—implicitly recognizing the relationships among brothers/sisters-in-law. These four quota preferences are very important to the long-term flow of Mexican immigrants to the United States, but they have such lengthy delays—on the order of years, even a decade—that they cannot easily be used by cross-border families to solve short-run problems of helping a relative enter the United States openly and securely.

There are also kinship ties that are not recognized in U.S. law but are of great importance among Mexicans. These include uncle and aunt with niece and nephew; cousins, who may be quite important kin allies if close in age; and, above all, fictive kinship (*compadrazgo*), a basic link for kinship assistance in Mexican life. Assistance in immigration to more distant or nonrecognized kin must be extralegal. It is against U.S. law to transport or shelter a person without documents. The fact that many ties have to be extralegal, or are most frequently that way, is best understood in light of the risks involved in undocumented crossing.

Contrary to common notions of a border "out of control", the U.S.–Mexican border has been placed under steadily increasing state control since the 1950s, especially in the 1970s and 1980s. This state control includes the actual physical barrier at the border, the placement of a chain-link fence in the 1940s and surveillance equipment (movement sensors, night vision, etc.) in the 1970s and 1980s; strengthening of enforcement arms, the Border Patrol along the open border and Customs and the INS at crossing gates; and the increasing elaboration of bureaucratic requirements—proof of residence, taxes, utility bills, homeownership, steady employment—required of Mexicans to visit the United States.

Undocumented crossing entails substantial investment, expenses, and risks. Those who enter in this way have to have money, sometimes borrowed at high interest, to get to the border, to find a place to stay there, and to pay for bus fare or other transportation from the U.S. side of the border to a more secure interior destination. In addition, the crosser may pay a smuggler, which reduces risks of being apprehended but increases risks of being cheated or abandoned. All of this may go for naught if the crosser is apprehended. He or she will probably be "voluntarily deported" to a border port distant from the one where he or she was caught, so he or she has to have money either to cross again or to return home. Every crossing also entails the danger of being robbed by thieves who prey on fearful immigrants, as well as of dying from thirst in the open desert or a closed boxcar. Once in the United States, the undocumented alien may be stranded because an employer fails to pay, or because of bad luck in a harvest, or because he or she is apprehended and the INS is not able to obtain the pay due from the employer (Samora, 1971:Chapter 6).

The border enforcement mechanism exacerbates the dangers and risks that undocumented aliens face. The extralegal entrant is more vulnerable to violence because he or she avoids regulated areas, and is more likely to put himself or herself in the potentially treacherous hands of a smuggler. U.S. enforcement, of course, heightens the risks of being caught and losing the investment.

The key to reduction of risk and investment is kin and personal networks that cross the border (Kearney, 1986), as well as a home base at the border in the case of local residents. For instance, Tomás used kinship connections in each of the three major locations where he worked in the United States: a trip accompanying a brother-in-law to New Mexico; repeated trips to stay with his sister living, without documents, in California; and repeated trips to Tucson to stay with a sister and U.S. citizen brother-in-law. When he was twice deported ("voluntarily departed") and other times when he left of his own volition, he could easily return to the United States from his parents' house in Agua Prieta. Tomás told me that he never borrowed money before he came to the United States, nor did he ever pay a smuggler, reflecting the strength of his kinship network.

Current cross-border kinship differs from the open kinship of an earlier era because it bends in specific ways in response to border power arrangements. The families of the turn of the century could freely switch legal residence between the United States and Mexico with little risk; thus they took the form of mobile, entire households. Today, constant side switching can be done only by legal commuters with U.S. permanent residence; in general persons have a definite legal right on one side or the other. Movement outside these rights can be done only at considerable risk. This has not stopped immigration either of individuals or of fragments of families seeking to reunite (Chavez, 1988), but it has changed the meaning of their kinship aid from open arms to hidden helping hands.

Among the Durazos in 1984–1986, there were two centers of gravity: one in Mexico (Agua Prieta), where the parents, a divorced son, and two married sons lived; the other in the United States (Tucson), where two daughters had immigrated by marriage, one daughter had regularized her status, and one son had immigrated by request of his employer. There was also a married son living in Douglas, Arizona. At the time Tomás was working in the United States, it would have been very unlikely that he could have immigrated legally in the narrow quota of his siblings, but they made it possible for him to pass frequently between Mexico and the United States as an undocumented immigrant.

Only a narrow range of ties forms part of the nuclear family model of the U.S. kinship preferences, and relatively close and important kinship ties are left outside the law. And border enforcement simply worsens the risks of undocumented entry without eliminating the needs that compel it, whether for young men, young women, or small families. Since kinship is a valuable way for undocumented immigrants to reduce risk of capture, robbery, or even death, today's powerful border enforcement has the ironic result of strengthening cross-border family ties in order to defy it.

FACING THE FUTURE ON THE BORDER

The U.S.–Mexican border gives the appearance of unquestioned boom: a region, though surrounded by Latin America's impoverishment, favored by corporations in the export war of all against all. Why, then, for the ordinary people of the border, was this not all it seemed? Each person judges his or her life against certain standards—what parents had, what one grew up admiring and wishing for, what rewards honest efforts should bring. For several decades after families arrived at Agua Prieta, their dreams were realistic, or at least they saw themselves on an upward path toward them.

What, then, can the young Córdobas, Durazos, and other border families expect as they mature into the dominant generation? Let us look briefly at the single most important goal in life, owning a house. The number of weeks of work as an operative in a maquiladora required to buy the construction materials for a small home has doubled from roughly 80 to 160 weeks if pay is devoted to that exclusive purpose (Heyman, 1988:374–377). Can the younger generation help but look at what their parents have, and wonder if they have any hope of matching it? They ask such questions amid seeming well-being, with jobs going for the asking and flashy consumer goods crying for money. The proportion of work in life has grown, not declined; the relation between effort and reward has been broken.

The sense of place in social life also has become more difficult. While one can say without fear of contradiction that the industrial working class of the maquiladoras has grown in size and density, there are complicating tendencies. The urban office and factory economy has opened white-collar jobs for the somewhat more educated children of families whose sisters, brothers, or cousins are factory operatives (the Aguirre kindred being a perfect example). The clear sense of working classness of northern Mexican industrial people has frayed. Automotive and sewing skills, for example, once raised industrial Mexicans above displaced peasants whose options were day labor and domestic service; today cars and sewing machines are commonplace in the slums of Mexican cities, and formal education offers the main hope against poverty. Yet education, which pulls children from the life of the barrio, brings with it ambivalent loyalties, humiliations, and ambitions.

Nor, in this social and cultural sense, is immigration a safety valve, as is so often unthinkingly stated. Immigration is less a matter of release than of insecurity and fear engendered each time a lonely person defies the powerful means of enforcement at the boundary. Yet people cross, because life patterns of immigrant labor created in railroads, mines, and fields cannot be easily erased, so long as American employment, now in cities and suburbs, meets a real need to renew life in Mexico. It may be that Mexicans will continue to immigrate despite the barriers being placed against them, but they cannot help but feel a tension between the America that draws them and the America that denies them.

7. A Border Working Class

Working classes have to sell their labor for wages with which they buy their daily needs. The effort they sell is managed through factory or industrial discipline. Not only do they lack much in the way of productive capital, but through their work and pay they enter into a relationship with those who do hold the reins of critical resources. The relationship may be one of dependence or submission to coercion, or it may be active effort to change the conditions of work and life. It is fundamentally a relationship of unequal power.

People have worked under such conditions at many times and in many places. Their ways of life have differed considerably with respect to who works and what they do, how pay and consumption are arranged, the origins of the population and how it was drawn together, and other vital questions. In *Europe and the People Without History* Eric Wolf contends that the diversity among wage laborers is inherent, and he calls for the use of the plural "working classes" (1982:358).

Each category of the definition outlines a basic pattern, but in each pattern there is much room for complexity. It is inadequate to impute working-class lives and actions on the basis of a speculative reading of definitions. We need to get underneath the skin of the generalizations to work out their manifestations. For example, one reads that necessary standards of living are historically determined, but how in fact do they become established in a time and a place? Such questions require ethnographic investigation of "working classes," whether done by anthropologists or by historians.

My strategy for ethnography was to look for ordered sequences of events in life courses set amid a changing industrial landscape. This strategy has been broader than studies of industrial workplaces or other single aspects of working-class life. I argue that the study of actual lives shows that diverse activities, some of which we would not ordinarily think to be part of the capital–wage labor relationship, did share historical dynamics imparted by the very great power of capital. Moreover, this was not an abstract kind of power, but one that was distinctive to the location and period of this working class.

For the northern regions of Mexico, the critical relationship has been with the U.S. border. The border divides Mexicans from ownership of the most important pieces of productive property, whether agriculture and industry inside the United States or U.S.-owned companies in Mexico. It has separated their homes from the North American sources of consumer needs, and thus has impelled their movements and labors to obtain these items. The border also divides the Mexican people from the rights of U.S. citizenship, and thus separates their conditions of life from the political arena in which conditions are determined.

The border relationship is distinct from other working-class relationships because of the radical disjuncture between power and politics (including informal as well as organized class actions). To border Mexicans, the power from the north is palpable every day, yet it seems far removed—indeed, unreachable. (Important elements of life do get determined inside of Mexico—the case of urban house lots being a good example—and border politics, disconnected from the largest issues, does address those quite openly.)

The U.S. border relationship created or re-created a working class at three turning points. Not only did large numbers of people hire on in primary product industries after 1880 (as occurred in many parts of the world at that time), but from across the border flowed money, manufactured goods, and special activities, as well as a counterflow of workers and families, all of which acted to dissolve frontier society into a new laboring, consuming way of life that we call "border culture."

In the 1940s, 1950s, and 1960s, massive U.S. labor demand drew people to the border, yet the U.S. government, by such policies as the bracero and commuter programs, did not permit them to follow the logical course of residing and establishing a secure, human community close to work. Families figuratively piled up against the border fence, dependent on cash earnings yet removed from the sources of that money. They were potential wage labor soon realized for use in the maquiladoras; indeed, Fernández-Kelly (1983:Chapter 2) has shown that concern over the buildup of population and the end of the bracero program motivated the policy decisions that led to the Border Industrialization Program in 1965. What is interesting is that the obvious industrialization in the maquiladoras was contingent on a prior period best summarized as the border version of separating people from their means of making a living.

A similar sequence is recounted by Robert Alvarez, Jr. (1987). He discusses the movement of a group of interrelated families through the following steps: isolated frontier mestizo farming communities in the interior of Baja California; foreign industrial mines of the Porfiriato; the closing of those mines and resettlement, via small mines and temporary immigrant work, to the U.S. side of the California border after 1900; and subsequent pulling of new groups of kin across the border. I had researched and formulated the Sonoran histories before I read Alvarez's work; our parallel results provide confirmation that the working-class processes are general to the border, not isolated results particular to one or another area of northern Mexico.

WAGED LIFE

In the study of life and family histories, I looked at the links—changes, alternatives, repetitions, and conflicts—between various wage-based situations. This contrasts with each job considered as a segregated "type," whether type of occupation, of relation of production, or of workplace. The objective was to define a patterned relationship to the labor market within complex ethnographic material about many forms of work.

I proposed a contrast in two male courses. One sequence is characteristic of rural production in areas of Mexico connected to the U.S. market for temporary manual labor. A young man may work for wages, but he will drop out of the labor market at certain key junctures to resume nonwaged labor on his land or on his father's behalf. These times can include marriage, land inheritance at his father's death, seasonal cycles, or layoffs from waged jobs. In this case wage labor is limited within an overall sequence of succession of nonwaged farming from generation to generation of men.

The alternative life course occurs when wage labor at key moments is followed by more wage labor. A man may be tossed out of the labor market by cyclical unemployment or a global crisis, but he will move his residence to find a new job. He may return from the United States to Mexico (or, within Mexico, return to the countryside) to marry, but he will form his new household in an urban, wage-earning location. Shifting in search of continued sources of paid employment in northern Mexico means moving closer and closer to the U.S. border. This sequence allows for frequent changes in type of labor—formal to informal, even paid to unpaid—but it requires that spatial and social movements renew involvement with wages over a lifetime, and into succeeding generations. I call this course the waged life.

Life course patterns started to change at the beginning of the industrial era, but the crisis of unemployment and repatriation in the 1930s tested and confirmed the shift. After bitter disputes within families between the older and younger generations of men, with women for reasons of their own weighing in on the side of the urban consuming locations, families left the Sonoran countryside for the border. The border was a place where jobs could be found and purchased material culture could be used. To a great extent, all future wage labor, whether in the Mexican border cities or within the United States, derived from this critical juncture around 1940.

UNPAID LABOR

The labor history of unpaid, reproductive labor can be written as part of the history of a working class; household work as much as industrial work undergoes initial wage and commodity formation and subsequent transformations. Two sets of questions have proven useful. One, which can be labeled consumption, addresses the changing means (cash, credit, peddlers, and traders in secondhand goods) and locations (mine company towns, U.S. border ports) of obtaining goods. The other addresses activities, uses, and the gender and age structure of purchased material culture.

The turn-of-the-century formation of the working class went beyond the assembling of a labor force for the mines, dramatic though that was. Frontier Mexican patterns were completely reworked.

Trucks and sewing machines were integrated into the daily labors, gender roles, and life courses of men and women. Manufactured goods came from the United States, they were obtained by selling one's labor either in the Sonoran mines or in the United States, and the skills they represented could best be utilized by urban, money-earning activities.

The value of the oral histories provided by widows and their daughters is that these accounts explicitly show that women's household activities were completely altered during the early industrial period. The widows' economic needs meant that they had to draw on the new appliance skills for their small businesses and marginal occupations. The experiences of wives of miners were similar, but they were masked by the dominant male paycheck system of the mine corporations.

Since the sources of female material culture lay in the United States, and since products were sold in urban, cash-earning areas, women were drawn toward the border at key junctures when family moves were decided. This occurred in two sets of cases: the relocations of widows, accompanied by their children; and the generation that relocated to the border when male wage earning was disrupted by the closing of the mines. In each movement toward a commodity center, the next generation was left in position to enter the industrial work force. These consumption-driven moves bridged gaps in employment at critical times in the waged life histories.

Women's life patterns were set in the first industrial generation to utilize U.S.–manufactured appliances, and were perpetuated through each generation of daughters. Daughters learned appliance skills from mothers and were then equipped at the time of marriage. Businesses operated out of houses were organized according to intergenerational relationships among women. The cohort of young women working in the maquiladoras, however, has a mixed, even contradictory, life path in contrast with that of men. Women enter and leave paid labor, always remaining obliged to household labor imperatives.

The use of purchased, manufactured material culture, even at home in nonwage activities, entails subtle and powerful social commitments. It draws people toward cash earning, buying, and selling locations. Women feel these new commitments particularly strongly, and may have different interests in migration than men, whose ability to use saved wages to buy farms or invest in small commerce may pull them back from such places. These commitments are best discerned over the course of time, by looking at the alternatives chosen in family histories.

POWER RELATIONS

There are two basic ways to look at power relationships: to examine the relationships of workers with powerholders and political situations in a delineated period, and to examine power relationships over long stretches of time by looking at the unequal capacity to determine the course at key junctures. Although the ethnographer remains but a contributor of on-the-ground observations to the study of important moments in Mexican political and labor history, he or she has a special opportunity to analyze the way that unequal power shapes the course of people's lives, how it creates and then denies hopes cherished over a lifetime.

Guadalupe Hernández, a miner, fought for the cause of a revolutionary chieftain, Plutarco Elías Calles. It seems clear that Hernández was motivated by the peasant goal of recovering land for the villages of Pivipa and San Clemente de Terapa, and he sought this through the patronage of Calles, who was not otherwise noted for his interest in land reform. Besserer, Novelo, and Sariego generalize that Mexican miners fought for regional chieftains, in contrast to the organized brigades of Mexico City workers (1983:24). In Sonora this is understandable, because the formative process recruited the bulk of the mine work force from nearby peasant villages. At the time of the revolution, workers at Pilares de Nacozari and the other giant mines were at most a decade removed from the countryside. They were not isolated from involvement in continuing rural land conflicts.

At the same time, the miners attempted to improve the conditions of their work and life in the face of severe repression. Only in the 1930s was the climate propitious in the Mexican presidency and the world depression for lasting labor union organization. The social-racial relationship of American and Mexican pervaded every aspect of the mine community, whether the supervisory hierarchy of the workplace or the residential segregation of the company town. Sonorans had a tradition of anti-American nationalism dating to the border conflicts of the mid-nineteenth century. The strength of mine labor unionism in northeastern Sonora can be explained by coordinating these three factors: the unity of the mine community and workplace; the tradition of opposition to American power combined with the fact that the U.S. mine corporations operated precisely on the basis of discrimination against Mexicans; and the specific political moment of the 1930s.

There are many work and social situations in the heterogeneous working class of the border cities: casual, full, and self-employment; male and female; older and younger; work on the U.S. side and in Mexico. Personalized dependence is complex and open to maneuver, not frozen as in the countryside. Many potential alignments of relationships exist, but only some of them are activated in politics. The rest lie ignored. Male economic relationships with elites are activated, as well as some senior women who speak for the household to political authorities for housing and neighborhood needs. Mobilizing young working women, on the other hand, has been avoided.

Regional political elites and maquiladora personnel managers control rewards that are significantly greater than the minimum wage: well-paid male jobs, patronage of small businesses, and municipal benefits. These rewards and downward linkages have enabled party politicians to recruit entire networks and families, including young women and men whose interests are not directly represented. Regional elites wanted to keep municipal party politics a quiet inside game from 1949 to 1979; the distribution of urban rewards served this goal. After the elite split into pro-government and populist right-wing parties in 1979, the same heterogeneous social structure served their need to mobilize adherents among the mass of Agua Prieta residents.[1]

The party politics and nonpolitics of the border city, Agua Prieta, contrast with those of the militant mine towns that lie in the same region and are populated by people of the same traditions. The Sonoran case demonstrates that contexts for action or inaction are as important as cultures of resistance. The historical and social-structural differences between Sonoran miners and border townsmen usefully address an injunction by Herbert Gutman about the study of working-class politics:

> The full history of subordinate groups—all of them—involves far more than studying these irregular outbursts of collective, democratic protest. A central tension exists within all modern dependent groups between individualist (utilitarian) and collective (mutualist) ways of dealing with and sometimes overcoming historically specific patterns of dependence

and inequality. That tension changes over time. It differs from group to group. It reveals itself in very diverse ways, reflecting regional, racial, ethnic, gender, and other differences. It is little understood, but it always is there and awaits thoughtful historical analysis. (1983:193)

The other approach to power asks who has the ability to determine what happens in a person's life, the individual or someone else. People strive toward cherished goals: a work career, secure or advancing jobs, income for old age, or tools and skills for independent production; education or at least a better labor market position for their children; houses, appliances, and other standards of a "decent" life; and, in the case of the border, legal (more secure) access to the United States, with its higher standard of living. These goals can be recognized in several ways: People may articulate some of them (especially after informed questioning), but others are apparent only through induction from the life historical materials by the ethnographer. They differ between men and women, and according to the life cycle. Some are at least partly in the autonomous power of working people, but most are contingent upon the decisions of those who control the productive enterprise and the border agencies. The question of power over life courses is a question of whose goals prevail, and whose lose out. The life histories show a modicum of achieved goals, but more often they show powerlessness.

An important case has been the establishment and undermining of decent standards of living. Economic evidence such as peso–dollar exchange rates and real wage levels is coordinated with sequences of family histories (including appliance histories). This shows exactly when patterns of so-called historically determined working-class standards of living are established, what goods are involved, and what relationships with U.S. border markets are entailed.

There were two periods of rising consumer buying power: the mid-1930s, when labor unions and the Cárdenas presidency dramatically improved pay scales in the mine cities; and the long ascent in the urban real wage from the early 1950s until the peso devaluation of 1976. Standards of life were created and consolidated during these two eras of prosperity; this is seen in the houses, material possessions, and small businesses that families such as the Aguirres, the Córdobas, and the Hernándezes accumulated after moving to Agua Prieta.

Each time that a decent life seemed secured, however, the buying power of the peso and the urban wage collapsed. Nacozari closed permanently in 1949, Cananea slowed employment, the peso was devalued several times between 1947 and 1953, and real wages hit bottom in 1947–1948. The standards of mine families were destroyed because they required that men be able to earn a paycheck sufficient to support an entire household. The border standard of living that followed required a stable exchange rate between the dollar and peso, because so many goods were either purchased in the United States or resold in Mexico. An entire way of life was wrapped up with American imports: Women's and men's small manufactures depended on inputs of U.S. materials such as auto parts and cloth yard goods, while the trade in secondhand items was both an important way of earning income and a basis for personal networks.

The devaluation of the peso to a hundredth of its value over the course of the 1980s, a power decision required for the redirection of Mexico to a low-real-wage, strong export economy, destroyed this cross-border way of life. It was replaced with factory drudgery for paychecks that hardly allow shopping on the American side. Important life goals, owner-built housing, and children's education are much more expensive in terms of weekly work; they appear to be slipping out of the reach of the younger generation.

U.S. immigration and border policies have been another major determinant of Mexican life goals. The open border prior to 1929, in combination with a new border way of life based on moving about, earning cash, initiated a male life course in which a voyage to the United States was an expected part of youth before marriage. This life pattern was perpetuated from father to son because the polarized Mexican social system has permitted little intergenerational accumulation among working and rural families. Meanwhile, Americans continue to hire successive generations of Mexican workers in agriculture, construction, and urban services.

While young Mexican men justifiably expect to work in the United States at some point in their lives, the U.S. government has sought complete mastery over the movement of persons across the border. This has not, in fact, been achieved; but in the attempt, crossing the line has become more chancy, and the side effects of undocumented entry, smugglers, and accidental deaths, harsher. The Mexican people are powerless to determine the terms of their entry into the United States.

TOWARD AN ANTHROPOLOGY OF WORKING PEOPLES

Although anthropology has provided a scattering of important ethnographies of working peoples, the discipline is only beginning to confront the topic of working classes as a whole, just as in the past it has confronted peasants and cities. Each case presents special circumstances that seem impossible to reconcile, even when certain features resonate from study to study. The fundamental dynamic of northern Mexican working people has been the U.S.–Mexican border, a feature that could hardly be encountered elsewhere, though it may resemble other cross-national migratory working situations.

However, if we abstract from this case key patterns—the renewal of waged life, activities and life patterns based on purchased material culture, and powerlessness in life courses—it may be possible to compare these with abstractions derived from other ethnographic cases. Our goal should be to discover recurrent phenomena of waged life since the advent of industry, labor, and capital.

Notes

Chapter 1

1. In writing this work I had to make a strategic decision to concentrate on border residents of the Mexican side. I refer to the U.S. side of the border insofar as they have worked there, shopped there, lived there, or have had kin there. One cannot isolate phenomena of one side of the border from those of the other side. While I was in Agua Prieta, I did fieldwork in Douglas, Arizona, across the line. Nevertheless, I have chosen not to discuss this material. While noting the identities and linkages of Mexicans in both countries, there are too many fundamental differences of context to be encompassed in one book: a different national history, political scene (in the case of Douglas, the labor union in the smelter), and especially the systematic discrimination and segregation against Mexican Americans.

2. One certainly could argue that kin forgetting is purely determined by genealogical distance. In most of the cases I am using, however, the various kin lines should be equivalent—descendants of father's siblings, for example. Kin forgetting as a function of physical proximity should be regarded as much the same as resource bases; this is indicated by my discussion of alternative economies as areas of the border region.

3. The idea of appliance histories was first developed by James Greenberg in Agua Prieta (Greenberg 1981–82; see also Lewis 1969).

Chapter 2

1. Owen (1959) found in his study of a small rural town in the Río San Miguel that while no openly Opata population existed, indigenous ancestry was recognized and that present-day stratification included an element of attributed social race: Certain families were known as autochthonous, were poorer, and generally had less status in the town. However, in Agua Prieta (and as best I can reconstruct for mine towns) the attribution of "race" or

descent played no social role, even among the families who recalled they had Opata ancestry.

2. This study was completed before the passage of the Immigration Control and Reform Act of 1986. This act provided for an amnesty for certain undocumented aliens already in the country, for special immigration preferences for undocumented agricultural workers, for making employment of an undocumented alien a crime, and for added proof of legal residence or citizenship rights to employment. It does not change the actual legal structure of immigration, but it does conform to the proposal that border enforcement is growing harsher over time.

Chapter 3

1. My informant, Antonio, obtained knowledge of his mother's siblings because he stayed with his mother at her widowed sister's home in Nacozari during the late 1930s and early 1940s.

2. A copy of this document and other items describing Guadalupe's role in the revolution, written at that time and many years later by his commanding officers for a legal case, are in the possession of the author; they are used with the kind permission of the family. The translation into English is mine.

3. It may have been that Hernández's recruiting in the Nacozari area was facilitated by the Phelps Dodge Corporation and its executives in Sonora–Arizona, who assisted Calles in many instances. Although his relationship to Horton makes this seem plausible, I have uncovered no evidence to this effect.

4. In Sanderson, the ejido is named Tonibabi. The hacienda of Tonibabi included the lands of Pivipa and Terapa.

5. Corroborating evidence of Guadalupe's close association with Calles can be found in Horton's account of the 1929 military rebellion against Calles, when Guadalupe suddenly arrived at her home in Pilares seeking refuge, fearing that he would be captured by the anti-Calles rebels who then controlled Agua Prieta and Nacozari. He also boasted to her that he would bring 150 men with rifles from his village if he could avoid capture, which he did not. He was later released (Horton, 1968:Chapter 18).

6. Although it would be desirable, I could not reliably reconstruct the nature of the dispute from the partial accounts provided by Guadalupe's son, Antonio.

7. Detailed information about company store and mine consumption (levels of credit, the interest rates and markup, and the distributions of purchases) is greatly needed.

8. These ethnographies obviously date much later than the period dealt with here. In addition, both were done in circumstances of heated commercial production in the Sonoran countryside (the mid-1950s cotton boom for Marobavi; the cattle boom for Cucurpe, and all Sonora since the 1970s), which may have influenced family relationships.

9. Luis also worked shoveling rock at the mine face and as a helper to the plumber who placed water lines, earning 3.15 pesos a day.

10. Another informant, a former miner and a composer of renown, told me that the Holy Cross was decorated with little wooden carvings of miners' tools, cloth, and flowers.

11. Beginning in the 1920s, the Mexican government began to push mine companies to train and use Mexican professionals. This policy began to be effective in the 1930s as the Cárdenas government put pressure on foreign investors, and in succeeding decades the strict racial power system disappeared in "nationalized" mines (Bernstein, 1964). Cananea was nominally nationalized in 1971 but Anaconda was assigned 49 percent of the stock; within these last several years the Mexican government's share of Cananea's stock was turned over to a private domestic owner. The exercise of power in the mine hierarchy was transferred from the sphere of nationality (Americans dominating Mexicans) to the sphere of domestic inequality (Mexicans dominating Mexicans, with the American role hidden behind investment and technology).

Chapter 4

1. I suspect that another factor which made widowhood so frequent in the family histories was that wives were younger than their husbands, and may have survived longer. All of the qualitative points are, of course, ripe for quantitative demographic history.

2. Of course, it is impossible to diagnose his ailment in retrospect from such general descriptions, so all one can do is report the informant's words, and the likely general conditions of health at the time.

3. Just after her husband died, she made one brief move there. That was her first of three attempts at the border.

4. In this case, my material strongly contrasts with the Bolivian material of Guillermo Delgado (1985). In Bolivia, widows, abandoned wives, and women who suffer from the chronic economic crisis of Bolivia's mines have had recourse to peasantlike strategies of agricultural production, marketing, and cooperation; and they tend to retreat from proletarian and urban locations. Possibly the difference between Sonora and Bolivia was the opportunity and pressure exerted by the heated economy of the border.

5. Carlos, describing his apprenticeship, reported learning both by direct instruction and by observation with imitation. It may prove that one development toward the modern working class was a change in learning from observation and imitation to direct instruction in person and by books and schools.

6. Women were mentioned doing weeding in the main fields, and they helped with the labor crunch at harvest; plowing, sowing, and irrigating were male labor.

Chapter 5

1. For the Romero family I had three informants: a daughter, Mercedes Romero, now in her seventies and living in Agua Prieta; her first cousin, (FaBrDa), who provided added and confirming information about the paternal side of the family in Sonora; and two of Mercedes's uncles (much youn-

ger brothers of her mother, Carmela), who provided information on the maternal branch.

2. The economic relationship between the farming and industrial branches of this family is of considerable interest, but it is difficult to reconstruct retrospectively. From Mercedes's remarks, it seems that there was some food coming from San Pedro to Pirtleville, such as cheese and dried meat, but that mainly aid in the form of money and purchased goods (such as cloth) went from Pirtleville to San Pedro, since, she said, "We were rich and they were poor" (that is, in cash). Likewise, during the 1930s, Carmela's siblings in Pirtleville sent her clothes and other such help.

3. Recorded by the author from pay stubs, medical reports, and union documents in the possession of Mr. Hernández.

4. This resembles patterning of oral history that occurred after similar events in a New Hampshire textile mill center (Hareven and Langenbach, 1978).

5. The walls of the house had been put up by a brother of Petra's when they let him live on the lot for a short period before they moved there.

6. Angelita Aguirre and Petra Hernández managed all aspects of their houses, and Mercedes Hernández managed most of hers. The father and sons in the Córdoba family dealt with credit from hardware firms and obtaining municipal land, but Francisca Córdoba was publicly active in petitioning the city for sewer service and repair of a flooding arroyo. Francisco Durazo presents the most completely male-organized case of housebuilding in Agua Prieta, but his wife Juanita was in charge of the construction of a house in the town where they resided before they moved to Agua Prieta.

7. My summary of politics is based on the Agua Prieta newspaper *El Sol* for 1953–1955 and 1960–1979, notes on which are in the possession of the author, as well as on interviews.

Chapter 6

1. The resident daughter who was most directly involved in the household economy—contributing money and drawing on her mother for babysitting while she was at the factory—was not visibly represented in displayed gifts. My guess is that daughters who were more removed might have had to cement their relationship with the core family household in symbolic ways.

2. Although it does not appear in this instance, it seems to me likely that future research will discover that unequal amounts of schooling for boys and girls is an important factor in dividing male and female careers.

3. Two caveats must be added. The study was made in 1972, prior to the onset of peso devaluations in 1976. After the devaluation, one would expect substitution of peso-denominated items for dollar-denominated ones; the degree of change, however, is unknown. Second, in 1972 Agua Prieta still purchased its water and electricity from Douglas, increasing U.S. expenditures. Since 1979 the utilities have been part of the Mexican national system.

4. This is based on an interview with a now retired dealer in secondhand materials, who started his business in 1954 and was active during those years corresponding to the influx of new households to Agua Prieta.

5. The noncontacted households almost entirely were renters who had moved and could not be located. This reduced the number of young couples and new immigrants to the border who were part of the resurvey, biasing the second sample toward families who were homeowners in Agua Prieta, further in the developmental cycle, and therefore possibly with more earners and thus more prosperous. The households providing incomplete information were typically headed by widows receiving in-kind aid from married children, so their income could not be calculated.

6. 26.26 pesos per dollar in January 1982; 500 as a reasonable approximation of a sliding rate in spring 1986. Their ratio is 19.0.

7. Other notes on the method not otherwise recounted in the text: In the counting of adults of working age, I dropped fourteen persons in 1982 and twelve in 1986 who were either too old to work or were disabled. One of the sixty-three households in 1982 that was recontacted in 1986 had merged into a daughter's household, so there are only sixty-two cases in 1986 as far as wage earning is concerned. (I kept this household in 1986 for other purposes.) I classified households according to the primary criterion of whether they contained "working children" as defined in the text; three households contained both unmarried and married "children" who were included in the former category, not the joint category (Table 3) where they would otherwise be placed—this resulted in two more maquiladora workers in 1982 and none more in 1986. Working female heads of households, because of the construction of my tables, are counted under the rubric "working parents only." There were four such households in 1982 and 1986; one of these women worked in a maquiladora both in 1982 and in 1986.

8. I consider it likely that other households failed to report income withholding by children because of the tendency for survey interviews to elicit formalistic responses by stating income as the total paycheck.

9. However, my interviews confirm Peña's observation that workers in maquiladoras resist raising piece-rate levels by dragging out work, stockpiling work, and other such tactics (Peña, 1987).

10. Unfortunately, the tendency among respondents was to state the simplest facts—"My son makes the minimum," for instance—and therefore to fail to include bonuses even when I knew from other interviews that the particular factory was paying them.

11. Mexican law mandates a fairly large severance payment. In summary form, the payment is twenty days' pay per year worked plus three months' pay in a lump sum; in addition, workers with more than fifteen years' tenure in one firm receive an extra twelve days' pay per year; and all paid vacations and the Christmas bonus come due (*Nueva ley federal de trabajo*, 1986:*Artículos* 50 and 162). Let us say that an employee making the minimum wage was laid off after five years (a long period for a maquiladora). His or her severance pay would be 384,450 pesos, or 769 dollars. On the other hand, there is no unemployment insurance in Mexico.

12. Power is fluid, however, and the situation in the factories can change. Allow me to put forth a speculative line of reasoning. If in the future there is a wave of strikes along the border, following Peña it is likely to arise from informal grievances. It is likely to spread along the lines of a shared generation—*los jóvenes*, young people—which could reduce the tensions between women and men, leading them at least temporarily to identify mutual interests. Possibly it will have a nationalist content, for the division between largely (not entirely) American ownership and completely Mexican work force is one thing all the border has in common.

13. For the purpose of maintaining confidentiality on the subject of undocumented entry, certain identifying details in these two histories have been changed.

14. In contradiction to my argument, however, Balán, Browning, and Jelin (1973) found significant intergenerational mobility from fathers to sons.

Chapter 7

1. The reader should be aware that this was the state of affairs as of 1986. For the first time in many years an effective Left coalition emerged in the presidential election of 1988. I cannot say what effect this has had on alignments of social and political activity/nonactivity.

Bibliography

Aguiar, Neuma.
    1983   "Household, Community, National, and Multinational Industrial Development." In *Women, Men, and the International Division of Labor,* June Nash and María Patricia Fernández-Kelly, eds., pp. 117–137. Albany: State University of New York Press.

Aguilar Camín, Héctor.
    1977   *La frontera nómada: Sonora y la revolución mexicana.* México, D.F.: Siglo Veintiuno Editores.

Aguirre, Manuel J.
    1958   *Cananea: Las garras del imperialismo en las entrañas de México.* México, D.F.: Libro Mex Editores.

Alvarez, Robert R., Jr.
    1987   *Familia: Migration and Adaptation in Baja and Alta California, 1800–1975.* Berkeley: University of California Press.

Arizona Daily Star (Tucson).
    1982   "Lean Times Put Squeeze on Border Plants." June 20, p. B1–2.

————.
    1985   "List of Maquiladora Plants with Over 100 Employees." February 19, Section 4, p. 2.

————.
    1986   "Forty Foreign-Owned Maquiladoras Employ 100 or More in Sonora." February 25, p. E6.

Arizona Republic (Phoenix).
    1983   "Mexico." September 25, p. A20.

Babb, Florence E.
    1986   "Producers and Reproducers: Andean Marketwomen in the Economy." In *Women and Change in Latin America,* June Nash and Helen Safa, eds., pp. 53–64. South Hadley, Mass.: Bergin and Garvey.

Baer, Roberta Dale.
   1984   "The Interaction of Social and Cultural Factors Affecting Dietary
          Patterns in Rural and Urban Sonora, Mexico." Ph.D. dissertation,
          Department of Anthropology, University of Arizona.
Balán, Jorge, Harley L. Browning, and Elizabeth Jelin.
   1973   *Men in a Developing Society: Geographic and Social Mobility in
          Monterrey, Mexico.* Austin: University of Texas Press.
Balmori, Diana, Stuart F. Voss, and Miles Wortman.
   1984   *Notable Family Networks in Latin America.* Chicago: University
          of Chicago Press.
Banco de México (Subdirección de Investigaciones Económicas).
   1986   *Indicadores económicas,* May. México, D.F.: Banco de México.
Bandelier, Adolf F.
   1970   [1883–1884]. *The Southwestern Journals of Adolf F. Bandelier,
          1883–1884,* Vol. 2. Charles H. Lange and Carroll L. Riley, eds. Al-
          buquerque: University of New Mexico Press.
Barrera, Mario.
   1979   *Race and Class in the Southwest: A Theory of Racial Inequality.*
          Notre Dame, Ind.: University of Notre Dame Press.
Bender, Donald.
   1967   "A Refinement of the Concept of the Household: Families, Co-
          residence, and Domestic Functions." *American Anthropologist*
          69:493–504.
Bennholdt-Thomsen, Veronika.
   1984   "Subsistence Production and Extended Reproduction." In *Of Mar-
          riage and the Market: Women's Subordination Internationally
          and Its Lessons,* 2nd ed., Kate Young, Carol Wolkowitz, and Roslyn
          McCullagh, eds., pp. 41–54. London: Routledge and Kegan Paul.
Bernstein, Marvin D.
   1964   *The Mexican Mining Industry, 1890–1950.* Albany: State Univer-
          sity of New York Press.
Besserer, Federico, José Díaz, and Raúl Santana.
   1980   "Formación y consolidación del sindicalismo minero en Cananea."
          Revista mexicana de sociología 42(4):1321–1353.
Besserer, Federico, Daniel González, and Laura Pérez Rosales.
   1979   "El conflicto de 'La Caridad.'" *Antropología y marxismo* 1(1):73–
          86.
Besserer, Federico, Victoria Novelo, and Juan Luis Sariego.
   1983   *El sindicalismo minero en México, 1900–1952.* México, D.F.: Edi-
          ciones Era.
Bortz, Jeffrey.
   1986   "Wages and Economic Crisis in Mexico." In *The Mexican Left, the
          Popular Movements, and the Politics of Austerity,* Barry Carr and
          Ricardo Anzaldua Montoya, eds., pp. 33–46. Monograph Series no.
          18. San Diego: Center for U.S.–Mexican Studies, University of
          California, San Diego.

Brown, Judith K.
  1985   "Introduction." In *In Her Prime: A New View of Middle-Aged Women*, Judith K. Brown and Virginia Kerns, eds., pp. 1–12. South Hadley, Mass.: Bergin and Garvey.
Buechler, Judith-Maria.
  1986   "Women in Petty Commodity Production in La Paz, Bolivia." In *Women and Change in Latin America*, June Nash and Helen Safa, eds., pp. 165–188. South Hadley, Mass.: Bergin and Garvey.
Burawoy, Michael.
  1979   "The Anthropology of Industrial Work." *Annual Review of Anthropology* 8:231–266.
Burkhalter, S. Brian, and Robert F. Murphy.
  1989   "Tappers and Sappers: Rubber, Gold and Money Among the Mundurucu." *American Ethnologist* 16(1):100–116.
Byrkit, James W.
  1982   *Forging the Copper Collar: Arizona's Labor–Management War of 1901–1921*. Tucson: University of Arizona Press.
Cafferty, Pastora San Juan, et al.
  1983   *The Dilemma of American Immigration*. New Brunswick, N.J.: Transaction.
Camarillo, Albert.
  1979   *Chicanos in a Changing Society: From Mexican Pueblos to American Barrios in Santa Barbara and Southern California, 1848–1930*. Cambridge, Mass.: Harvard University Press.
Cardoso, Lawrence A.
  1980   *Mexican Emigration to the United States, 1897–1931*. Tucson: University of Arizona Press.
Carillo, Jorge, and Alberto Hernández.
  1985   *Mujeres fronterizas en la industria maquiladora*. México, D.F.: SEP-CEFNOMEX.
Carter, Anthony T.
  1984   "Household Histories." In *Households: Comparative and Historical Studies of the Domestic Group*, Robert McC. Netting, Richard R. Wilk, and Eric J. Arnould, eds., pp. 44–83. Berkeley: University of California Press.
Catron, William.
  1930   *Mining Methods, Practices, and Costs of the Cananea Consolidated Copper Company*. U.S. Bureau of Mines Information Circular no. 6247. Washington, D.C.: U.S. Government Printing Office.
Chavez, Leo R.
  1988   "Settlers and Sojourners: The Case of Mexicans in the United States." *Human Organization* 47(2):95–108.
Cockcroft, James D.
  1968   *Intellectual Precursors of the Mexican Revolution, 1900–1913*. Austin: University of Texas Press.

Cornelius, Wayne A.
1986   *The Political Economy of Mexico Under De la Madrid: The Crisis Deepens, 1985–1986.* Research Report no. 43. San Diego: Center for U.S.–Mexican Studies, University of California, San Diego.
Cumberland, Charles C.
1972   *Mexican Revolution: The Constitutionalist Years.* Austin: University of Texas Press.
Delgado P., Guillermo.
1985   "Industrial Stagnation and Women's Strategies for Survival at the Siglo XX and Uncia Mines." In *Miners and Mining in the Americas*, Thomas Greaves and William Culver, eds., pp. 162–170. Manchester, U.K.: Manchester University Press.
DeWind, Adrian.
1975   "From Peasants to Miners: The Background to Strikes in the Mines of Peru." *Science and Society* 39(1):44–72.
Dinerman, Ina R.
1982   *Migrants and Stay-at-Homes: A Comparative Study of Rural Migration from Michoacán, Mexico.* Monograph no. 5. San Diego: Center for U.S.–Mexican Studies, University of California, San Diego.
Douglas Chamber of Commerce.
1986   *Manufacturers Directory: Douglas, Arizona; Agua Prieta, Sonora, Mexico.* Douglas, Ariz.: Douglas Chamber of Commerce.
Dumke, Glenn S.
1948   "Douglas, Border Town." *Pacific Historical Review* 7:283–298.
Dunnigan, Timothy.
1969   "Subsistence and Reciprocity Patterns Among the Mountain Pimas of Sonora, Mexico." Ph.D. dissertation, Department of Anthropology, University of Arizona.

————.
1981   "Adaptive Strategies of Peasant Indians in a Biethnic Mexican Community." In *Themes of Indigenous Acculturation in Northwestern Mexico*, Thomas B. Hinton and Phil C. Weigand, eds., pp. 36–49. University of Arizona Anthropological Papers no. 38. Tucson: University of Arizona Press.
Elder, Glen H., Jr.
1978   "Family History and the Life Course." In *Transitions: The Family and Life Course in Historical Perspective*, Tamara K. Hareven, ed., pp. 17–69. New York: Academic Press.
Eller, Ronald D.
1982   *Miners, Millhands, and Mountaineers: Industrialization of the Appalachian South, 1880–1930.* Knoxville: University of Tennessee Press.
Epstein, A. L.
1958   *Politics in an Urban African Community.* Manchester, U.K.: Manchester University Press.

Escandón, Patricia.
1985 "La nueva administración misional y los pueblos de indios." In *Historia general de Sonora*, vol. 2, *De la conquista al estado libre y soberano de Sonora*, Sergio Ortega Noriega and Ignacio del Río, eds., pp. 249–272. Hermosillo: Gobierno del Estado de Sonora.

Fernández, Raul.
1977 *The United States–Mexico Border: A Politico-Economic Profile*. Notre Dame, Ind.: University of Notre Dame Press.

————.
1989 *The Mexican–American Border Region: Issues and Trends*. Notre Dame, Ind.: University of Notre Dame Press.

Fernández-Kelly, María Patricia.
1983 *For We Are Sold, I and My People: Women and Industry in Mexico's Frontier*. Albany: State University of New York Press.

Ferree, Myra Marx.
1984 "Sacrifice, Satisfaction, and Social Change: Employment and the Family." In *My Troubles Are Going to Have Trouble with Me*, Karen Brodkin Sacks and Dorothy Remy, eds., pp. 61–79. New Brunswick, N.J.: Rutgers University Press.

Figueroa Valenzuela, Alejandro.
1985 "Los indios de Sonora ante la modernización porfirista." In *Historia general de Sonora*, vol. 4, *Sonora moderno: 1880–1929*, Cynthia Radding de Murrieta, ed., pp. 140–163. Hermosillo: Gobierno del Estado de Sonora.

Flores Clair, Eduardo, Cuauhtémoc Velasco Avila, and Elia Ramírez Bautista.
1985 "Estadísticas mineras de México en el siglo XIX." In *Recopilación de estadísticas económicas del siglo XIX en México*, vol. 2. México, D.F.: Instituto Nacional de Antropología e Historia.

Fortes, Meyer.
1949 "Time and Social Structure." In *Social Structure: Essays Presented to A. R. Radcliffe-Brown*. Meyer Fortes, ed., pp. 54–84. Oxford: Oxford University Press.

Friedrich, Paul.
1986 *The Princes of Naranja: An Essay in Anthrohistorical Method*. Austin: University of Texas Press.

Frobel, Folker, Jurgen Heinrichs, and Otto Kreye.
1979 *The New International Division of Labor*. Cambridge: Cambridge University Press.

Furtado, Celso.
1970 *Economic Development of Latin America*. Cambridge: Cambridge University Press.

Galarza, Ernesto.
1964 *Merchants of Labor: The Mexican Bracero Story*. Santa Barbara, Calif.: McNally and Loftin, West.

Gamio, Manuel.
   1930   *Mexican Immigration to the United States.* Chicago: University of Chicago Press.
García, Mario T.
   1981   *Desert Immigrants: The Mexicans of El Paso, 1880–1920.* New Haven: Yale University Press.
Gates, Hill.
   1987   *Chinese Working-Class Lives: Getting by in Taiwan.* Ithaca, N.Y.: Cornell University Press.
Gilbert, James Carl.
   1934   "A Field Study in Mexico of the Mexican Repatriation Movement." M.A. thesis, Department of Sociology, University of Southern California.
Gildersleeve, Charles R.
   1978   "The International Border City: Urban Spatial Organization in a Context of Two Cultures Along the United States—Mexico Border." Ph.D. dissertation, Department of Geography, University of Nebraska, Lincoln.
Gómez-Quiñones, Juan.
   1979   "The Origins and Development of the Mexican Working Class in the United States: Laborers and Artisans North of the Río Bravo, 1600–1900." In *El trabajo y los trabajadores en la historia de México,* Elsa Cecilia Frost, Michael C. Meyer, and Josefina Zoraida Vázquez, eds., pp. 463–505. México, D.F., and Tucson: Colegio de México and University of Arizona Press.
Goody, Jack.
   1972   *Domestic Groups.* Addison-Wesley Modular Publications, Module 28. Menlo Park, CA: Cummings.
Gordon, Robert J.
   1977   *Mines, Masters, and Migrants: Life in a Namibian Mine Compound.* Johannesburg: Ravan Press.
Gracida Romo, Juan José.
   1985   "Génesis y consolidación del Porfiriato en Sonora (1883–1895)" and "El Sonora moderno (1892–1910)." In *Historia general de Sonora,* vol. 4, *Sonora moderno, 1880–1929,* Cynthia Radding de Murrieta, ed., pp. 19–138. Hermosillo: Gobierno del Estado de Sonora.
Greenberg, James B.
   1981–1982   Field Notes of Interviews Conducted in Agua Prieta in 1981 and 1982. Originals in possession of James B. Greenberg.
Gregory, Peter.
   1986   *The Myth of Market Failure.* Baltimore: Johns Hopkins University Press.
Griswold del Castillo, Richard.
   1984   *La Familia: Chicano Families in the Urban Southwest 1848 to the Present.* Notre Dame, Ind.: Notre Dame University Press.

Guadarrama, Rocío.
1987 "Elections in Sonora." In *Electoral Patterns and Perspectives in Mexico,* Arturo Alvarado, ed., pp. 43–80. Monograph no. 22. San Diego: Center for U.S.–Mexican Studies, University of California, San Diego.

Gutman, Herbert G.
1977 *Work, Culture, and Society in Industrializing America.* New York: Vintage.

——.
1983 "Interview with Herbert G. Gutman." In *Visions of History,* MARHO (Henry Abelove et al.), eds., pp. 185–216. New York: Pantheon.

Hansen, Edward C.
1977 *Rural Catalonia Under the Franco Regime.* Cambridge: Cambridge University Press.

Hansen, Roger D.
1971 *The Politics of Mexican Development.* Baltimore: Johns Hopkins University Press.

Hareven, Tamara K.
1982 *Family Time and Industrial Time.* Cambridge: Cambridge University Press.

Hareven, Tamara K., and Randolph Langenbach.
1978 *Amoskeag: Life and Work in an American Factory-City.* New York: Pantheon.

Hellman, Judith Adler.
1983 *Mexico in Crisis,* 2nd ed. New York: Holmes and Meier.

Herrera-Sobek, María.
1979 *The Bracero Experience: Elitelore vs. Folklore.* Los Angeles: UCLA Latin American Center.

Hewes, Leslie.
1935 "Huepac: An Agricultural Village of Sonora, Mexico." *Economic Geography* 11(3):284–292.

Heyman, Josiah McC.
1986 "The History of the Mexican American Community of Douglas, Arizona, 1901–1942." Paper presented at meeting of the Arizona Historical Society, Douglas, Arizona, May.

——.
1988 "The Working People of the United States–Mexico Border in the Region of Northeastern Sonora, 1886–1986." Ph.D. dissertation, Ph.D. Program in Anthropology, City University of New York.

Hinton, Thomas B.
1959 *A Survey of Indian Assimilation in Eastern Sonora.* University of Arizona Anthropological Papers no. 4. Tucson: University of Arizona Press.

——.
1976 Estado de la investigación etnográfica sobre la región del río Sonora

y la del alto Yaqui." In *Sonora: Antropología del desierto, la primera reunión de antropología e historia del Noroeste,* Beatriz Braniff C. and Richard S. Felger, eds., pp. 229–233. Colleción Cien tífica Diversa no. 27. México, D.F.: Instituto Nacional de Antropología e Historia–SEP.

──────.

1983   "Southern Periphery: West." In *Handbook of North American Indians,* vol. 10, *Southwest,* Alfonso Ortiz, ed., William Sturtevant, gen. ed., pp. 315–328. Washington, D.C.: Smithsonian Institution Press.

Hoffman, Abraham.

1974   *Unwanted Mexican Americans in the Great Depression: Repatriation Pressures, 1929–1939.* Tucson: University of Arizona Press.

Horton, Inez.

1968   *Copper's Children: The Rise and Fall of a Mexican Copper Mining Camp.* New York: Exposition Press.

Hrdliĉka, Aleŝ.

1904   "Notes on the Indians of Sonora, Mexico." *American Anthropologist* n.s. 6(1):51–89.

Hu-DeHart, Evelyn.

1980   "Immigrants to a Developing Society: The Chinese in Northern Mexico, 1875–1932." In *The Chinese Experience in Arizona and Northern Mexico,* Lawrence Michael Fong, et al., eds., pp. 49–86. Tucson: Arizona Historical Society.

──────.

1985   "La comunidad china en el desarrollo de Sonora." In *Historia general de Sonora,* vol. 4, *Sonora moderno: 1880–1929,* Cynthia Radding de Murrieta, ed., pp. 195–211. Hermosillo: Gobierno del Estado de Sonora.

Iglesias Prieto, Norma.

1985   *La flor más bella de la maquiladora: Historias de vida de la mujer obrera en Tijuana, B.C.N.* México, D.F.: SEP/Centro de Estudios Fronterizos del Norte de Mexico.

Ingersoll, Ralph McA.

1924   *In and Under Mexico.* New York: Century.

Instituto Nacional de Estadística, Geografía, e Informática.

1984   *Manual de estadísticas básicas del estado de Sonora.* México, D.F.: Secretaría de Programación y Presupuesto, Instituto Nacional de Estadística, Geografía, e Informática.

Jayawardena, Chandra.

1962   "Family Organization in Plantations in British Guiana." *International Journal of Comparative Sociology* 3(1):43–64.

Jeffrey, Robert S.

1951   "The History of Douglas, Arizona." M.A. thesis, Department of History, University of Arizona.

Jiménez Ornelas, Roberto.
  1985 "La tecnología en la modernización de Sonora." In *Historia general de Sonora*, vol. 4, *Sonora moderno: 1880–1929*, Cynthia Radding de Murrieta, ed., pp. 167–192. Hermosillo: Gobierno del Estado de Sonora.
Johnson, Jean B.
  1950 *The Opata: An Inland Tribe of Sonora.* University of New Mexico Publications in Anthropology no. 6. Albuquerque: University of New Mexico Press.
Katz, Friedrich.
  1980 *La servidumbre agraria en México en la época porfiriana.* México, D.F.: Ediciones Era.
———.
  1981 *The Secret War in Mexico: Europe, the United States, and the Mexican Revolution.* Chicago: University of Chicago Press.
Kearney, Michael.
  1986 "From the Invisible Hand to the Visible Feet: Anthropological Studies of Migration and Development." *Annual Review of Anthropology* 15:311–361.
Kiser, George C., and Martha Woody Kiser, eds.
  1979 *Mexican Workers in the United States.* Albuquerque: University of New Mexico Press.
Knight, Rolf.
  1975 *Work Camps and Company Towns in Canada and the United States.* Vancouver, B.C.: New Star Books.
Kornblum, William.
  1974 *Blue Collar Community.* Chicago: University of Chicago Press.
Ladman, Jerry R., and Mark O. Poulson.
  1972 *The Economic Impact of the Mexican Border Industrialization Program: Agua Prieta, Sonora.* Special Study no. 10. Tempe: Center for Latin American Studies, Arizona State University.
Laite, Julian.
  1981 *Industrial Development and Migrant Labor in Latin America.* Austin: University of Texas Press.
Langness, L. L., and Gelya Frank.
  1981 *Lives: An Anthropological Approach to Biography.* Novato, Calif.: Chandler and Sharp.
Leach, E. R.
  1961 *Pul Eliya: A Village in Ceylon.* Cambridge: Cambridge University Press.
Leland, Everard.
  1930 *Mining Methods and Costs at the Pilares Mine, Pilares de Nacozari, Sonora, Mexico.* U.S. Bureau of Mines Information Circular no. 6307. Washington, D.C.: U.S. Government Printing Office.
León-Portilla, Miguel.
  1972 "The Norteño Variety of Mexican Culture: An Ethnohistorical Ap-

proach." In *Plural Society in the Southwest*, Edward H. Spicer and Raymond H. Thompson, eds., pp. 77–114. Albuquerque: University of New Mexico Press.

Lewis, Oscar.
1969   "Possessions of the Poor." *Scientific American* 221 (October): 114–124.

Lloyd, Peter.
1982   *A Third World Proletariat?* London: Allen and Unwin.

Lomnitz, Larissa, and Marisol Pérez-Lizaur.
1984   "Dynastic Growth and Survival Strategies: The Solidarity of Mexican Grand-Families." In *Kinship Ideology and Practice in Latin America*, Raymond T. Smith, ed., pp. 183–195. Chapel Hill: University of North Carolina Press.

Lumholtz, Carl.
1973   [1902]   *Unknown Mexico: A Record of Five Years' Exploration Among the Tribes of the Western Sierra Madre*. 2 vols. Glorieta, N.M.: Rio Grande Press.

Machado, Manuel.
1981   *The Northern Mexican Cattle Industry, 1910–1975*. College Station: Texas A&M Press.

Mackintosh, Maureen.
1984   "Gender and Economics: The Sexual Division of Labor and the Subordination of Women." In *Of Marriage and the Market: Women's Subordination Internationally and Its Lessons*, Kate Young, Carol Wolkowitz, and Roslyn McCullagh, eds., pp. 3–17. London: Routledge and Kegan Paul.

Martínez, Oscar J.
1977   "The Peso Devaluation and the Border: Some Historical Observations." *El Paso Economic Review* 15(1):1–5.

Massey, Douglas S., Rafael Alarcon, Jorge Durand, and Humberto Gonzalez.
1987   *Return to Aztlan: The Social Process of International Migration from Western Mexico*. Berkeley and Los Angeles: University of California Press.

Meinig, D. W.
1971   *Southwest: Three Peoples in Geographical Change, 1600–1970*. New York: Oxford University Press.

The Mexican American Tapes.
1984   *The Mexican American Tapes: A Chronicle of Life Outside the Law.* Videocassette produced by Louis Hock. San Diego: L. Hock.

Meyer, Eugenia, et al.
1980   *La lucha obrera en Cananea, 1906*. México, D.F.: Instituto Nacional de Antropología e Historia.

Mines, Richard.
1981   *Developing a Community Tradition of Migration to the United States: A Field Study in Rural Zacatecas, Mexico, and California Settlement Areas*. Monograph Series no. 3. San Diego: Center for U.S.–Mexican Studies, University of California, San Diego.

Mintz, Sidney W.
1960   *Worker in the Cane: A Puerto Rican Life History.* New York: Norton.
Moncada O., Carlos.
1985   "El escenario político en Sonora." In *Municipios en conflicto,* Carlos Martínez Assad, ed., pp. 27–53. México, D.F.: Instituto de Investigaciones Sociales, UNAM.
Montgomery, David.
1979   *Workers' Control in America.* Cambridge: Cambridge University Press.
Multinational Monitor.
1987   "Largest Maquila Employers in Mexico," February, p. 6.
Nash, June.
1979   *We Eat the Mines and the Mines Eat Us: Dependency and Exploitation in Bolivian Tin Mines.* New York: Columbia University Press.

——.
1980   "A Critique of Social Science Roles in Latin America." In *Sex and Class in Latin America,* June Nash and Helen Icken Safa, eds., pp. 1–24. Brooklyn, N.Y.: J. F. Bergin.

——.
1983   "The Impact of the Changing International Division of Labor on Different Sectors of the Labor Force." In *Women, Men, and the International Division of Labor,* June Nash and María Patricia Fernández-Kelly, eds., pp. 3–38. Albany: State University of New York Press.
Nolasco Armas, Margarita.
1979   *Migración municipal en México (1960–1970),* 2 vols. México, D.F.: Instituto Nacional de Antropología e Historia–SEP.
North, Diane M. T.
1980   *Samuel Peter Heintzelman and the Sonora Exploring and Mining Company.* Tucson: University of Arizona Press.
Nueva ley federal del trabajo (México).
1986   *Nueva ley federal del trabajo 1986,* Jacinto Lobato, ed. México, D.F.: Librería Teocalli.
Officer, James E.
1987   *Hispanic Arizona, 1536–1856.* Tucson: University of Arizona Press.
Onselen, Charles Van.
1976   *Chibaro: African Mine Labour in Southern Rhodesia, 1900–1933.* London: Pluto Press.
Owen, Roger C.
1959   *Marobavi: A Study of an Assimilated Group in Northern Sonora.* Anthropological Papers of the University of Arizona no. 3. Tucson: University of Arizona Press.
Park, Joseph F.
1961   "The History of Mexican Labor in Arizona During the Territorial

Period." M.A. thesis, Department of History, University of Arizona.

Peña, Devon Gerardo.

1980   "Las Maquiladoras: Mexican Women and Class Struggle in the Border Industries." *Aztlán: International Journal of Chicano Studies Research* 11(2):159–230.

————.

1987   "Tortuosidad: Shop Floor Struggles of Female Maquiladora Workers." In *Women on the U.S.–Mexico Border: Responses to Change,* Vicki L. Ruiz and Susan Tiano, eds., pp. 129–154. Boston: Allen and Unwin.

Peña, Elsa M., and J. Trinidad Chávez.

1985   "Aspectos de la vida en los minerales: 1929–1980," "Organización obrera de los minerales: 1929–1980," and "Ganadería y agricultura en la sierra: 1929–1980." In *Historia general de Sonora,* vol. 5, *Historia contemporánea de Sonora: 1929–1980,* Gerardo Cornejo Murrieta, ed., pp. 237–282. Hermosillo: Gobierno del Estado de Sonora.

Pennington, Campbell W.

1979   *The Material Culture of the Pima Bajo of Central Sonora, Mexico,* vol. 1. Salt Lake City: University of Utah Press.

Peterson, Herbert B.

1975   "A Twentieth Century Journey to Cibola: The Tragedy of the Bracero in Maricopa County, Arizona, 1917–1921." M.A. thesis, Department of History, Arizona State University.

Piore, Michael J.

1979   *Birds of Passage: Migrant Labor and Industrial Societies.* Cambridge: Cambridge University Press.

Portes, Alejandro, and Robert L. Bach.

1985   *Latin Journey: Cuban and Mexican Immigrants in the United States.* Berkeley: University of California Press.

Powdermaker, Hortense.

1962   *Copper Town: Changing Africa.* New York: Harper & Row.

Quijada Hernández, Armando.

1985   "Integración política del nuevo estado." In *Historia general de Sonora,* vol. 3, *Período de México independiente: 1831–1883,* Juan Antonio Ruibal Corella, ed., pp. 57–70. Hermosillo: Gobierno del Estado de Sonora.

Radding de Murrieta, Cynthia.

1981   "La acumulación originaria de capital agrario en Sonora: La comunidad indígena y la hacienda en la Pimería Alta y Opatería, 1768–1868." In *Memoria, VI simposio de historia de Sonora,* pp. 198–224. Hermosillo: Instituto de Investigaciones Históricas.

————.

1984   "El espacio sonorense y la periodificación de las historias municipales." In *Memoria, VIII simposio de historia de Sonora*, pp. 75–87. Hermosillo: Instituto de Investigaciones Históricas.

———.

1985   "El Maderismo en Sonora y los inicios de la Revolución (1910–1913)," and "El triunfo constitucionalista y las reformas en la región (1913–1919)." In *Historia general de Sonora*, vol. 4, *Sonora moderno: 1880–1929*, Cynthia Radding de Murrieta, ed., pp. 215–311. Hermosillo: Gobierno del Estado de Sonora.

Ramírez, José Carlos, Ricardo León, and Oscar Conde.

1985   "El último auge," "Una época de crisis económica," "La estrategía económica de los Callistas," "Cárdenas y las dos caras de la recuperación," and "La nueva economía urbana." In *Historia general de Sonora*, vol. 5, *Historia contemporanea de Sonora, 1929–1984*, Gerardo Cornejo Murrieta, ed., pp. 19–35, 53–66, 69–78, 113–128, 197–215. Hermosillo: Gobierno del Estado de Sonora.

Rapp, Rayna.

1983   "Peasants into Proletarians from the Household Out: An Analysis from the Intersection of Anthropology and Social History." In *Social Anthropology of Peasantry*, Joan P. Mencher, ed., pp. 32–47. Bombay: Somaiya Publications.

Ribeiro, Gustavo Lins.

1985   "Proyectos de gran escala: Hacia un marco conceptual para el análisis de una forma de producción temporaria." In *Relocalizados: Antropología social de las poblaciones desplazadas*, Leopoldo Bartolomé, ed., pp. 23–47. Buenos Aires: IDES.

Roberts, Bryan R.

1978   *Cities of Peasants: The Political Economy of Urbanization in the Third World*. Beverly Hills, Calif.: Sage.

Romo, Ricardo.

1983   *East Los Angeles: History of a Barrio*. Austin: University of Texas Press.

Rosaldo, Renato.

1980   *Ilongot Headhunting, 1883–1974*. Stanford, Calif.: Stanford University Press.

Rothstein, Frances Abrahamer.

1983   *Three Different Worlds: Women, Men, and Children in an Industrializing Community*. Westport, Conn.: Greenwood.

Ruíz, Ramón Eduardo.

1976   *Labor and the Ambivalent Revolutionaries: Mexico, 1911–1923*. Baltimore: Johns Hopkins University Press.

———.

1988   *The People of Sonora and Yankee Capitalists*. Tucson: University of Arizona Press.

Samora, Julian.

1971   *Los Mojados: The Wetback Story*. Notre Dame, Ind.: University of Notre Dame Press.

Sanderson, Steven E.
  1981   *Agrarian Populism and the Mexican State: The Struggle for Land in Sonora.* Berkeley: University of California Press.
Sandomingo, Manuel.
  1951   *Historia de Agua Prieta.* Agua Prieta: Imprenta Sandomingo.
Sanjek, Roger.
  1983   "Female and Male Domestic Cycles in Urban Africa: The Adabraka Case." In *Female and Male in West Africa,* Christine Oppong, ed., pp. 330–343. London: Allen and Unwin.
Schneider, Jane.
  1980   "Trousseau as Treasure: Some Contradictions of Late Nineteenth Century Change in Sicily." In *Beyond the Myths of Culture,* Eric Ross, ed., pp. 323–356. New York: Academic Press.
Secretaría de Programación y Presupuesto.
  1983   *X censo general de población y vivienda, 1980: Sonora, tomo 26,* vols. 1 and 2. México, D.F.: Secretaría de Programación y Presupuesto.
Seligson, Mitchell A., and Edward J. Williams.
  1981   *Maquiladoras and Migration: Workers in the Mexico–United States Border Industrialization Program.* Austin: Mexico–United States Border Research Program and University of Texas Press.
Sheridan, Thomas E.
  1983   "Economic Inequality and Agrarian Conflict in the Municipio of Cucurpe, Sonora, Mexico." Ph.D. dissertation, Department of Anthropology, University of Arizona.

————.
  1986   *Los Tucsonenses: The Mexican Community in Tucson, 1854–1941.* Tucson: University of Arizona Press.

————.
  1988   *Where the Dove Calls: The Political Ecology of a Peasant Corporate Community in Northwestern Mexico.* Tucson: University of Arizona Press.
Simonelli, Jeanne.
  1985   "Markets, Motherhood, and Modernization: Fertility and Economic Change in a Rural Mexican Municipio." Ph.D. dissertation, Department of Anthropology, University of Oklahoma.
Solórzano-Torres, Rosalía.
  1987   "Female Mexican Immigrants in San Diego County." In *Women on the Border: Responses to Change,* Vicki L. Ruiz and Susan Tiano, eds., pp. 41–60. Boston: Allen and Unwin.
Sonnichsen, C. L.
  1974   *Colonel Greene and the Copper Skyrocket.* Tucson: University of Arizona Press.
Spicer, Edward H.
  1962   *Cycles of Conquest: The Impact of Spain, Mexico, and the United States on the Indians of the Southwest, 1533–1960.* Tucson: University of Arizona Press.

————.

1969 "Northwest Mexico: Introduction." In *Handbook of Middle American Indians*, Robert Wauchope, gen. ed., *Ethnology*, vol. 8, Evon Vogt, ed., pp. 777–791. Austin: University of Texas Press.

Stoddard, Ellwyn R.

1987 *Maquila: Assembly Plants in Northern Mexico.* El Paso: Texas Western Press.

Strickon, Arnold, and Sidney M. Greenfield, eds.

1972 *Structure and Process in Latin America.* Albuquerque: School of American Research–University of New Mexico Press.

Taylor, Paul S.

1933 *Mexican Labor in the United States: Migration Statistics IV.* University of California Publications in Economics, vol. 12, no. 3. Berkeley: University of California Press.

Thompson, E. P.

1963 *The Making of the English Working Class.* New York: Vintage.

Tilly, Louise A., and Joan W. Scott.

1978 *Women, Work, and Family.* New York: Holt, Rinehart, and Winston.

Twin Plant News.

1986 "History of Cost per Hour in Dollars Based on a 48 Hour Work Week—Juarez, Chihuahua," February, p. 12.

Ugalde, Antonio.

1970 *Power and Conflict in a Mexican Community.* Albuquerque: University of New Mexico Press.

————.

1974 *The Urbanization Process of a Poor Mexican Neighborhood.* Austin: Institute of Latin American Studies, University of Texas.

Urquidi, Víctor, and Sofía Méndez Villarreal.

1978 "Economic Importance of Mexico's Northern Border Region." In *Views Across the Border*, Stanley R. Ross, ed., pp. 141–162. Albuquerque: University of New Mexico Press.

Valencia Ortega, Ismael.

1986 "Formas de propiedad y explotación agraria en el Río de Sonora." Paper presented at XI Simposio de Historia y Antropología de Sonora, Hermosillo, February 19–22.

Vélez-Ibáñez, Carlos G.

1983 *Rituals of Marginality: Politics, Process, and Culture Change in Central Urban Mexico, 1969–1974.* Berkeley: University of California Press.

Vidargas de Moral, Juan Domingo.

1982 "Un caso de contradando en Sonora y su repercusión en los consulados de comercio de Nueva España." In *Memoria: VII Simposio de historia de Sonora*, pp. 147–163. Hermosillo: Instituto de Investigaciones Históricas.

Villa, Eduardo.

1984 [1938]. *Historia del estado de Sonora.* Hermosillo: Gobierno del Estado de Sonora.

Wiest, Raymond.
    1973   "Wage-Labor Migration and the Household in a Mexican Town."
            Journal of Anthropological Research 29:180–209.

——.
    1979   "Implications of International Labor Migration for Mexican Rural
            Development." In *Migration Across Frontiers: Mexico and the
            United States*, Fernando Camara and Robert Van Kemper, eds., pp.
            85–97. Contributions of the Latin American Anthropology Group,
            vol. 3. Albany, N.Y.: Institute for Mesoamerican Studies, State
            University of New York at Albany.
Wilson, Godfrey.
    1941–1942   *An Essay on the Economics of Detribalization in Northern
            Rhodesia.* Rhodes-Livingstone Papers nos. 5 and 6. London:
            Oxford University Press for the Rhodes-Livingston In-
            stitute.
Winn, Peter.
    1979   "Oral History and the Factory Study: New Approaches to Labor
            History." *Latin American Research Review* 14(2):130–140.
Wolf, Eric R.
    1959   *Sons of the Shaking Earth.* Chicago: University of Chicago Press.

——.
    1966   "Kinship, Friendship, and Patron–Client Relations in Complex So-
            cieties." In *The Social Anthropology of Complex Societies*, Mich-
            ael Banton, ed., pp. 1–21. A.S.A. Monographs 4. London: Tav-
            istock.

——.
    1982   *Europe and the People Without History.* Berkeley: University of
            California Press.
Young, Kate, Carol Wolkowitz, and Roslyn McCullagh, eds.
    1984   *Of Marriage and the Market: Women's Subordination Interna-
            tionally and Its Lessons.* London: Routledge and Kegan Paul.
Young, Otis E., Jr.
    1970   *Western Mining.* Norman: University of Oklahoma Press.
Zapata, Francisco.
    1977   "Enclaves y sistemas de relaciones industriales en América Lat-
            ina." *Revista mexicana de Sociología* 39:719–731.

Index

Agrarian reform. *See* Sonora: agrarian reform in

Agua Prieta, Sonora, 5, 7, 8, 28, 35, 43, 94, 125, 128–31, 156–61, 174, 215n.3; battle of, 51; broomstraw factories in, 149; ejido of, 156–57; elite families of, 146, 150, 157; house lots in, 148, 156–58; immigrants to, 128–29; maquiladora industry in, 5, 8, 41–43, 162; meat-packing plant in, 38, 150; politics in, 154, 155, 157–58, 217n.1; population of, 38–39; unions of the unemployed at, 37. *See also* Barrio Ferrocarril; Border cities, family settlement in; Colonia Ejidal; Consumption: at border city

Aguiar, Neuma, 161

Aguirre family history, 65–73, 74–75, 131–43; Angelita, housework of, 139–41; Angelita, managerial role of, at Agua Prieta, 140–43, 215n.6; Angelita, sewing skills of, 70, 92, 105, 133–34, 139; Angelita, stores of, 141; kinship of, 134–35; kinship of, in mine town, 66–68, 74–75; Luis, bracero work of, 136–39; Luis, child-

hood of, 69; Luis, unemployment and prospecting at El Tigre mine of, 131–33; Luis, work at El Tigre mine of, 69–70, 213n.9; Luis and Angelita, children of, 140, 141–42; Luis and Angelita, consumption by, 72–73, 140; Luis and Angelita, household arrangements of, during male migration, 139, 141, 143; Luis and Angelita, marriage of, 71; Luis and Angelita, move to Agua Prieta by, 134; Luis and Angelita, retirement investments by, 137, 141–42; Santiago, origins and work of, 66, 133. *See also* León family history: Angelita, childhood and work; Peralta family, origins of

Alamos, District of, Sonora, 27, 55, 86

Alvarez, Roberto, Jr., 204

American-Mexican relations: ambiguity in, 18, 201; American ownership of Mexican resources and, 25–26, 28–30; border as power in, 5, 18, 197–200, 203–4, 210; in maquiladoras, 189–90, 217n.12; Mexican nationalism and, 23–24, 29, 79, 217n.12; social race dur-

dency of, 36, 44, 81, 209, 214n.11
Cardoso, Lawrence, 24
Cars. *See* Automotive and mechanical skills: cars and trucks and
Cash, circulating paper, 43, 60; effects of, on labor relationships, 53, 59–60; in rural economy, 37–38; women's activities and, 85, 92, 134
Chavez, Leo, 195
Chicanos. *See* Arizona, Mexican labor in; California; Douglas, Arizona; Kinship: cross-border; Mexican immigrants to U.S.; Pirtleville, Arizona
Children. *See* Men, childhood of; Women: role of, in household as working children
Chinese, in Sonora, 54, 103
Christmas, 88–89
Churunibabi, Sonora, 28, 35, 96
Clifton-Morenci, Arizona, 24, 64
Colonia Ejidal (Agua Prieta), 135, 156–57, 176
Company towns, 10, 29–30; housing in, 71–72, 86; neighborhoods and segregation in, 71–72; payroll credit system in, 59, 72, 146; scrip in, 60; stores in, 30, 72–73, 79; unitary structure of, 10, 73–79
Compañeros. *See* Labor relationships: personalized, before industry
Construction projects. *See* Large-scale projects
Consumption, 17–18, 58, 60, 104–5, 107–8; at border cities, 44, 89, 94, 129, 174–78; credit, general patterns of, 59, 158–59, 175; credit, instances of, 72, 142, 148, 167–68; fashion and, 88–89, 105; immigration to U.S. and, 59, 96; in mine centers, 59; peddlers and, 58; responses to inflation and economic crisis and, 185–86; role of, in family consumer/wage

economy, 163, 178–84; role of, in formative working class, 53, 56, 58–60, 91–93; standards of living and, 175, 200–201, 209–10; of used goods, 175; U.S. sources of goods and, 58–59, 88–89, 174; youth and, 187–88. *See also* Aguirre family history: Luis and Angelita, consumption by; Automotive and mechanical skills; Cash, circulating paper; Cooking skills; Córdoba family history: consumption at border by; Encinas de Acosta family history: consumption and fashion of; Furnishings; Galaz family history; Hernández (José) family history; Material culture; Radios and televisions; Sewing: skills and businesses
Cooking skills, 84–86, 140; refrigerators and, 140, 167, 175; restaurants and, 84, 92; stoves and, 73, 84, 114, 140, 167
Córdoba family history, 93–97, 164–74; Carlos, apprenticeship of, 94, 214n.5; Carlos, migration and work in U.S. by, 94–96, 113; Carlos, machine shop of, 167; Carlos, work in Sonoran mines of, 78–79, 96–97, 164–66; Carlos and Francisca, marriage of, 86; children's education, 164–66, 169–70; Consuela Hoyos de, family and residential arrangements of, as widow, 93–94; consumption by, at border, 167; cross-border kinship of, 169–70; Francisca, managerial roles at border of, 215n.6; Francisco, work in maquiladoras of, 169–72; household arrangements of, 164–66, 168–69, 215n.6; Jorge, work career of, 166, 169–72; Luisa, work in maquiladoras of, 169–70, 173; move to Agua Prieta by, 164–66; Teresa, work in ma-

Material culture (*cont.*)
85–86, 92–93, 105; long-term
consequences of, 85–86, 92, 105–
6, 107–9, 113–15, 134, 142, 147,
206–7; regional vs. outside manufactures in, 107–8; of repatriates, 114; role of, in working-
class formation, 83, 93, 103–4,
107–9. *See also* Automotive and
mechanical skills; Cooking
skills; Furnishings; Houses; Mementos; Radios and televisions;
Sewing: machines; Shoes; Washing machines
Maytorena, José María, 31, 51
Mechanical and metal-working
skills. *See* Automotive and mechanical skills
Mementos, 168, 215n.1
Men: career patterns of, 159–60,
170–73, 184, 190; childhood of,
69; education of, 69, 124, 141,
201; father-son conflict between,
112–16; friendships between,
149, 151–55; learning and skills
of, 94, 97, 106–7, 147, 153, 169–
71; life courses of, 16, 107–9,
204–5; marriage of, 103, 169,
195; migration to the U.S. by, 95,
96, 101–3, 126–28, 196–97; old
age and, 142, 152; patron-client
relationships between, 149–51,
154–55, 159–60; personalized relationships between, in maquiladoras, 172–73, 189–91; role
of, in household economy of, 71,
160–61, 171, 187; work of, 69,
183–84; workshops owned by,
152–53. *See also* Automotive and
mechanical skills; Border balance
households
Meresichic, Sonora (Marobavi,
pseudonym), 61, 105, 213n.8
Mestizos, 7, 22–23, 55–56, 86–87,
104, 147
Mexican Americans. *See* Arizona,
Mexican labor in; California;

Douglas, Arizona; Kinship: cross-
border; Mexican immigrants to
U.S.; Pirtleville, Arizona
Mexican immigrants to U.S., 18;
during 1920s, 95; in agricultural
labor, 101–3, 136–39; as braceros,
136–39; effects of legal structure
on, 23, 64, 118–20, 126–28; experiences of, in U.S. labor markets,
124; families of, 195–96; female,
122, 147–48, 194–96; green-cards
and, 122–25; male, 96, 101, 102–
3, 126–27, 183, 194–96, 196–97;
in mining and construction, 95–
96, 194; nineteenth century, 23,
53; permanent resident, 126, 195;
risks and dangers to, 198–99; undocumented aliens, 193–96; in
urban occupations, 122–24, 194–
95. *See also* Border balance
households; Kinship: cross-
border; Railroads
Mexican nationalism. *See*
American-Mexican relations
Mexican revolution, 30, 207;
Batallon Pilares, 31, 49–51; cross-
border population during, 65;
leadership of, 30–31, 51; mine
cities during, 32; in San Pedro de
la Cueva, 100; side effects of, 31–
32; Sonoran populace in, 31, 50.
See also Calles, Plutarco Elías;
Hernández (Guadalupe) family
history
Mexico, economy of: 1980s debt
crisis and export development, 9,
42, 45, 176; crisis in, 185, 200–
201; inflation-beating strategies
used in, 186; peso devaluations
and, 9, 42–43, 43–45, 176–78;
real wages in, 43–45, 176–78, 184.
See also Employment and unemployment; Income, 1982–1986;
Maquiladora industry; Mining industry; Sonora
Mexican history. *See* Border region,
U.S.–Mexico: history of; Cár-

manent, 57, 59, 61–62, 63, 68;
women's role in, 83, 85, 93
Working class transformation, 8,
128–31, 142–43, 145, 155; complexity as a result of, 158–60;
kinship evidence for, 134–36; personalized relationships in, 149–
55. *See also* Maquiladora
workers; Work, 1940–1965
Working class uprooting, 8, 74,
110–16. *See also* Aguirre family
history; Employment and unemployment; Repatriation; Romero
family history

Working parents, 179; female, 182;
male, 182–84
Work places and skills. *See* Automotive and mechanical skills;
Cooking skills; Housework; Maquiladora industry; Mining industry; Prospecting and small
mining; Sewing: skills and businesses; Work, 1940–65; Workshops
Workshops: men's, 152–54;
women's, 154

Zenith, Inc., 43